AF707592

■ The Alabama State Constitution

The Oxford Commentaries on the State Constitutions of the United States
G. Alan Tarr, Series Editor

Professor G. Alan Tarr, Director of the Center on State Constitutional Studies at Rutgers University, serves as General Editor for this important new series which in its entirety will cover each of the fifty states. Each volume of *The Oxford Commentaries on the State Constitutions of the United States* contains a historical overview of the state's constitutional development, plus a section-by-section analysis of the state's current constitution. Other features included in the volumes are the text of the state's constitution, a bibliographic essay, table of cases, and index. This series provides essential reference tools for those investigating state constitutional development and constitutional law.

The Alabama State Constitution

Second Edition

William H. Stewart

THE OXFORD COMMENTARIES ON THE STATE CONSTITUTIONS OF THE UNITED STATES
G. Alan Tarr, Series Editor

OXFORD
UNIVERSITY PRESS

OXFORD
UNIVERSITY PRESS

Oxford University Press is a department of the University of Oxford. It furthers the University's objective of excellence in research, scholarship, and education by publishing worldwide. Oxford is a registered trademark of Oxford University Press in the UK and certain other countries.

Published in the United States of America by Oxford University Press
198 Madison Avenue, New York, NY 10016, United States of America.

© Oxford University Press 2016

All rights reserved. No part of this publication may be reproduced, stored in a retrieval system, or transmitted, in any form or by any means, without the prior permission in writing of Oxford University Press, or as expressly permitted by law, by license, or under terms agreed with the appropriate reproduction rights organization. Inquiries concerning reproduction outside the scope of the above should be sent to the Rights Department, Oxford University Press, at the address above.

You must not circulate this work in any other form
and you must impose this same condition on any acquirer.

Library of Congress Cataloging-in-Publication Data

Names: Stewart, William Histaspas, 1939- writer of added commentary. |
Alabama. Constitution (1901)
Title: The Alabama state constitution / William H. Stewart.
Description: Second edition. | New York : Oxford University Press, 2016. |
Series: The Oxford commentaries on the state constitutions of the United States |
Includes bibliographical references and index.
Identifiers: LCCN 2015047145 | ISBN 9780199896394 (hardback)
Subjects: LCSH: Constitutions—Alabama. | Constitutional law—Alabama. |
Constitutional history—Alabama.
Classification: LCC KFA401 1901.A6 S738 2016 | DDC 342.76102—dc23 LC record available at
http://lccn.loc.gov/2015047145

Note to Readers

This publication is designed to provide accurate and authoritative information in regard to the subject matter covered. It is based upon sources believed to be accurate and reliable and is intended to be current as of the time it was written. It is sold with the understanding that the publisher is not engaged in rendering legal, accounting, or other professional services. If legal advice or other expert assistance is required, the services of a competent professional person should be sought. Also, to confirm that the information has not been affected or changed by recent developments, traditional legal research techniques should be used, including checking primary sources where appropriate.

(Based on the Declaration of Principles jointly adopted by a Committee of the American Bar Association and a Committee of Publishers and Associations.)

You may order this or any other Oxford University Press publication by visiting the Oxford University Press website at www.oup.com

This book is dedicated to Connie, Trey, Susan, and Wes.

CONTENTS

SERIES FOREWORD

In 1776, following the declaration of independence from England, the former colonies began to draft their own constitutions. Their handiwork attracted widespread interest, and draft constitutions circulated up and down the Atlantic seaboard, as constitution-makers sought to benefit from the insights of their counterparts in sister states. In Europe, the new constitutions found a ready audience seeking enlightenment from the American experiments in self-government. Even the delegates to the Constitutional Convention of 1787, despite their reservations about the course of political developments in the states during the decade after independence, found much that was useful in the newly adopted constitutions. And when James Madison, fulfilling a pledge given during the ratification debates, drafted the federal Bill of Rights, he found his model in the famous Declaration of Rights of the Virginia Constitution.

By the 1900s, however, few people would have looked to state constitutions for enlightenment. Instead, a familiar litany of complaints was heard whenever state constitutions were mentioned. State constitutions were too long and too detailed, combining basic principles with policy prescriptions and prohibitions that had no place in the fundamental law of a state. By including such provisions, it was argued, state constitutions deprived state governments of the flexibility they needed to respond effectively in changing circumstances. This—among other factors—encouraged political reformers to look to the federal government, which was not plagued by such constitutional constraints, thereby shifting the locus of political initiative away from the states. Meanwhile, civil libertarians concluded that state bills of rights, at least as interpreted by state courts, did not adequately protect rights and therefore looked to the federal courts and the federal Bill of Rights for redress. As power and responsibility shifted from the states to Washington, so too did the attention of scholars, the legal community, and the general public.

During the early 1970s, however, state constitutions were "rediscovered." The immediate impetus for this rediscovery was former President Richard Nixon's appointment of Warren Burger to succeed Earl Warren as Chief Justice of the U.S. Supreme Court. To civil libertarians, this appointment seemed to signal a decisive shift in the Supreme Court's jurisprudence, because Burger was expected to lead the Court away from the liberal activism that had characterized the Warren Court. They therefore sought ways to safeguard the gains they had achieved for defendants, racial minorities, and the poor during Warren's tenure from erosion by the Burger Court. In particular, they began to look to state bills of rights to secure the rights of defendants and to support other civil-liberties claims that they advanced in state courts.

This new judicial federalism, as it came to be called, quickly advanced beyond its initial concern to evade the Burger Court. Indeed, within two decades after it originated, it had become a nationwide phenomenon, and it has continued to be so to the present day. This is not surprising for when judges and scholars turned their attention to state constitutions, they discovered an unsuspected richness. They found not only provisions that paralleled the federal Bill of Rights but also constitutional guarantees—of the right to privacy and of gender equality, for example—that had no analogue in the U.S. Constitution. Careful examination of the text and history of state guarantees revealed important differences between even those provisions that most resembled federal guarantees and their federal counterparts. Looking beyond state declarations of rights, jurists and scholars discovered affirmative constitutional mandates to state governments to address such important policy concerns as education and housing. Taken altogether, these discoveries underlined the importance for the legal community of developing a better understanding of state constitutions.

Yet the renewed interest in state constitutions has not been limited to judges and lawyers. State constitutional reformers have renewed their efforts with notable success: since 1960, ten states have adopted new constitutions and several others have undertaken major constitutional revisions. These changes have usually resulted in more streamlined constitutions and more effective state governments. Also, in recent years political activists on both the left and the right have pursued their goals through state constitutional amendments, often enacted through the initiative process, under which policy proposals can be placed directly on the ballot for voters to endorse or reject. Scholars too have begun to rediscover how state constitutional history can illuminate changes in political thought and practice, providing a basis for theories about the dynamics of political change in America.

In this second edition, William Stewart updates his original study of the hefty Alabama Constitution as part of *The Oxford Commentaries on the State Constitutions of the United States*, a series which reflects the renewed interest in state constitutions and will contribute to our knowledge about them. Because the constitutional tradition of each state is distinctive, the volume begins with the history and development of constitutionalism in Alabama. It then provides the complete text of the state's current constitution, with each section accompanied with commentary that explains the provision and traces its origins and its interpretation by the courts and by other governmental bodies. Finally, the book concludes with a bibliography, a table of cases cited in the volume, and a topical index.

G. Alan Tarr

ACKNOWLEDGMENTS

I have been working on this second edition of the reference guide to the Alabama Constitution almost from the time the first edition came off the press. The Alabama legislature, which is the sole proposer of formal constitutional changes, is regularly sending amendments of one sort or another to the voters for their consideration (most of which are approved), and I have endeavored to keep up with them.

The influence of my parents and immediate family members was mentioned in the Acknowledgments section of the first edition and I will not repeat what I said there. Since the publication of the first edition, my former state senator, the Honorable Ryan deGraffenried has, sadly, passed away. Most of the constitutional materials he graciously made available to me when I was working on the first edition are now accessible online at the Alabama legislative website, ALISON. For data not so readily available I am indebted to Secretary of State John Merrill and his very able staff headed by a former student of mine, David Brewer. Assistance from an author's university library is always indispensable and, in the writing of this second edition, I have had the help most frequently of Kevin Walker and Michael Pearce of the University of Alabama's Gorgas Library.

Without question I am most indebted to Professor Michael DeBow of the Cumberland School of Law at Samford University. Professor DeBow has been the source of both information on case law and encouragement during the long process of putting the frequently arcane language of jurists into understandable English. Steven Noles, a practicing attorney, in Fort Payne, Alabama, has also been of assistance in providing additional perspectives on complex court rulings.

Let me conclude by repeating what I said in the Acknowledgments section of the first edition: I take full responsibility for the accuracy of the materials presented in this book and for the judgments I base upon them. If the reader discovers any errors, I am to blame for them.

PART ONE

The History of the Alabama Constitution

What follows is a commentary on the Alabama Constitution of 1901 from the perspective of a political scientist. It is not difficult to discern common themes historically and contemporaneously in the Alabama Constitution, and it is these that will be stressed here.

Alabama has had six Constitutions since it entered the Union. The first, the Constitution of 1819, was drafted as part of the admissions process and was among the most progressive of the states of the New West. An illustration of the Constitution's forward-looking character can be found in its granting of the right to vote to all free white males. There was no property-owning requirement. The original Constitution served the state well for forty-two years.

Each of the succeeding five Constitutions was closely tied to the relations between whites and African Americans in Alabama. The Constitution of 1861 is known as the "Secession Constitution," and it sought to legitimize the state's exit from the Union in the year the Civil War began. The failure of the Confederacy is reflected in the Constitution of 1865, which was adopted pursuant to the moderate postwar policies of President Andrew Johnson, successor to the assassinated President Abraham Lincoln. This Constitution prohibited slavery, declared the state's ordinance of secession null and void, and repudiated all debts incurred in the Civil War.

The collapse of the postwar Johnson program is reflected in the "Reconstruction Constitution" of 1868. This is the only Alabama Constitution which African Americans had a significant role in drafting. It was the most progressive of the six fundamental laws adopted between 1819 and 1901. Blacks participated freely in all aspects of Alabama political life and, along with liberally minded whites, were a vital element in the dominant Republican Party.

The failure of the program of Radical Reconstruction is reflected in the Constitution of 1875. Conservative whites were once again in charge of Alabama government, and they were determined to undo as much of the change in race relations as they could as soon as they could. By this time federal commitment to racial equality had greatly lessened, and white elites were able to take a number of measures to try to prevent future coalitions of Republicans, including both blacks and whites, from governing the state. The judgment had still not been made to try to totally rid the state of its new black electorate, however. It was not sufficiently clear how the U.S. Supreme Court would react to stringent disfranchising moves in the face of the clear language of the Fourteenth and especially the Fifteenth Amendments. Also, African-American voters were still seen as useful by white elites, who held many of them in their economic and social sway. The document the 1875 framers produced and proclaimed in effect reflected a strong desire to curb what they deemed to be the extravagant expenditures of the late 1860s and early 1870s.

By 1901 the hesitancy to effectively disfranchise blacks could be and was dispensed with. The Constitution drafted in Montgomery kept much of the 1875 document but added an elaborate panoply of measures to make sure that governing Alabama would be the business of white men only, especially white men from the southern areas of the state where human slavery had been most prominent before the Civil War. We will resume our discussion of the origins of the 1901 Constitution later.

The analysis which follows will focus on those provisions of the 1901 Constitution which have survived a total change in attitude regarding black political rights. The latter are null and void, as this Introduction will show. Also, in the years since 1901, Alabama's has become the nation's and possibly the world's longest Constitution, and many of the original sections have been replaced by amended versions. (Amendments pertaining to specific local areas are excluded from analysis here.)

CONSTITUTIONAL CHANGE IN A TRADITIONAL CULTURE

Constitutional change and development have occurred in Alabama in a culture of substantial nonparticipation of the masses in these processes. Inevitably identified as an example of a traditionalistic culture, Alabama is a state where the average citizen generally is expected to and normally does defer to elites in most decision-making activities (see Daniel J. Elazar, *American Federalism: A View from the States*, 2d ed. [New York: Thomas Y. Crowell Co., 1972], pp. 93ff.). Thus the

Alabama Constitution contains no provisions whereby the people themselves may undertake to change it or even begin the process of change. All proposals for change must first win the support of the legislature.

Of course, substantial change has occurred since 1901. While many post-1901 revisions are the result of processes envisaged by the framers, much crucial change has come about as the federal government has functioned as a safety valve for groups, most notably African Americans, who were unable to obtain relief through the normal constitutional channels. The whole edifice of discriminatory voting regulations was designed to maintain a system of elite rule which is an integral part of traditionalistic political culture. Following its being declared unconstitutional or superseded by federal law, a new Article VIII was adopted in 1996 to replace the discredited one. Even though racial barriers have crumbled, elites have continued to use their political clout and regularly employ the Constitution as a means of improving the extrinsic rewards they receive from public service. One of the major formal constitutional changes came in 1968 when the Constitution was amended (Section 116) to allow the governor and other constitutional executive officers to succeed themselves in office.

The kind of piecemeal constitutional change that Alabama has experienced since 1901 has been facilitated because of the ease with which the document may be formally amended. As this volume goes to press, there have been 893 amendments to the Constitution which emerged from the Montgomery convention of 1901. The last amendment is numbered 892, but there was a mistake in numbering many years ago. Approximately 70 percent of the amendments are local in character. Passing such amendments through the legislature usually has not been difficult if members from the local areas affected were supportive. Until 1982 such amendments nevertheless had to be ratified in a statewide referendum. However, under terms of Section 284.01 (Amendments 425 and 555, 1982 and 1994) if an ex officio commission classifies amendments as local, they are voted on only by the areas mentioned in the proposals. Because the original procedure was held to be racially discriminatory by the U.S. Justice Department, the revision article itself was revised to remove the possibility that proposed amendments could be differentiated as statewide or local based on racial grounds.

Alabama courts have generally encouraged legislative development of the Constitution by not demonstrating eagerness to declare their enactments unconstitutional. For example, in 1939 the Court said, "When an act is susceptible to two constructions, one of which would render it offensive to the Constitution and the other would not, the construction most favorable to the Constitution should be given though the less natural one." (J. Blach & Sons v. Hawkins, 189 So. 726)

The fact that the legislative article comes first and is longer than those dealing with the executive and judiciary points to the legacy of legislative supremacy in the American states. A year before the present Constitution went into effect, the

Court observed that the states' reserved powers under the U.S. Constitution are exercisable by the legislature, except for the limitations contained in either the federal or state constitutions. (Sheppard v. Dowling, 28 So. 791 (1900))

The judiciary has also facilitated the process of constitutional change in Alabama by at times making rulings which otherwise would appear to be irrational. For example, the Court holds that the acts of public corporations set up to perform particular government functions, especially as related to economic development, are not state acts. (See Curtis v. Alabama River Development Agency, 372 So. 2d 353 (Civ. App. 1979).) The state Supreme Court has also held, "Public hospital corporations . . . are not political subdivisions of the state of Alabama." (Alabama Hospital Association v. Dillard, 388 So. 2d 903 (1980)) Further, "debts of a public corporation or quasi-corporation are not debts against the state . . . and do not constitute indebtedness of a county or municipality." (See Opinion of the Justices, 49 So. 2d 175 (1950).)

This pattern of constitutional accommodation has not been altogether consistent. For example, the Court has been unwilling to expand gubernatorial power by its decisions to the extent that the governor could appropriate funds when the legislature, as sometimes happens, adjourns its regular legislative session with basic public appropriations still not made. (See Wallace v. Baker, 336 So. 2d 156 (1976).) Section 71.01 (Amendment 448, 1984) confirms the executive budget; however, with so much earmarking as Alabama utilizes (about 90 percent), its meaning is greatly constricted. Traditionally, the judiciary has foresworn itself of any power to levy taxes. The decision of the Court in Bozeman v. Conecuh County Board of Education is the controlling one. There the Court observed: "The imposition of taxes is a legislative prerogative. Certainly the courts have no such power." (213 So. 2d 388 (1968)) Also, in the mid-1970s the Alabama Supreme Court declared: "The authority to determine the amount of appropriations necessary for the performance of the essential functions of government is vested fully and exclusively in the legislature." (Morgan County Commission v. Powell, 293 So. 2d 830 (1974))

Possibly the most significant formal constitutional change made since 1901 was the article dealing with the courts (VI), the judicial reform article ratified in 1973 as Amendment 326. This amendment provided for a much more unified judicial system than previously and one better organized to guide constitutional development in the state.

CONSTITUTIONAL CONTINUITY

In the sense that the Constitution of 1901 reflected a continuation of the white supremacist sentiment behind the immediately preceding Constitution of 1875, there are close linkages between these two documents. However, the Constitution of 1901 also reflects continuity with preceding state constitutions as well as a body of law dating back many centuries.

Section 11, for example, which deals with the right to a jury trial, is defined in a distant historical context. Despite what the Constitution seems to say here, the Alabama Supreme Court ruled many years ago that this right did not apply to every situation in which an individual might be put on trial and face the possibility of punishment or loss of property. Instead, the right was more circumscribed than this, being limited to the types of cases in which the right to a jury trial existed under the common law, or in which it was guaranteed when the original 1819 Constitution went into effect. (Boring v. Williams, 17 Ala. 510 (1850)) This decision, although rendered in 1850 and based on the original Constitution of 1819 is still good constitutional law. Indeed, the Court of Criminal Appeals reasserted in 1984 that the purpose of Section 11 was "to preserve the right to trial by jury as it existed in the English common law." (Crowe v. State, 485 So. 2d 351 (Crim. App.)) It was "not intended to extend the right of trial by jury beyond that which existed prior to the [1819] Constitution." (Ibid.)

The common law also influences the regular operations of governmental institutions. For example, under the current interpretation of common law a state legislator cannot serve simultaneously as an officer in a local political subdivision. (See 89 American Law Reports, Annotated 632.) In the view of the ancient authors of the common law, these offices would be mutually incompatible. With regard to Section 89, which very generally declares, "The Legislature shall not have power to authorize any municipal corporation to pass any laws inconsistent with the general laws of the state," the Alabama Supreme Court observed in 1966 that this language was "merely reiteration of a common law rule and an application of that rule to the legislature." (Winter v. Cain, 187 So. 2d 237 (1966))

The common law influence on Alabama constitutional development would in time begin to weaken. For example, in 1931 the Alabama Court of Appeals said that Section 3, which reads in part "that no religious test shall be required as a qualification to an office of public trust," did away with the common law rule which asserted that witnesses could not be regarded as credible unless they believed in a God who rewarded truth and condemned falsehood. (Wright v. State, 135 So. 636 (App.)) Also, in interpreting Section 111.01 (390, 1980), authorizing termination of alimony upon the remarriage or cohabitation of the receiving spouse, the court observed that divorce was not a right enjoyed by couples under the common law; it had a solely statutory basis. (Note that when two numbers are presented in parentheses as in the previous sentence the first number is that of the applicable constitutional amendment, the second is the year in which it was ratified.) (Oliver v. Oliver, 431 So. 2d 1271 (Civ. App. 1983))

Section 13, which is the state Constitution's version of the U.S. Constitution's due process clause as contained in the Fifth and Fourteenth Amendments, goes back to the original Constitution of 1819. But it goes back much further than this. The Alabama Supreme Court observed in 1885 that it grew out of "the existing evil of anciently holding courts in clandestine sessions, and of paying fines to the king and his officers for delaying or expediting lawsuits and for obtaining justice." (Swann v. Kidd, 79 Ala. 431) Section 14, which requires some of the most extensive commentary presented in this volume, dealing as it does with the complex question of the liability of governments and their agents for lawsuits, also traces back to the English monarchy. The Alabama Supreme Court observed in the 1980s that, as English constitutional law developed, the idea took hold that, "while the king himself could not be charged with wrongdoing, his ministers were personally responsible when they acted illegally." (Quoted in DeStafney v. University of Alabama, 413 So. 2d 391 (1981))

There is precious little in the Alabama Constitution, original or amended, of direct benefit to the poor. However, the Court observed during the depths of the Great Depression that, in situations such as prevailed in the 1930s, where there was a pervasive hardship facing the population generally, the legislature did not have to justify its actions on the basis of any particular constitutional provisions but could take action under its police power to relieve suffering. (Beeland Wholesale Co. v. Kaufman, 174 So. 516 (1937).) Section 88 specifically gives the legislature the right to require counties to assist the poor. However, an amendment to the Constitution (425, 1957), identified in the recompiled document as Section 215.04, was required to give them the specific authority to pay their hospital bills. (See Opinion of the Justices, 95 So. 2d 923 (1957).)

■ BLACK-WHITE RELATIONS

The reader who is at all familiar with the Constitution knows that it is impossible to separate Alabama constitutionalism from issues of race relations. As we observed at the outset of this Introduction, the initial motivations for the Constitutions of 1861, 1868, 1875, and 1901 pertained mostly to race. One cannot presume to understand the Constitution without an appreciation of the politics of race. To be sure, this is not the only theme in Alabama constitutionalism, but it is the one that it would be most perilous to underemphasize. Space demands related to the extraordinary length of the Alabama Constitution prevent giving any particular theme, including race, the attention it deserves. However, the Bibliography lists works that contain excellent and lengthy discussions to which the reader should refer.

By 1901 the U.S. Supreme Court had indicated that it would tolerate a great deal in the way of white efforts to prevent black Americans from voting. Thus Alabama elites were anxious to join other southern states in framing and adopting a constitution that would, in a relatively short period of time, do just that. Since substantial numbers of blacks were still casting ballots, it would be necessary to manipulate the black electorate in the campaign to ratify the 1901 Constitution. Blacks would need to be used to endorse their own disfranchisement in order to counter the correctly anticipated opposition to the Constitution among whites in north Alabama.

The Alabama courts provided little if any protection to blacks who resisted efforts to politically emasculate themselves. For example, when in 1903, the state Supreme Court was asked to abrogate discriminatory voting regulations as antithetical to the Fourteenth and Fifteenth Amendments, they supported almost complete discretion in the hands of local (white) boards of registrars. (See Giles v. Teasley, 33 So. 820.) In the same year (1903), the U.S. Supreme Court said that a federal circuit court in Alabama lacked the authority to require a local board of voter registrars to sign up Jackson W. Giles, an African American who was being unconstitutionally denied his right to vote. The decision was written by Justice Oliver Wendell Holmes (Giles v. Harris, 189 U.S. 475). The framers of the Alabama Constitution were definitely of the opinion that it should never be too convenient to register and vote, even for whites. Alabama would be one of the states most affected by the "motor voter" bill passed by Congress in 1993 at the urging of President Bill Clinton. This legislation has greatly facilitated the registration of voters.

Ironically, even though the overweening importance of race to understanding the Alabama Constitution is stressed here, readers will not observe a great amount of constitutional language pertaining to race as they read this book. As previously pointed out, explicitly racial provisions of the Constitution have repeatedly been declared unconstitutional (or are patently illegal today) and thus are not operable parts of the current Alabama Constitution. Original and subsequent provisions of the 1901 Constitution which have been voided as a result of federal actions are not included here.

It is a fundamental principle of the American federal system that state laws are subject to central review, ultimately by the Supreme Court of the United States, and, as this Court became more vigilant in the mid-twentieth century to enforce both the letter and spirit of the federal Constitution, more and more of Alabama's 1901 constitutional infrastructure against the exercise of equal rights by blacks crumbled under the federal weight.

The early dual federalism which assisted Alabama in maintaining racial segregation in public facilities and an overwhelming white electorate eventually gave way to a national federalism reflected in judicial validations of constitutional protections dating from Reconstruction days and executive and legislative initiatives of more recent date that put real teeth into these constitutional guarantees.

Some of the Alabama constitutional provisions which are not explicitly racial have, nonetheless, been used in an effort to maintain the racial status quo. For example, Section 131, which makes the governor the commander in chief, was interpreted during the massive resistance era in 1963 to allow then-Governor George C. Wallace to close down the public schools if, in his opinion, such a step was necessary to preserve order. (See Opinion of the Justices, 156 So. 2d 639.) There was an equation of peace with the suppression of black political rights. However, Section 131 also reflects the reality that the president can take control of the state National Guard at his discretion. This happened most spectacularly, also in 1963, when President John F. Kennedy federalized the Guard to facilitate the integration of the University of Alabama after Governor Wallace's infamous "stand in the schoolhouse door."

At the beginning of the massive resistance era in 1956, the Constitution was amended (Amendment 111) to remove the "right" to a public education. This change was later ruled invalid, thus paving the way in 1993 for Montgomery Circuit Judge Eugene Reese to find that thousands of Alabama children, both black and white, were being denied an "adequate" public education as guaranteed by the original 1901 Constitution. (Alabama Coalition for Equity v. Hunt (1993 WL, 204083 (Ala. Cir.)) In 1962 a more passive judge had said that, given the adoption of Amendment 111 as part of the massive resistance program, "Alabama [was] under no constitutional obligation to provide public schools." (Mitchell v. Metcalf, 143 So. 2d 629)

The era of using the Constitution and laws of Alabama to foster and protect a particular, white-dominated system of race relations came to an official end later in the 1960s. In one of the most important federal cases decided during this period, Lee v. Macon, the federal court took notice of the fact that Alabama state officials had for many years done all within their power to maintain racial segregation in state schools. (267 F. Supp. 458 (1967)) This could no longer be tolerated, however, and these officials would now have to discharge a higher constitutional responsibility than that to the state. They would have to fulfill their federal constitutional obligation to help rid the state of the now constitutionally discredited dual public school system.

In the area of voting, Congress and the federal courts finally, over a period of years, struck down virtually every discriminatory barrier standing in the path of full and free African-American suffrage. For example, the Alabama Constitution once contained a long list of petty criminal offenses which would bar an individual from voting. In requiring Alabama to forsake some of its prejudices, the U.S. Supreme Court held that the original inclusion of such language in the Alabama Constitution "was motivated by a desire to discriminate against blacks on account of race, and [it] continues to this day to have that effect." Thus most of Section 182 could not measure up to the standard of the equal protection clause of the Fourteenth Amendment. (Hunter v. Underwood, 471 U.S. 222 (1985))

The primary way Alabama's constitutional development in the area of political participation was federally influenced was through congressional enactment and successive strengthening reenactments of the Voting Rights Act of 1965 (VRA). This crucial law, among other provisions, required preclearance of all proposed new state and local legislation impacting on voting. (This mandate was struck down by the U.S. Supreme Court in 2013. (Shelby County v. Holder, 133 S. Ct. 2612)) The VRA also suspended the literacy tests which were still in effect when this law was originally passed.

Another area closely related to race in which federal officials (primarily federal judges) influenced constitutional development under the 1901

Constitution dealt with legislative reapportionment. Despite the mandate contained in Section 199 to have legislative reapportionment after each decennial census, the legislature never responded until the judicially inspired "reapportionment revolution" of the 1960s. The reapportionment requirements of the Constitution were defective with regard to the strict use of population as the basis for representation (e.g., the provision that each county regardless of population would have at least one member of the House of Representatives). However, the failure of the legislature to make any changes at all for such a long time probably contributed to the radical character of the changes which were ultimately imposed by the federal courts. In the Tennessee case of Baker v. Carr (369 U.S. 186 (1962)) and the Alabama case of Reynolds v. Sims (377 U.S. 533 (1964)), the U.S. Supreme Court required both houses of the state legislature to be apportioned strictly on the basis of population. While the federal district court would give some weight to state constitutional standards, if a conflict was found between federal and state constitutional provisions, the supremacy clause of the U.S. Constitution would have to prevail, and any inconsistent language in the Alabama Constitution would yield. (Sims v. Frink, 205 F. Supp. 245 (M.D. Ala. 1962)) The state judiciary had been unwilling to take a leadership role here. For example, in 1950 the Alabama Supreme Court rejected the argument that "the legislature could make no law nor do any act since it [had] not complied with [the Constitution] by reapportioning the membership of the legislature." (Bonds v. State Department of Revenue, 49 So. 2d 280) Also, the Court advised five years later that a bill which would have established a board of apportionment and given it authority to effect legislative reapportionment after each census would amount to an unacceptable delegation of legislative power. (Opinion of the Justices, 81 So. 2d 697 (1955))

Although the Alabama Constitution originally called for multimember districts in counties rather than single-member districts, the federal courts would conclude in the early 1970s that this arrangement, although not avowedly racial, nevertheless worked against blacks having fair opportunities to be elected to public office. This was because of polarized voting among blacks and whites. (See Sims v. Amos, 336 F. Supp. 924 (M.D. Ala. 1972).) As will be observed, the weight of Alabama constitutional law is still stacked against progressive and liberal legislation, the impact of which would redound primarily to the benefit of lower income blacks and whites. The Alabama traditional political culture continues to reflect the belief that an elite ought to rule and that the masses of people should not take much of a part in politics. The Alabama Constitution continues to be a formidable barrier to its own use as any kind of device of popular democracy.

Before concluding this section, however, one should note state constitutional evidences of movement toward a more racially sensitive society. The Alabama courts have responded to decisions of the Supreme Court of the United States in the area of jury selection, such as Batson v. Kentucky (479 U.S. 79 (1986)), in a very favorable way. For example, the Alabama Supreme Court, also in 1986, ruled that the prosecution must present legitimate nonracial reasons for peremptory jury strikes. (See Jackson v. State, 516 So. 2d 768.) Even affirmative action has made its ways into the Alabama Constitution. The Forever Wild Amendment (Section 219.08) specifically provides that, as far as the governing board of the program is concerned, "at least one appointee by the Governor, at least one appointee by the Lieutenant Governor and at least one appointee by the Speaker of the House of Representatives shall be black."

THE ALABAMA AND U.S. CONSTITUTIONS

In considering the general subject of Alabama constitutional development, special attention must be given to the influence of the federal Constitution on Alabama Constitutions, particularly the Constitution of 1901. This is obvious from the highly inclusive racial context as illustrated in the immediately preceding paragraphs, but perspectives from other areas are also needed.

In some cases, state constitutional language represents only a slight modification of the language found in the U.S. Constitution. For example, Section 123: "The governor shall, from time to time, give to the legislature information of the state of the government." Compare this to: "He [the president] shall from time to time give to the Congress information of the state of the Union." (Article II, Section 3, U.S. Constitution)

There is a natural tendency in the case of a state such as Alabama to stress the asymmetries between the state and federal constitutions, primarily because of extremely abrasive relations in the area of race relations over a period of many years. However, it is also important to try to identify consistent patterns of constitutional development, particularly in recent times as the race issue has ceased to be as divisive as it was either when the Constitution of 1901 went into effect or in the era of massive resistance following the Supreme Court's decision in Brown v. Board of Education (347 U.S. 483 (1954)).

In a 1978 case, the Court of Criminal Appeals stressed that the Alabama Constitution "afford[ed] no less protection to its citizens than that afforded by the United States Constitution." (Ford v. Sims, 356 So. 2d 720 (Crim. App.)) The court was particularly concerned with the procedural safeguards of Section 6 in this case. Whether or not this statement is true, it does indicate more of an orientation toward individual rights than used to be the case. In the context of the notorious Scottsboro Boys trials of the 1930s, the Alabama Supreme Court ruled in 1932 that one of the African Americans accused, who was placed on trial on April 8, 1931, for a rape alleged to have taken place on March 25, 1931, had not been denied his rights to a fair and impartial trial. Nor had he been tried too speedily. (Powell v. State, 141 So. 201)

The pace of constitutional development in Alabama in the area of civil liberties has generally been behind federal development. Aside from crucial cultural factors, the constitutional language with which state judges have had to work (and which importantly reflects cultural values) has been more limiting. For example, Section 4, which recognizes the freedom of speech and of the press, cautions that the exerciser is "responsible for the abuse of that liberty." Section 12, while stating a reasonably stringent standard to prove libel, also speaks about information related to public affairs which "is proper for public information." One of the pathbreaking U.S. Supreme Court decisions in the area of freedom of the press came when the nation's highest Court reversed an Alabama Supreme Court ruling against the editor of the *Birmingham Post-Herald* for editorializing on election day. (See State v. Mills, 176 So. 2d 884 (1965), rev'd in 384 U.S. 214 (1966).)

Much of the increasing symmetry between the Alabama and U.S. Constitutions, as observed particularly in the second half of the twentieth century, was not because of a sudden coalescing of thought among Alabama and federal Constitution makers and interpreters. It was because Alabama Constitution provisions were found inconsistent with federal guarantees, and federal authorities simply would not tolerate the kind of conduct demonstrated in the Scottsboro cases just mentioned.

Again in the area of criminal procedure, the appellate court recognized in 1964 that, "[i]nasmuch as Mapp v. Ohio [367 U.S. 643 (1961)] brings the Fourth Amendment to bear upon state trials, it would seem that the minimum degree of proof established under the Fourth Amendment would necessarily be the minimum for the issuance of a state search warrant." (Brown v. State, 167 So. 2d 281 (App.)) In 1971 the Supreme Court of Alabama held that "the privilege against self-incrimination afforded by the Fifth Amendment to the Constitution of the United States applies to state actions." (International Board of Teamsters v. Hatas, 252 So. 2d 7) The Alabama Court of Criminal Appeals acknowledged in 1973, "When rules of state practice and procedure conflict with the due process clause of the Fourteenth Amendment they must yield to the commandments of that amendment." (Nelson v. State, 278 So. 2d 734 (Crim. App.)) And, in the mid-1980s, showing the new harmony between the federal and Alabama Constitutions in the area of procedural safeguards, the Alabama appeals court noted, "The use of the post-arrest, post-Miranda warning silence of the accused as evidence of his guilt is a violation of the Due Process Clauses of both the Fourteenth Amendment to the Constitution of the United States and Section Six of the Alabama Constitution." (Quoted in Mead v. State, 472 So. 2d (Crim. App.)) Before the Miranda ruling, Section 6 of the Alabama Constitution was not viewed so stringently.

In 1971 the federal court reminded the state that the attorney general was "required by his oath of office to support and defend the Constitution of the United States of America." (Delchamps v. Alabama State Milk Control Board, 324 F. Supp. 117) "When and if there is a conflict between the state law and the federal law in areas where the federal law is applicable," the court continued, "the [U.S.] supremacy clause controls." (Ibid.) In the same year (1971), the Alabama Supreme Court observed that even though Section 232 (now updated by Section 211.03, Amendment 662, 2000) defines what "doing business" in Alabama means, ultimately "federal authorities would be controlling on the question of what constitutes 'doing business.'" (City Stores v. Williams, 252 So. 2d 45) Neither of these was a race-related case.

In the area of taxation, the federal courts have taken Alabama to task because of faulty assessment practices. In 1971 the federal judges said the state should have lived up to its then operating constitutional commitment, namely, that "the property of private corporations, associations, and individuals of this state shall forever be taxed at the same rate." (old Section 217) The failure of the state to adhere to this commitment "offend[ed] the Due Process and Equal Protection clauses of the Fourteenth Amendment" of the U.S. Constitution. (Weissinger v. Boswell, 330 F. Supp. 615 (M.D. Ala.)) This decision necessitated constitutional change which, as will be seen, was in the direction of a federally acceptable classification plan.

In 1978 the Alabama Supreme Court held that a law which offered governmental immunity from damage suits but used a population figure that applied only to the city of Birmingham did not have a sufficiently reasonable relationship to the supposed object of the legislation and thus failed to satisfy the equal protection requirements of the U.S. Constitution. (Peddycoart v. Birmingham, 354 So. 2d 808 (1978))

DEBT AND TAXES

Reconstruction and its resulting unpaid debts were still in the minds of the framers of the 1901 Constitution at the time of its adoption. Even the amended Section 215 (208), ratified as recently as 1962, made reference to the long-cleared carpetbag debt. The framers of the Constitution of 1901 were very eager to obstruct the creation of new debt.

The Court's "review of the proceedings of the constitutional convention of 1901 . . . evidence[d] a purpose on the part of the framers of the Constitution to prevent the counties and cities of the state from loading themselves, by local legislation, with bond or security issues and thereby placing undue burdens on the local taxpayers and citizens without their having a voice in the matter." (Newton v. Tuscaloosa, 36 So. 2d 487 (1948)) Local governments must be restrained should they be tempted to begin programs which men of property would have to pay for. To overcome the original restrictions, many constitutional changes in the form of hundreds of local amendments would be needed. The Constitution originally required new indebtedness, particularly for capital improvements, to be legitimated by a statewide constitutional amendment.

Local governments in Alabama are held not to have any inherent powers. Thus to increase their powers it frequently has been necessary to amend the Constitution. The Court held in 1888 that local governments in this state did not have any inherent power to tax. Any power they had in this area was a result of grants from the legislature. (Hare v. Kennerly, 3 So. 683) But, despite the absence of any inherent power, due to the ease with which the Alabama Constitution could be amended, local governments were frequently able to get permission to engage in those activities which a governing elite consensus had grudgingly decided could be done, if they must—at the local level.

Section 222.04 (26, 1933) reflects the continuing commitment of the state to a balanced budget. It calls for proration of funds when revenues received do not equal amounts appropriated by law. The Court observed in 1946 that Section 213 requires "the annual financial operations of the State to be on a balanced budget and prevents any department of the State from making a State Debt." (Norton v. Lusk, 26 So. 2d 849)

Section 222.04 (228, 1965), dealing with the issuance of bonds by municipalities to encourage economic development, provides local governments with the debt flexibility to enable them to engage in the very kinds of activities which the framers of 1901 wished to forbid. In the case last noted, the Alabama Supreme Court accommodated the expansion of debt by making the artificial distinction between public corporation debts and "regular" debts. "When a state corporation is set up to perform an important public purpose," the Court ruled, "it may be given the power to, and may, create a debt on its own account, without any liability or debt imposed on the state." (Norton v. Lusk, 26 So. 2d 849 (1946))

As the framers of 1901 opposed new debt, so they also opposed new taxes. Presumably, new taxes would not be needed if state and local debt could be held down. However, new debt has been incurred to an extent which would have horrified the 1901 framers, and evading original limits has also been the cause of constitutional change in the form of numerous bond issues. They have not been included here because the bonds have already been issued. More of these amendments related to the docks than to any other governmental activity.

Additional property taxes were most opposed by the framers of 1901. Thus the stress from the beginning has been to keep property taxes low. Section 214 of the original Constitution specified that the legislature would "not have the power to levy in any one year a greater rate of taxation than sixty-five one-hundredths of one percentum on the value of the taxable property within this state." Provisions such as this one meant that constitutional amendments would be required to authorize specific new property taxes for designated purposes. Also, reliance would have to be placed increasingly on regressive taxes, especially sales and income taxes. The latter are potentially progressive but, because of the specificity of rates contained in the amendments authorizing them, much less so than tax reformers desire. Sales taxes are not mentioned in the original Constitution and thus have not required constitutional amendments for their imposition. There has also been an emphasis on sin taxes (particularly on cigarettes and alcoholic beverages) to finance bond issues for various kinds of public improvements and facilities, as well as the application of user fees. For example, Section 219.01 (272, 1972) established the game and fish fund. It provides for a strict earmarking of all funds collected from the primary beneficiaries of the programs authorized through Amendment 272.

Even though Alabama already had very low property taxes, the state was nevertheless caught up in the anti–property tax mood in the United States in the late 1970s, best symbolized by California's "Proposition 13" movement. Section 217 (373), adopted in 1978 and popularly known as the "lid bill," continued the anti-tax theme, as will be seen when the reader examines this section. Rates of property taxes remain minimal, and it is difficult for local elites desiring to raise them to act. All new local initiatives relative to property taxes also require state legislative action. To increase local property taxes for a specific county/community/district, it is mandatory not only to have a local popular vote (a favorable outcome of which is highly problematic), but it is also necessary to have a favorable vote of the entire legislature. (The wishes of the local legislative delegation would be crucial here.)

■ RELIGION AND THE CONSTITUTION

It is impossible to discuss constitutional development in Alabama without an understanding of the role religion has played in this state. The Constitution both reflects and regulates this role. Alabama is one of the states of the traditional "Bible Belt," and religion has always been an important aspect of the state's constitutional system. The language of the 1901 Constitution reflects a lesser commitment to the principle of separating church and state than does the federal Constitution. Section 3 uses language which the U.S. Supreme Court specifically rejects as an appropriate basis for defining the relationship between religion and government in the United States: "that no preference shall be given by law to any religious sect, society, denomination, or mode of worship."

Because of the traditional lack of responsiveness on the part of the state in this area, most controversies related to church and state in Alabama do not go to state court on the basis of Section 3 but to federal court on the foundation of the First Amendment of the U.S. Constitution. While several provisions of the Constitution are sympathetic toward a blending of church and state, there has been little support for direct state aid to parochial schools, which would have been, until relatively recently, aid essentially to the small number of Catholic schools.

At present, the dominant Protestant strain of religious values is most apparent in the debate over whether constitutional changes should be made which would allow for a state lottery. Proposals to rescind the ban on lotteries contained in Section 65 have been made frequently in recent years. The now-dominant Republican Party has been mostly opposed to a state lottery, however. In continuing bans from previous constitutions (see Buckalew v. State, 62 Ala.

334 (1878) and Loiseau v. State, 22 So. 138 (1897)), the framers of 1901 had sought to prevent legalized gambling in Alabama.

The most salient public policy reflective of Alabama's religious environment for the longest time was that of alcoholic beverage policy. The Constitution of 1901 was written when Prohibition sentiment was very strong and gaining further momentum, if not always consistently. Thus numerous provisions in the Constitution relate to the sale of alcoholic beverages. The courts have frequently tempered zealous regulatory sentiment with their decisions. For example, in 1975 the Alabama Supreme Court held that a $5,000 annual city beer license was not valid since "the only conceivable purpose [was] to totally prohibit the sale of beer." (Lawrence v. Gayle, 312 So. 2d 385) But the Court, in interpreting the Constitution, also rules that "[t]he legislative power to regulate the sale of liquor is absolute. [It] may regulate it as it sees it, or prohibit it entirely." (Ebony Club v. State, 318 So. 2d 282 (1975))

Even as there was for many years a very strong desire to minimize the availability of alcoholic beverages and to use the Constitution to achieve this objective, there was also much evidence of a schizophrenic situation in this area of public policy. Public officials were frequently involved in cases clearly involving abuse of the supposedly scarce liquor. In 1915 the Alabama Supreme Court found that a judge of probate had been "a very near constant alcoholic drinker" over a period of many years and that this greatly diminished his "mental and moral faculties and more normal sensibilities." (State v. Pratt, 68 So. 255) Thus his removal from office was in order under Section 173, which identifies alcohol abuse as one of the grounds for impeachment.

Many cases that have come before the courts in the area of search and seizures have involved alcoholic beverages. At present they are more likely to involve illegal drugs.

INTEREST GROUPS

It is impossible to discuss constitutional development in Alabama without recognizing the power of interest groups, both organized and unorganized. All of the concerns addressed thus far reflect interest concerns. In some important respects, moreover, they also reflect the activities of highly structured, quasi-public groups. For example, the promotion amendments to the Constitution were passed at the behest of particular agricultural groups. The power of higher educational interests is reflected in the Constitution, particularly the University of Alabama and Auburn University. Long before the Alabama Education Association (AEA) was a powerhouse in Alabama politics, the Alabama Medical Association was held to be an appropriate constitutional depository of power so far as medical policy was concerned (reiterated in Evers v. Board of Medical Examiners, 516 So. 2d 650 (Civ. App. 1987)). In the area of taxation, the current Section 217 (Amendment 373) very much reflects the interests of such groups as the Alabama Farmers Federation and large timber companies. All businesses benefit from Section 211.03 (212, 1963; 662, 2000), which guarantees that they will "always" be permitted to deduct federal income taxes when computing their state tax liability. Private power influence is reflected, for example, in Section 93.13 (227, 1965), which forbids the use of its provisions to allow any more public power, despite the fact that this was not even an issue at the time the amendment was being debated.

■ EXTRA-CONSTITUTIONAL CHANGE

Ironically, most of the changes made in the Constitution since 1901 as a result of state action are probably not as important as state actions which have taken other forms such as gubernatorial leadership and legislative policy making. The Alabama executive branch, for example, still bears the marks of the highly significant reorganization implemented during the administration of Governor Frank M. Dixon (1939–43). These changes occurred for the most part through executive order and legislative enactment; they did not require changes in the formal Constitution document. Specialized statutory provisions were able to circumvent presumably more sacrosanct constitutional language. Professionalization and increasing bureaucratization of government did an end run around the Constitution.

■ FUTURE CONSTITUTIONAL CHANGE

As far as future constitutional change in Alabama is concerned, it is unlikely that a convention will be assembled to replace the one that is the subject of this volume. Constitutional change has not been an issue in the most recent campaigns for major state offices, and political leaders, currently wrestling particularly with controversies pertaining to financial shortfalls, appear to believe they have quite enough on their respective plates. Thus, one can expect that constitution-related matters will continue to be dealt with on an incremental, piecemeal basis.

As will be noted later in the book related to language dealing with constitutional change, the Alabama Supreme Court resisted efforts of the formerly Democratic legislature to simply clean up the present Constitution. It also gave the opinion that, contrary to the practice in some other states, it would not be possible to assemble a convention to deal with only named subjects. (See Opinion of the Justices, 81 So. 2d 678 (1955).) Republicans in the legislature, in the majority since 2010, have shown little interest in constitutional reform, although they have recompiled the Constitution to include amendments within appropriate articles rather than simply being tacked on at the end.

The most serious effort directed toward systematic constitutional change came in 1969 when, under the leadership of then-Governor Albert P. Brewer, the legislature created the Alabama Constitutional Commission to study the existing

Constitution and make recommendations for needed changes. Unfortunately for the cause of constitutional change, Governor Brewer remained in office only until early 1971. At that time George C. Wallace returned to the governorship, and this issue was not one in which he was interested. Nevertheless, a reformed judicial article did pass in 1973, and in 1975 voters did approve annual legislative sessions, both of which had been endorsed by the constitutional commission. (The work of the Commission is discussed at length in William H. Stewart, Jr., The Alabama Constitutional Commission [Tuscaloosa: University of Alabama Press, 1975].)

More recently, Republican Governor Bob Riley named a constitutional commission shortly after he assumed office in 2003. However, its modest proposals for change were not greeted warmly by the still-Democratic legislature. Finally, another Brewer-led commission was created by a now Republican-majority legislature, and it continues to work with little publicity as this volume goes to press. On a positive note, voters have approved new constitutional articles dealing with voting, corporations, and banking, none of which were controversial.

▪ A FINAL WORD ABOUT CONSTITUTIONAL LENGTH

The most obvious characteristic of constitutional change in Alabama has been growth in the length of the Constitution itself, irrespective of the particular subjects of the additions as briefly surveyed in this Introduction.

The Constitution began as a long document and has grown increasingly longer ever since. It is a horror story as far as state constitutional purists are concerned. The Alabama Constitution is the very opposite of what normativists believe a state constitution should be. In a document as long as the Alabama Constitution, there would be many candidates for the "worst," most "unconstitutional" provision. The present author's candidate would probably be Clause 2 of Section 219.02 (450, 1985) related to the Alabama trust funds, which says: "All corporate securities shall at the time of purchase by the [trust fund] Board carry a rating of 'A' or better by Moody and/or Standard and Poor's."

At this point we will begin a section-by-section analysis of the Official Recompilation of the Alabama Constitution of 1901. Readers familiar with the first edition of this book will note that its amendments have been placed where they best fit within the subject-matter articles. An explanation of the reasons for the exclusion of particular sections from the analysis that follows immediately may be found in the Appendix.

PART TWO

The Alabama Constitution and Commentary

Preamble

> We, the people of the State of Alabama, in order to establish justice, insure domestic tranquility, and secure the blessings of liberty to ourselves and our posterity, invoking the favor and guidance of Almighty God, do ordain and establish the following Constitution and form of government for the State of Alabama.

The preamble of any constitution is generally considered to be an unenforceable, generalized statement of the source of governmental power and the fundamental goals actuating the writing of the document. (See Justin Orlando, *Constitutional Preambles: At a Crossroads between Politics and Law*, Santarcangelo: Maggoli Editore, 2012, esp. Ch. 2.) This preamble is most similar to that which introduced the 1865 Constitution.

Article I

Declaration of Rights

That the great, general, and essential principles of liberty and free government may be recognized and established, we declare:

SECTION 1.

That all men are equally free and independent, that they are endowed by their Creator with certain inalienable rights; that among these are life, liberty and the pursuit of happiness.

This section, along with Sections 6 and 22, collectively, are sometimes said to be the equivalents of the equal protection clause of the Fourteenth Amendment of the U.S. Constitution. (See Pickett v. Matthews, 192 So. 261 (1939).) Where possible, the citation is to the more generally available Southern reports of decisions. The language here is exactly that which appeared in the 1875 Constitution. The clause is also held to guarantee due process of law and to bar unalterable, monopolistic awards of governmental favor. (This was the ruling in the Pickett case.) To make matters more confusing, however, the Court of Civil Appeals used the fact that Alabama has no "equal-protection provision" to decide the case of Melof v. James in 1998. (735 So. 2d 1166) Freedom of the press, freedom of movement, and the opportunity to earn a living are also included within the protections offered by this section. The language here is, of course, very reminiscent of the Declaration of Independence. If there is a discrepancy between a couple of sections of the Alabama Constitution, the provision which is part of the Declaration of Rights will be the controlling one. (Henderson by and through Hartsfield v. Alabama Power Co., 627 So. 2d 878 (1993)) This is similar to the approach the U.S. Supreme Court takes with respect to the Bill of Rights. In 1983 the Alabama Supreme Court (or, the Court, which hereinafter always refers to Alabama's highest court unless otherwise indicated) held that taxing gummed cigarette paper quite a bit higher than ungummed papers was an unequal classification that violated this section. (Robert Burton Associates v. Eagerton, 432 So. 2d 1267)) A close approximation to the clause was also included in the 1868 Constitution, and on this foundation the Court ruled in 1871 that married women were "the peer and equal" of their mates "in all [their] great rights of life, liberty and the pursuit of happiness." (O'Neal v. Robinson, 45 Ala. 526) In the area of race relations, the state is bound by Batson v. Kentucky which held that potential jurors cannot be struck even peremptorily on the basis of ethnicity. (476 U.S. 79 (1986)) (See the Alabama case of Oblander v. USAA Cas. Ins. Co., 792 So. 2d 1103 (2000).)

SECTION 2.

That all political power is inherent in the people, and all free governments are founded on the authority, and instituted for their benefit; and that, therefore, they have at all times an inalienable and indefeasible right to change their form of government in such manner as they may deem expedient.

This section makes explicit the state's commitment to the principle of popular sovereignty. It harks back to the Declaration of Independence and the right of the people to change their government arrangements. The Supreme Court has interpreted this provision to means that any provision of the Constitution is subject to amendment, even those included in this Declaration of Rights which are supposedly to "forever remain inviolate." (Opinion of the Justices, 81 So. 2d 882 (1955). Interpretation of Section 36.)

SECTION 3.

That no religion shall be established by law; that no preference shall be given to any religious sect, society, denomination, or mode of worship; that no one shall be compelled by law to attend any place of worship; nor to pay any tithes, taxes, or other rate for building or repairing any place of worship, or for maintaining any minister or ministry, that no religious test shall be required as a qualification to any office of public trust under this state, and that the civil rights, privileges, and capacity of any citizen shall not be in any manner affected by his religious principles.

This provision calls for less of a "wall of separation" between church and state than the First Amendment is currently held to require. It says that "no preference" is to be given to one faith over another. The "no preference" doctrine, however, has been specifically rejected as far as the First Amendment is concerned by the federal judiciary. Also, this Constitution's religion section is more detailed regarding the kinds of things which are to remain unaffected by one's religious beliefs and associations or their absence.

Modern case law relating to free exercise and establishment of religion has been mostly federally developed. However, at least one state case is worth mentioning. Early in the 1990s the Court of Criminal Appeals ruled against a claim that one could not be convicted of possessing controlled substances if the plants involved were used in religious services. (Rheuark v. State, 601 So. 2d 135) (1992)) Free exercise of religion did not extend this far.

In a strongly religious state such as Alabama, disputes within churches have been frequent and sometimes extremely bitter. The courts are held to be appropriate forums for handling such disputes as, for example, those related to property and which are otherwise justiciable through the use of secular legal principles. However, judges will not attempt to reconcile disputes over which side is adhering most closely to orthodox religious doctrine. (Trinity Presbyterian Church v. Tankersley, 374 So. 2d 861 (1979))

SECTION 3.01.

Section I. The amendment shall be known as and may be cited as the Alabama Religious Freedom Amendment.

Section II. The Legislature makes the following findings concerning religious freedom:

(1) The framers of the United States Constitution, recognizing free exercise of religion as an unalienable right, secured its protection in the First Amendment to the Constitutio n, and the framers of the Constitution of Alabama of 1901, also recognizing this right, secured the protection of religious freedom in Article I, Section 3.

(2) Federal and state laws "neutral" toward religion may burden religious exercise as surely as laws intended to interfere with religious exercise.

(3) Governments should not burden religious exercise without compelling justification.

(4) In Employment Division v. Smith, 494 U.S. 872 (1990), the United States Supreme Court virtually eliminated the requirement that the government justify burdens on religious exercise imposed by laws neutral toward religion.

(5) The compelling interest test as set forth in prior court rulings is a workable test for striking sensible balances between religious liberty and competing governmental interests in areas ranging from public education (pedagogical interests and religious rights, including recognizing regulations necessary to alleviate interference with the educational process versus rights of religious freedom) to national defense (conscription and conscientious objection, including the need to raise an army versus rights to object to individual participation), and other areas of important mutual concern.

(6) Congress passed the Religious Freedom Restoration Act, 42 U.S.C., § 2000bb, to establish the compelling interest test set forth in prior federal court rulings, but in City of Boerne v. Flores, 117 S.Ct. 2157 (1997), the United States Supreme Court held the act unconstitutional stating that the right to regulate was retained by the states.

Section III. The purpose of the Alabama Religious Freedom Amendment is to guarantee that the freedom of religion is not burdened by state and local law; and to provide a claim or defense to persons whose religious freedom is burdened by government.

Section IV. As used in this amendment, the following words shall have the following meanings:

(1) Demonstrates. Meets the burdens of going forward with the evidence and of persuasion.

(2) Freedom of religion. The free exercise of religion under Article I, Section 3, of the Constitution of Alabama of 1901.

(3) Government. Any branch, department, agency, instrumentality, and official (or other person acting under the color of law) of the State of Alabama, any political subdivision of a state, municipality, or other local government.

(4) Rule. Any government statute, regulation, ordinance, administrative provision, ruling guideline, requirement, or any statement of law whatever.

Section V.

(a) Government shall not burden a person's freedom of religion even if the burden results from a rule of general applicability, except as provided in subsection (b).

(b) Government may burden a person's freedom of religion only if it demonstrates that application of the burden to the person:

(1) Is in furtherance of a compelling governmental interest; and

(2) Is the least restrictive means of furthering that compelling governmental interest.

(c) A person whose religious freedom has been burdened in violation of this section may assert that violation as a claim or defense in a judicial, administrative, or other proceeding and obtain appropriate relief against a government.

Section VI.

(a) This amendment applies to all government rules and implementations thereof, whether statutory or otherwise, and whether adopted before or after the effective date of this amendment.

(b) Nothing in this amendment shall be construed to authorize any government to burden any religious belief.

(c) Nothing in this amendment shall be construed to affect, interpret, or in any way address those portions of the First Amendment of the United States Constitution permitting the free exercise of religion or prohibiting laws respecting the establishment of religion, or those provisions of Article I, Section 3, of the Constitution of Alabama of 1901, regarding the establishment of religion.

Section VII.

(a) This amendment shall be liberally construed to effectuate its remedial and deterrent purposes.

(b) If any provision of this amendment or its application to any particular person or circumstance is held invalid, that provision or its application is severable and does not affect the validity of other provisions or applications of this amendment.

Like other recently adopted symbolic provisions of the Constitution, the Religious Freedom Amendment adopted as Amendment 622 in 1999 arose out of a belief that government (especially the federal government and, within this sphere, the federal judiciary) was becoming increasingly hostile toward religion. Most specifically, it was a response to the U.S. Supreme Court's decision in City of Boerne v. Flores (117 S. Ct. 2157 (1997)) where the Religious Freedom Restoration Act had been declared unconstitutional because the Court said Congress lacked authority to compel states to honor the concept of religious freedom. That act, in turn, had been a response to a previous High Court decision (Employment Division v. Smith, 494 U.S. 872 (1992)) which was viewed as hostile to religious exercise. Other states besides Alabama had also adopted their own Religious Freedom Restoration laws.

As is typical with many amendments to the Alabama Constitution, Amendment 622, after its overwhelming ratification by the voters, was virtually forgotten about. In the sixteen years since its ratification it has provided the basis for no implementing legislation or state Supreme Court decisions and, in fact, has not even been cited by the Court.

SECTION 4.

That no law shall ever be passed to curtail or restrain the liberty of speech or of the press, and any person may speak, write, and publish his sentiments on all subjects, being responsible for the abuse of that liberty.

This section is a more extended version of the First Amendment's guarantees of freedom of speech, writing, and press. However, the "being responsible" clause adds a note of conservatism and restraint to what is otherwise a liberating section.

Again, Alabama constitutional law has not been as sensitive to rights of freedom of expression as recent federal interpretations. Probably the dominant theme was expressed in the case of State v. Mills (176 So. 2d 884 (1965), rev. on other grounds, 384 U.S. 214 (1966)) where the Court asserted that "the freedom of speech and of the press . . . does not confer an absolute right to speak or publish, without responsibility, whatever one may." (The Court here quoted from Barton v. Bessemer, 173 So. 626 (1937).) The U.S. Supreme Court has not upheld an unlimited freedom of expression either, but the emphasis has been more often on vindication than denial of rights in this area. In the mid-1990s the

Alabama Court held that a local ordinance forbidding nudity (complete or partial) where alcoholic beverages are served regulates conduct instead of speech and thus is not violative of this section. (Ranch House, Inc. v. City of Anniston, 678 So. 2d 745 (1996))

SECTION 5.

That the people shall be secure in their persons, houses, papers, and possessions from unreasonable seizure or searches, and that no warrants shall issue to search any place or to seize any person or thing without probable cause, supported by oath or affirmation.

The language of this section is almost identical with that of the Fourth Amendment. There appears to be a greater similarity between federal and state approaches to constitutional interpretation in this area than in the area of freedom of expression. With the steady definition of the procedural safeguards of the U.S. Bill of Rights as state protections as well via the Fourteenth Amendment, this became even more pronounced. And the appellate court recognized in Brown v. State (167 So. 2d 281 (App. 1964)) that, "[i]nasmuch as Mapp v. Ohio [367 U.S. 643 (1961)] brings the fourth amendment of the federal Constitution to bear upon state trials, it would seem that the minimum degree of proof established under the fourth amendment would necessarily be the minimum for the issuance of a state search warrant." Based on an examination of numerous cases it may safely be said that there has been more congruence between the state and federal judiciaries in this area of criminal procedure than in any other. As in the Brown case just noted, and in others as well, the Alabama appellate court has mentioned both state and federal constitutional provisions related to searches and seizures. (See, for example, Eggers v. State, 2004 Ala. Crim. App.) Nevertheless, the Alabama appellate courts have never said that the state and federal provisions are identical. The circumstances of each case are at least slightly different and interpretations of the state and federal constitutional language are continually evolving.

SECTION 6.

That in all criminal prosecutions the accused has a right to be heard by himself and counsel, or either; to demand the nature and cause of the accusation, and to have a copy thereof; to be confronted by the witnesses against him; to have compulsory process for obtaining witnesses in his favor; to testify in all cases, in his own behalf, if he elects to do so; and, in all prosecutions by indictment, a speedy public trial, by an impartial jury of the county or district in which the offense was committed; and he shall not be compelled to give evidence against himself, nor be deprived of life, liberty, or property, except by due process of law; but the legislature may, by a general law, provide for a change of venue at the instance of the defendant in all prosecution by indictment, and such change of venue, on application of the defendant, may be heard and determined without the personal presence of the defendant so applying therefor; provided, that at the time of the application for the change of venue, the defendant is imprisoned in jail or some legal place of confinement.

The subjects of this section relate to the provisions of the Sixth and Fifth Amendments of the U.S. Constitution, respectively. Its force is somewhat diluted by technical language in the last part of the section relating to changes of venue. Despite the fact that the greater commitment to individual rights has historically been demonstrated by federal rather than by Alabama courts, the Alabama Court of Criminal Appeals asserted in 1978 that, "The Alabama Constitution affords no less protection to its citizens than that afforded by the United States Constitution." (Ford v. State, 356 So. 2d 720)

This section contains Alabama's due process clause. The Constitution has no equal protection clause as such. However, as previously noted, Sections 1, 6, and 22 are held, collectively, to guarantee equal protection. (Hueytown v. Jiffy Chek Co., 342 So. 2d 761 (1977))

Space limitations prohibit elaboration of even the major interpretations of each of this section's numerous provisions. However, a brief sampling of interpretations will be provided.

In McClemore v. State (798 So. 2d 693 (2000)), the Criminal Appeals Court overturned a conviction where a trial judge had permitted the striking of two black members of the jury pool while a potential white juror with similar non-ethnic characteristics was retained.

In Blackmon v. State (462 So. 2d 1057 (1985)), the appellate court warned that it would "not tolerate comments by the prosecutor on the accused's privilege not to testify." Indeed, "The prosecutor who even inadvertently makes reference to the fact that the defendant can testify is inviting reversible error."

Showing the present degree of synchronization between the U.S. and Alabama Constitutions, the Court of Criminal Appeals held in Mead v. State (472 So. 2d 449 (1985)) that, "the use of the post-arrest, post-Miranda warning of silence of the accused as evidence of his guilt is a violation of the due process clauses of both the fourteenth amendment to the Constitution of the United States and Section Six of the Alabama Constitution of 1901." (The quote is from Houston v. State, 354 So. 2d 825 (Cr. App. 1977).)

Constitutional claims related to inadequacy of counsel are still relatively new in Alabama. It was one of the states most affected by the classic 1963 U.S. Supreme Court case, Gideon v. Wainwright (372 U.S. 335), which held that defendants must be provided counsel in all cases, not just capital cases, if they cannot afford it. Obviously counsel remains most important in capital cases and it is in this category that Yeomans v. State falls. (2013 Ala. Crim. App. LEXIS 23) The case is significant because it shows that the appellate judiciary in Alabama still lacks zeal as far as enforcing the right to effective counsel is concerned. For example, one of the grounds for rejecting Yeomans' claims of inadequate representation was that they had not adhered closely enough to the *Alabama Rules of Criminal*

Procedure. A stronger commitment to a defendant's rights would have shown less deference to these rules and more concern for whether the defendant had received justice. Even though the case was decided in 2013, it has already been cited by criminal appellate judges in seven cases.

With regard to changes of venue, it should be noted that Alabama law also allows requests for changes of venue to be made by public prosecutors. Whether such petitions are granted is, as Section 75 makes clear, for the judge to decide.

SECTION 6.01.
Basic rights for crime victims.

(a) Crime victims, as defined by law or their lawful representatives, including the next of kin of homicide victims, are entitled to the right to be informed, to be present, and to be heard when authorized, at all crucial stages of criminal proceedings, to the extent that these rights do not interfere with the constitutional rights of the person accused of committing the crime.

(b) Nothing in this amendment or in any enabling statute adopted pursuant to this amendment shall be construed as creating a cause of action against the state or any of its agencies, officials, employees, or political subdivisions. The Legislature may from time to time enact enabling legislation to carry out and implement this amendment.

Like Section 3.01, discussed earlier, this is another new symbolic addition to the Constitution. (567, 1994) It guarantees crime victims and/or their families the right to be informed whenever any criminal procedure pertaining to an alleged assailant is being heard. However, it specifically excludes any right of victims or their families to sue the state because of any negligence on its part in the course of criminal proceedings. Section 6.01 has not been the basis of any significant litigation. It has been mentioned in only one case. (See State v. Wheat, 907 So. 2d 461 (2005).) The Alabama Crime Victims Compensation Commission was not established pursuant to this section. It has been in operation since 1984.

SECTION 7.

That no person shall be accused or arrested, or detained, except in cases ascertained by law, and according to the form which the same has prescribed, and no person shall be punished but by virtue of a law established and promulgated prior to the offense and legally applied.

This section deals, inter alia, with the subject of ex post facto laws, which it prohibits. It promotes government based on rule of law rather than the whims of public prosecutors.

SECTION 8.

No person shall for any indictable offense be proceeded against criminally by information, except in cases arising in the militia and volunteer forces when in actual service, or when assembled under arms as a military organization, or, by leave of the court, for misfeasance, misdemeanor, extortion, and oppression in office, otherwise than is provided in the Constitution. In cases of misdemeanor, the Legislature may by law dispense with a grand jury and authorize prosecutions and proceedings before any inferior courts as may be by law established. In all felony cases, except those punishable by capital punishment, the Legislature may by law dispense with a grand jury and authorize prosecutions and proceedings in any manner as may be provided by law if the defendant, after having had the advice of counsel of his or her choice or in the event he or she is unable to employ counsel, the advice of counsel which shall be appointed by the court, makes known in open court to a judge of a court having jurisdiction of the offense that he or she desires to plead guilty.

The language here is that of Amendment 598 (1996), which replaced both the original Section 8 and Amendment 37 in 1939. The Court ruled in 1837 that the language (as contained in the Constitution of 1819) put the authority of the state behind the individual's right to be indicted before being brought to trial on felony charges. (State v. Middleton, 5 Port. 484 (1837)) The indictment permits a defendant to know specifically what offenses against the law he or she is alleged to have committed. People can be indicted for misdemeanors, but it is not constitutionally mandated. The Criminal Appeals Court reasserted the accused's right to have his or her conviction based solely on charges contained in a lawful indictment in 1999. (Gamble v. State, 758 So. 2d 1125, Crim. App.)

SECTION 9.

That no person shall, for the same offense, be twice put in jeopardy of life or limb; but courts may, for reasons fixed by law, discharge juries from the consideration of any case, and no person shall gain an advantage by reason of such discharge of the jury.

This provision has required a considerable amount of judicial interpretation. Of course, a person cannot be tried twice for "the same identical act and crime." (Johns v. State, 69 So. 259 (App. 1915)) (This quote is from *17 Am. & Eng. Ency. Law (2d ed.)* 596 et seq.) This is the classic definition of double jeopardy. The Court held nearly 120 years ago that jeopardy started when a jury had been impaneled and the indictment on which the defendant was being tried was read. (Scott v. State, 20 So. 468 (1896))

Being acquitted for embezzling currency, however, did not bar a subsequent prosecution for embezzling a check. (Christison v. State, 142 So. 2d 663 (1960)) Where multiple offenses have allegedly been committed simultaneously (of varying degrees of severity), where the individual is tried and acquitted on a lesser charge, he or she cannot subsequently be tried on more serious charges. (Baldwin v. State, 251 So. 2d 633 (App. 1971)) If an individual were tried for first degree murder, but was convicted in the second degree, he or she could not, of course, again be tried on the more serious charge. (Clark v. State, 318 So. 2d 805 (1974))

If one who is convicted appeals and wins a reversal, it is not double jeopardy for him to be tried once more. (State v. Hughes, 2 Ala. 102 (1841)) The same holds true if a guilty verdict appealed by a convicted person is remanded to the lower court because of some error in the trial. (Collins v. State, 385 So. 2d 1005 (1980)) A mistrial grounded in prosecutorial misconduct may be a bar to further prosecution. (Kinard v. State, 495 So. 2d 705 (Cr. App. 1986))

After the U.S. Supreme Court invalidated capital punishment as implemented in Alabama, all individuals then on death row were spared from electrocution (the form of execution then used). Despite the passage of a new law with constitutionally acceptable language, individuals who had been sentenced to death under the old act could not be resentenced without violating the prohibition against double jeopardy. Since the resumption of executions fifty-six people have been subjected to capital punishment. Alabama ranked sixth among the states still using the death penalty.

In the mid-1980s the Court summarized guarantees afforded by the no double jeopardy clause as follows: "(1) protection against a second prosecution for the same offense after acquittal; (2) protection against a second prosecution for the same offense after conviction; and (3) protection against multiple punishments for the same offense." (Wright v. Montgomery, 477 So. 2d 492 (1985)) Most recently, the Court of Criminal Appeals ruled that since capital murder, sexual abuse, and sexual torture were separate offenses and necessitated separating at trial, approving a man's conviction for more than one offense did not impinge on his protection against double jeopardy. (Kelley v. State, CR-0642 (Ala. Crim. App. 2014))

SECTION 10.

That no person shall be barred from prosecuting or defending before any tribunal in this state, by himself or counsel, any civil cause to which he is a party.

The accused is assured "the right to be heard on all questions of law and fact which may arise at any time during the prosecution." (Peaglar State, 20 So. 363 (1896))

The recognition of the right to counsel in even "the pettiest 'civil cause' that may be tried" goes back to at least 1860. (Withers v. State, 36 Ala. 252) Of course, counsel means a licensed attorney. (Ex parte Lamberth, 5 So. 2d 622 (1942)) In a relatively recent case, the Civil Appeals Court ruled that non-attorney parents lacked the legal credentials to pursue the interests of their daughter's grievance against her school principal and the local board of education. (Chambers v. Tibbs, 980 So. 2d 1010 (2007))

SECTION 11.

That the right of trial by jury shall remain inviolate.

As we have seen, Section 6 also seeks to guarantee an individual's right to trial by jury, which is required by that provision to be impartial.

A fundamental right such as this is never to be diluted by the "burdening, disturbing, qualifying or tampering" action of "the legislative, executive or judicial department, one or all." (Alford v. State, 54 So. 213 (1910))

The Court has declined to expand the right to a jury trial, however, holding that it is guaranteed only in those cases where juries were used under the common law or statute law as applied when the Constitution was adopted. (Gilbreath v. Wallace, 292 So. 2d 651 (1974)) In Woodmen of the World Life Ins. Soc'y v. Harris, 740 So. 2d 362 (1999), the Court held that because the insured had signed an arbitration agreement permitting non-jury settlement of disputed matters, the guarantee of this section was not contravened. Further, there is no right to a jury trial in a municipal court where one is accused of violating a city ordinance. (Birmingham v. Evans, 300 So. 2d 396 (App. 1974))

The Court of Appeals has declared that the essential features of a jury trial are a twelve-member jury, a jury which is impartial, and a unanimous jury verdict. (Dixon v. State, 167 So. 340 (App. 1936)) A defendant in a criminal case may waive his right to a trial by jury. (Rule 18.1, Alabama Rules of Criminal Procedure) A party in a civil action must demand a trial by jury. Failure to do so constitutes a waiver of such right. (Rule 38, Alabama Rules of Civil Procedure) While the U.S. Supreme Court allows states to vary the size of juries so long as there are at least six members, Alabama has not chosen to take advantage of this option.

This section is identical with one that appeared in the initial state Constitution approved in 1819. (noted in Crowe v. State, 485 So. 2d 351 (Crim. App. 1984))

SECTION 12.

That in all prosecutions for libel or for the publication of papers investigating the official conduct of officers or men in public capacity, or when the matter published is proper for public information, the truth thereof may be given in evidence; and that in all indictments for libel, the jury shall have the right to determine the law and the facts under the direction of the court.

This section has a narrow application. There are no recent court decisions that would be instructive.

SECTION 13.

That all courts shall be open, and that every person, for any injury done him in his lands, goods, person, or reputation shall have a remedy by due process of law; and right and justice shall be administered without sale, denial, or delay.

Courts are to be open, this section proclaims. (See preceding discussions for what constitutes an open court, especially in Section 10.) The last clause states a general ideal rather than a strict remedy of law.

Thirteen decades ago, the Court said that its study of history revealed "the chief purpose [of this section as being] . . . to assail the existing evil of anciently holding courts in clandestine sessions, and of paying fines to the king and his officers, for delaying or expediting law-suits and for obtaining justice." (Swann v. Kidd, 79 Ala. 431 (1885))

In Ex Parte Rice, the Court identified three bedrock elements of due process: (1) notice, (2) a hearing based on the notice, and (3) a decision pursuant to the notice and hearing. (92 So. 2d 16 (1957)) The case of Patricia Poffenberger v. Merit Energy Co. (972 So. 2d 792) held nearly a decade ago (2007) that limiting property owners to the recovery of damages only to the extent of recovering their loss did not deny them the remedy guaranteed by Section 13.

SECTION 14.

That the State of Alabama shall never be made a defendant in any court of law or equity.

This section is very unambiguous, but has been subject to much interpretation and adjudication, particularly in the contemporary litigious society. Judicial doctrines in this area are outgrowths of the medieval notion that, although to the monarch personally no charge of misfeasance could be attached, his minions were individually liable when they committed ultra vires acts. (DeStafney v. University of Alabama. 413 So. 2d 391 (1981))

The principle was stated in 1875 that the "State is not liable for the negligence, malfeasance, or torts of its agents or employees." (State v. Hill, 54 Ala. 67) In 1983, in Taylor v. Troy State University, the Court went so far as to say that, "Because of this section, Alabama has been held to have virtually complete sovereign immunity." (437 So. 2d 472 (1983)) Thus the Court has cautioned over the years, as it did in 1937: "All persons dealing with the state are charged with knowledge that no one has authority to subject the state to suit." (Dunn Construction Co. v. State Board of Adjustment, 175 So. 383)

As the functions of government have expanded in modern times, efforts have sometimes been made to distinguish between traditional governmental functions where the old doctrine of sovereign immunity should remain untouched and new areas where suits could legitimately be tolerated. Thus, in 1935, the Court ruled that this section sought to shield only "immediate and strict governmental agencies of the State" from litigation. (Ex Parte Board of School Commissioners, 161 So. 108) However, the line of judicial decisions in this area has not been consistent. In 1983 the Court appeared to grant broad immunity to both traditional and more modern business-type functions of state government. (Jones v. Alabama State Docks, 443 So. 2d 1902) The state docks, for example, are regarded as an "immediate and strict" public agency. (Foley v. Terry, 175 So. 2d 461 (1965))

The courts have been somewhat clearer regarding the susceptibility to suits of other public agencies. A public corporation does not enjoy the immunity of regular state agencies. (Curtis v. Alabama Elk River Development Agency, 372 So. 2d 353 (1979)) Further, municipalities do not possess the immunity from suits that the state enjoys. Indeed, in the case of Jackson v. Florence (320 So. 2d 68 (1975)), a sharply divided Court declared that it was abolishing the doctrine of municipal immunity. Jackson could legitimately seek to collect from the city for injuries inflicted upon him by police who were taking him into custody. Prior to this case the Court had unsuccessfully sought to make a distinction between strictly governmental activities (where suits would be impermissible) and corporate or proprietary activities (where they would not be). County governments are also subject to being sued. (Rutledge v. Baldwin County Commission, 495 So. 2d 49 (1986))

Of course, the generally negative view toward anti-state suits does not mean that those who suffer loss of some kind due to what amounts to state action have no recourse. The legislature, in its discretion, can pass relief measures and procedures. (Hutchinson v. Board of Trustees of University of Alabama, 256 So. 2d 281 (1971)) However, provision of relief does not mean that the state is waiving its immunity from lawsuits. This it cannot do. (Druid City Hospital v. Epperson, 378 So. 2d 696 (1979)) The usual procedure is for claims against the state to be made to the State Board of Adjustment.

Also, a distinction is made between the ministerial acts of public agents (which they must perform as a matter of course) and discretionary acts (which are not legally stipulated). The former are subject to suit whereas the latter are not. One will see instances in this volume where state officials are named as defendants in cases, even though the grievances alleged do not reflect the actions of these men and women as private citizens. Instead, they reflect the ban against suing the state itself. (See Ex Parte Ala. DOT (978 So. 2d 17) (2007).)

SECTION 15.

That excessive fines shall not be imposed, nor cruel or unusual punishment inflicted.

Traditionally, the methods of punishment in Alabama were hard labor (usually in behalf of the county), incarceration, or, at the extreme, death. In this area, as in many others related to the procedural safeguards, pathbreaking leadership more frequently has been taken by federal than by Alabama courts. It was a federal court which held that it was "cruel and unusual punishment" for prisoners not to receive adequate medical care. (Cf. Hart v. State, 274 So. 2d 614 (1973).)

Of course, most controversy has focused on capital punishment, which is still practiced in Alabama. In 1933 the Court held that execution was constitutionally authorized if it was "speedy and without undue pain or torture." (Lee v. State, 150 So. 164) Even in more recent years, there has been no inclination on the part of Alabama judges to find that "the sentence of death is [in and of itself] cruel and unusual punishment." (Harris v. State, 352 So. 2d 460 (1976))

Because of the likelihood that death sentences employing the electric chair would be overturned by federal judges, Alabama switched to the lethal-injection method, which thus far has survived federal challenges. (The drug protocols are still undergoing increasing scrutiny, however.) Also following the guidance of the federal courts, the Alabama appellate judiciary has held it unconstitutional to execute someone who was below the age of eighteen for murder. (Wimberly v. State, 931 So. 2d 60 (2005)) Finally, like their federal colleagues to whom they are accountable, Alabama judges are balancing aggravating and mitigating circumstances in considering whether a death sentence was appropriate in capital cases they are reviewing. (Deardorff v. State, 6 So. 3d 1205 (2004) (Ala. Crimp. App.)

As far as lesser sentences are concerned, as recently as 1977 the Court held that sentencing an individual to a jail term of twelve years upon conviction for heroin possession did not amount to "cruel and unusual punishment." (Cabble v. State 347 So. 2d 546) By 2001, however, the Court had decided that a sentence of life imprisonment with no chance of parole for trafficking in morphine did constitute such punishment. (Wilson v. State (830 So. 2d 765), Crim. App.)

SECTION 16.

That all persons shall, before conviction, be bailable by sufficient sureties, except for capital offenses, when the proof is evident or the presumption great; and that excessive bail shall not in any case be required.

This provision has its roots in the common law, under which "all charged crimes were bailable." (Turner v. State, 27 So. 2d 239 (1946)) The specific language used here goes back to Alabama's first Constitution. (See Ex Parte Simonton, 9 Port. 390 (1839).) This section excepts capital crimes under the conditions specified. Denial of bail must not be used as an indirect way of punishing someone accused but not convicted of a crime. (Johnson v. State, 10 So. 2d 298 (App. 1942)) Somewhat over a decade ago the Court ruled that a woman who had not been indicted for a capital offense but was still denied bail had not been treated fairly according to Section 16 and directed the trial court to establish a bail sum. (Ex parte Patel, 879 So. 2d 532 (2003))

The amount of bail may legitimately vary with the financial condition of the accused. (Ex parte Banks, 28 Ala. 89 (1856)) Guidelines related to the setting of bail are established in rules promulgated by the Court. Rule 2 of the Alabama Rules of Judicial Administration sets forth a discretionary bail schedule.

SECTION 17.

That the privilege of the writ of habeas corpus shall not be suspended by the authorities of this state.

The fundamental objective of this historic writ is "to secure . . . release, unless . . . [a person is] lawfully detained. (Luckie v. State, 502 So. 2d 870 (1986)) Note that the "State Constitution, unlike the Federal[,] admits of no power to suspend the writ of habeas corpus under any supposed requirement of the public safety." (Aaron v. State, 192 So. 2d 456 (App. 1966)) In Alabama a defendant has a narrow window of opportunity within which to apply for a habeas corpus review. If the accused delays, an extension of time will not be granted. (Williams v. Ala. (2012 U.S. Dist. LEXIS 51850, Civil Action No. 1:07-cv-1276 (United States District Court for the Northern District of Alabama, Eastern Division 2012))) and Williams v. Alabama, No. 12-14397 (United States Court of Appeals for the Eleventh Circuit 2015))

SECTION 18.

That treason against the state shall consist only in levying war against it, or adhering to its enemies, giving them aid and comfort, and that no person shall be convicted of treason, except on the testimony of two witnesses to the same overt act, or his own confession in open court.

This section goes back to the first state Constitution. It is practically identical with Article III, Section 3, of the U.S. Constitution. In 1837 the Court ruled that the state could go so far as to punish by death any who would plot or consult with the aim of encouraging insurrection or rebellion against the state. (State v. McDonald, 4 Port. 449) There was no twentieth-century litigation.

SECTION 19.

That no person shall be attainted of treason by the legislature; and no conviction shall work corruption of blood or forfeiture of estate.

Bills of attainder are clearly prohibited. What else is proscribed by this section has only infrequently been the subject of judicial inquiry. A bizarre case in 1945 affirmed the right of an insurance company to exclude from benefits the husband of a wife he was found guilty of murdering. (Weaver v. Hollis, 22 So. 2d 525) No cases have been decided on the basis of this section since 1945.

SECTION 20.

That no person shall be imprisoned for debt.

This section is "limited to contract liabilities." (Bray v. State, 37 So. 250 (1904); also Lavender v. Tuscaloosa, 198 So. 450 (App. 1940))

The Court ruled nearly 125 years ago that "an indefinite imprisonment until the fine and costs are paid" goes against this section, which first made its appearance in the 1868 Constitution. (Ex parte Russellville, 95 Ala. 19 (1891)) "Imprisonment [cannot be used] as a means of coercing the payment of fine and costs." (Ibid.) Recently there has been controversy related to privatization of collection of unpaid fines in Alabama municipalities. One of the results has been the jailing of people for these debts. (See "The Town [Harpersville] That Turned Poverty into a Prison Sentence," *Nation*, April 20, 2014. (Accessed online February 9, 2015).)

In 2005 the Civil Appeals Court ruled that an ex-husband delinquent on promises of payment in a property settlement could not be cited for contempt of court and subjected to imprisonment since such incarceration would conflict with Section 20. (Dolberry v. Dolberry, 920 So. 2d 573 (2005), Civ. App.) However, the same court had held at the beginning of the eighties that a husband could be jailed for contemptuous failure to make required alimony payments. (Smith v. Smith, 380 So. 2d 897 (Civ. App. 1980)) The most contentious problem in this area in recent years has not been alimony but child support payments.

Finally, the section does not mean that someone cannot be jailed for bouncing checks in return for goods or services. If there is found an intent to defraud, then the jail sentence for the check bouncer is an appropriate punishment. (This discussion is derived from Harris v. State, 378 So. 2d 257 (Crim. App. 1979). Harris was not a check bouncer.)

SECTION 21.

That no power of suspending laws shall be exercised except by the legislature.

This section provides a basis for a constitutional determination of the legitimacy of the delegation of legislative power. The Court held long ago that the legislature could specify that a law would start operating when something they designated actually happened, and that this determination could be made by an administrative official. (Stein v. Mobile, 24 Ala. 591 (1854)) This official may be the governor. (Norton v. Lusk, 26 So. 2d. 849 (1946))

SECTION 22.

That no ex post facto law, nor any law, impairing the obligation of contracts, or making any irrevocable or exclusive grants of special privileges or immunities, shall be passed by the legislature, and every grant or franchise, privilege or immunity shall forever remain subject to revocation, alteration, or amendment.

This section specifically prohibits ex post facto laws. It also bars the impairment of contracts. More democratic than the original U.S. Constitution, however, it directs the legislature not to make any irrevocable, unalterable, or unamendable grants of special privileges. (Section 95 also deals with the obligation of contracts.) Nevertheless, Sweet v. Wilkinson (40 So. 2d 427 (1949)) held that this section and the comparable U.S. Constitution language mean essentially the same thing.

Perhaps the longest interpretive history is associated with the matter of corporate charters being construed as contracts. By the original 1819 Constitution a corporate charter relieving the corporation of any tax burden was held to be permissible. However, beginning in the 1868 Constitution the language reproduced here was inserted specifically to authorize legislative alteration of corporate charters for the public good. (Explained in State v. Alabama Bible Society, 32 So. 1011 (1902)) The Court specifically held that this section was aimed at legislative granting of monopolistic privileges through corporate franchises. (Birmingham, etc. Railway Co. v. Birmingham Street Railway Co., 79 Ala. 465 (1885))

With regard to state-local relations, the Court held about 130 years ago that a municipality could not look to the obligation of contracts clause to protect itself from state intrusion into local affairs by revocation of its charter. (Smith v. Inge, 80 Ala. 283 (1885))

A major category of public employees, however, finds protection in the obligation of contracts clause. The Court has held that a tenured teacher's contract does enjoy the guarantees of this section of the Constitution. (Faircloth v. Folmar, 40 So. 2d 697 (1949))

On the most intimate level, the Court also held in the late nineteenth century that marriage does constitute a contract as contemplated by the Constitution, although it is much more than this. (Green v. State, 58 Ala. 190 (1877)) This case involved now-unconstitutional miscegenation laws. In mid-2015 the U.S. Supreme Court upheld the legitimacy of same-sex marriage in all states. This decision was not seen as a surprise because, as in the case of divorce, it is not practical in a federal system for one's marital status to depend on her or his state of residence. (See Obergefell v. Hodges, 576 U.S. ____, 2015 WL 2473451 (U.S. June 26, 2015).)

With respect to ex post facto laws, as in the case of the U.S. Constitution, the Alabama framers were held to have contemplated a ban only on criminal laws. (Elliott v. Mayfield, 4 Ala. 417 (1842)) In a recent case the Court rejected upping a defendant's charge from misdemeanor to felony because she had failed to comply with a rule related to change of residence applied to accused sex offenders. (The rule was not in place at the time of her indictment.) (State v. Livingston (8 So. 3d 1014, Crim. App.) (2008))

In the area of civil litigation, the Court held in 2013 that an act passed to rescue Alabama's financially endangered PACT (Prepaid Affordable College Tuition) program was not an unconstitutional ex post facto law even though it ultimately worked to the disadvantage of many participants in it. (Perdue v. Green, 127 So. 3d 343) The Court said that even though the change revised the powers of the PACT board of directors, the act itself did not diminish the contractual rights of PACT participants. (The newly empowered board section did diminish these rights, however.)

SECTION 23.

That the exercise of the right of eminent domain shall never be abridged nor construed to prevent the legislature from taking the property and franchises of incorporated companies, and subjecting them to public use in the same manner in which the property and franchises of individuals are taken and subjected, but

> private property shall not be taken for, or applied to public use, unless just compensation be first made therefor; nor shall private property be taken for private use, or for the use of corporations, other than municipal, without the consent of the owner; provided, however, the legislature may by law secure to persons or corporations of the rights herein reserved, but just compensation shall, in all cases, be first made to the owner, and provided, that the right of eminent domain shall not be so construed as to allow taxation or forced subscription for the benefit of railroads or any other kind of corporations, other than municipal, or for the benefit of any individual or association.

In the U.S. Constitution, the Fifth Amendment briefly provides for the exercise of the power of eminent domain with just compensation paid. In sharp contrast, the Alabama Constitution does not only this but specifies minutely the conditions under which eminent domain may and may not be exercised. The conditions are very particularly spelled out in Section 23 and require little interpretation here.

While there is much economic conservatism in the Constitution, there is also plenty of language that stresses the growth of fear, particularly in the latter part of the nineteenth century, of concentrated corporate economic power. The last sentence of this section also shows the fear of more reckless expenditures for which conservative elites blamed the Reconstruction era, and which would necessitate a higher burden of property taxes.

The Court also early in the twentieth century used this section to point out the particular nature of state constitutions. Jones v. Nashville, C. & St. L. Ry. (37 So. 677 (1904)) notes that any government possesses the power of eminent domain. What the Constitution does with these details is try to ensure that restraint is exercised in the use of this inherent governmental power. (From the early 1970s, see also Cooper v. Magic City Trucking Service, 264 So. 2d (1972).)

This section has been kept relatively up to date. In the expansive post–World War II period the Court advised that property could be taken for urban redevelopment projects. (Opinion of the Justices, 48 So. 2d 757 (1950)) Also in an urban context, the Court urged that "public use" be interpreted liberally. (Blankenship v. Decatur, 115 So. 2d 459 (1959)) On the other hand, the "taking" of property means only taking physical possession. The eminent domain protections did not apply to a municipal ordinance that made it impossible for a quarry owner to conduct his usual operations within city territory. (Town of Gurley v. M&N Materials, Inc., 143 So. 3d 1 (2012))

One of the most controversial aspects of the section is that which authorizes the legislature, in effect, to delegate the power of eminent domain to private corporations. This has most frequently involved utility companies which need rights of way for their lines. The Court has upheld a broad eminent domain power for public utilities, and the judiciary will not interfere with its exercise in the absence of very clear abuse. (Alabama Power Co. v. Hamilton, 342 So. 2d 8 (1977))

SECTION 24.

That all navigable waters shall remain forever public highways, free to the citizens of the state and the United States, without tax, import, or toll, and that no tax, toll, impost, or wharfage shall be demanded or received from the owner of any merchandise or commodity for the use of the shores of any wharf erected on the shores, or over the waters of any navigable stream, unless the same be expressly authorized by law.

Excerpted in the Alabama *Code* (a compilation of state laws made periodically, grouping laws on similar subjects together) is the case of Pollard v. Files (3 Ala. 47 (1841)), a time when most goods moved long distances by water. (In contrast with the Code, the *Acts of Alabama* volumes simply present laws in the order in which they were passed.) Railroads were still relatively unimportant. In the 2013 case of City of Irondale v. City of Leeds (122 So. 3d 1244), the Court held that the Cahaba River was navigable where Leeds wished to add to its territory. Therefore, its annexation attempt was unconstitutional under Section 24.

SECTION 25.

That the citizens have a right, in a peaceable manner, to assemble together for the common good, and to apply to those invested with the power of government for redress of grievances or other purposes, by petition, address, or remonstrance.

This is a longer version of the freedom of assembly clause of the First Amendment. It has not been the subject of any notable litigation. Some Alabama situations have indeed been critical to the development of assembly rights, but they have provided the basis for federal, not state, cases.

SECTION 26.

That every citizen has a right to bear arms in defense of himself and the state.

Even though the Alabama cultural environment is strongly supportive of the right to own and use firearms, the Court of Appeals did caution nearly six decades ago that "the constitutional right of every citizen to bear arms, in defense of himself and the state . . . is subject to reasonable regulation under the police powers of the state." (Mason v. State, 103 So. 2d 337 (App. 1956)) For example, cities have forbidden the possession of firearms in businesses serving liquor. (Ex parte Childers, 640 So. 2d 16 (1994))

SECTION 27.

That no standing army shall be kept up without the consent of the legislature, and, in that case, no appropriation for its support shall be made for a longer term than one year; and the military shall, in all cases, and at all times, be in strict subordination to the civil power.

This old section prohibiting military funding for longer than a year at a time reflects Thomas Jefferson's and the other early democrats' fear of standing armies and is more of an anachronistic curiosity today than anything else. The clause was cited during the Phenix City clean-up era of the mid-1950s when Governor Gordon Persons declared martial law following the assassination of attorney general nominee Albert L. Patterson. Russell County Deputy Sheriff Albert Fuller relied on this section in an unsuccessful attempt to challenge the legality of actions taken following the governor's supersession of local law enforcement officials. (Fuller v. State, 115 So. 2d 110 (App. 1958))

SECTION 28.

That no soldier shall, in time of peace, be quartered in any house without the consent of the owner; nor, in time of war, but in a manner to be prescribed by law.

This section is identical to the Third Amendment of the U.S. Constitution. It is totally devoid of any contemporary constitutional significance.

SECTION 29.

That no title of nobility or hereditary distinction, privilege, honor, or emolument shall ever be granted or conferred in this state; and that no office shall be created, the appointment to which shall be for a longer time than during good behavior.

Article I, Section 9, of the U.S. Constitution prohibits Congress from granting titles of nobility. This section proscribes the same action and also goes on to forbid lifetime appointments. As a result of the influence of Jacksonian democracy, more and more offices would be made elective for relatively brief terms. In Alabama's traditional culture, however, offices have, in effect frequently been handed down within the family, sometimes for generations, the younger offspring seeming to have an almost hereditary right to their fathers' (or mothers') offices.

SECTION 30.

That immigration shall be encouraged; emigration shall not be prohibited, and no citizen shall be exiled.

A sparsely populated state such as Alabama in earlier times wanted to encourage immigration. This provision lacks present-day relevance, however, and has not figured prominently in litigation for over a century. In 1882 the Court ruled that white plantation owners fearful that the former slave population would be siphoned off to other states as free laborers could not obstruct such attempts by a law licensing and regulating emigrant agents without contravening this section. (See Joseph v. Randolph, 72 Ala. 499.)

Attitudes toward immigration have changed radically in recent times. In 2011 the legislature adopted HB 56, which was identified as the most draconian any nativist state had yet passed. Challenges to the law occurred immediately and its harshest aspects were declared to be in violation of the U.S. Constitution. (See, for example, Hispanic Interest Coalition of Alabama v. Bentley (Case No. 5-11-cv-02484-SLB (N.D. Ala.)) (2011).)

SECTION 31.

That temporary absence from the state shall not cause a forfeiture of residence once obtained.

This section is self-explanatory. It has not been the subject of any constitutional controversy.

SECTION 32.

That no form of slavery shall exist in this state, and there shall not be any involuntary servitude, otherwise than for the punishment of crime, of which the party shall have been duly convicted.

This proscription against slavery has been a part of Alabama's basic law since the Civil War when the victory of the Union armies dictated an end to the enslavement of African Americans by whites. Nearly a decade ago the State of Alabama through the governor and legislature "apologiz[ed] for the wrongs of slavery" and "express[ed] profound regret for Alabama's role in slavery." (Acts 2007, No. 07-223) It was made clear, however, that this act should not be the basis for descendants of slaves seeking any monetary compensation.

SECTION 33.

The privilege of suffrage shall be protected by laws regulating elections, and prohibiting, under adequate penalties, all undue influences from power, bribery, tumult, or other improper conduct.

The right to vote, and the regulation thereof, have been the subject of intense constitutional controversy. Most of the emphasis, historically, was not on protecting "the privilege of suffrage," but on denying it to blacks. This section puts voting in the context of election day. It has not been the subject of judicial litigation.

SECTION 34.

Foreigners who are, or may hereafter become, bona fide residents of this state, shall enjoy the same rights in respect to the possession, enjoyment, and inheritance of property as native born citizens.

This is another section (along with Section 30) which sought to encourage the settlement of additional whites of European ancestry in Alabama by promising them the benefits of citizens.

SECTION 35.

That the sole object and only legitimate end of government is to protect the citizen in the enjoyment of life, liberty, and property, and when the government assumes other functions it is usurpation and oppression.

This section enshrines in the Constitution the Lockean philosophy of limited government. Its language rings very hollow when contrasted to later constitutional amendments involving state and local governments in many more than the rudimentary governmental functions contemplated here.

Perhaps surprisingly, this philosophical section has been the subject of a good bit of judicial interpretation. The most significant case bearing on the central thrust of this section was Churchill v. Board of Trustees (409 So. 2d 1382 (1982)), in which the Court employed the "compelling need" criterion to assess the constitutionality of governmental participation in a profit-making activity, here the sale of hearing aids by the University of Alabama to clinic patients, an activity the Court found sufficiently related to the institution's research and service mission.

In a case that attracted national notoriety, the Court held in 2010 that a legislative ban on the sale of certain devices designed to heighten sexual enjoyment did not unconstitutionally contravene the Section 35 guarantee to the citizen of the right to enjoy life free of governmental interference. (Montgomery Highway, Inc. v. City of Hoover (45 So. So. 310)) Also the challenged law was viewed as an acceptable use of the state's power to act to promote the morals and general welfare of its residents (i.e., the police power).

SECTION 36.

That this enumeration of certain rights shall not impair or deny others retained by the people, and, to guard against any encroachments on the rights herein retained, we declare that everything in this Declaration of Rights is excepted out of the general powers of government, and shall forever remain inviolate.

This section parallels what has been referred to as the "forgotten Ninth" Amendment of the U.S. Constitution. As noted above, the Court has held that despite the "shall forever remain inviolate" language, any provisions of the Constitution, including provisions of the Declaration of Rights itself, are potentially amendable. The Court declared in 1955 that Section 36 did "not put a limitation on the power of amendment of the Constitution." (Opinion of the Justices, 81 So. 2d 882, [numbers omitted] quoting from Downs v. Birmingham, 198 So. 231 (1940))

SECTION 36.01.

English is the official language of the state of Alabama. The legislature shall enforce this amendment by appropriate legislation. The legislature and officials of the state of Alabama shall take all steps necessary to insure that the role of English as the common language of the state of Alabama is preserved and enhanced. The legislature shall make no law which diminishes or ignores the role of English as the common language of the state of Alabama.

Any person who is a resident of or doing business in the state of Alabama shall have standing to sue the state of Alabama to enforce this amendment, and the courts of record of the state of Alabama shall have jurisdiction to hear cases brought to enforce this provision. The legislature may provide reasonable and appropriate limitations on the time and manner of suits brought under this amendment.

The English language amendment (509, 1990) was part of a national movement led by groups which claimed that successive waves of immigration, especially illegal, jeopardized the role of English as the lingua franca within the United States. Despite the amendment, the state is giving driver's license examinations in multiple languages, and private merchants frequently advertise their wares in both English and Spanish, Hispanics making up the largest group of immigrants. For the propriety of this practice, see Cole v. Riley, 989 So. 2d 1001 (2007).

SECTION 36.02.

(a) All persons shall have the right to hunt and fish in this state in accordance with law and regulations.

(b) This amendment shall be known as the "Sportsperson's Bill of Rights."

This is another new section of the Constitution (adopted as Amendment 597 in 1996) that seeks to prevent something that most observers would feel was not under attack. At the time it was attached, many Alabama hunters and fishermen were under the impression that animal rights activists were seeking to greatly restrict their freedom to do what this section asserts that they have a right to do, e.g., "to hunt and fish in this state in accordance with law and regulations." Since encroachment on this right was more of an imagined than a real fear, the section has not been litigated. A "bill" generally includes a list of items. This one has only two.

SECTION 36.03.
["Sanctity of Marriage" (774, 2006)]

[No longer in effect.]

This was voided by the U.S. Supreme Court when it upheld same-sex marriage in all states. (See Obergefell v. Hodges, 576 U.S. _____, 2015 WL 2473451 (U.S. June 26, 2015).)

SECTION 36.04.

[No longer in effect.]

This section sought to nullify major sections of the Affordable Health Care Act ("Obamacare"). It was emasculated when the U.S. Supreme Court upheld this legislation. See National Federation of Independent Business v. Sibelius (132 S. Ct. 603(2012)) and King v. Burwell (135 S. Ct. 475 (2015)).

Article II

State and County Boundaries

SECTION 37.

The boundaries of this state are established and declared to be as follows, that is to say: Beginning at the point where the thirty-first degree of north latitude crosses the Perdido river; thence east, to the western boundary line of the State of Georgia; thence along said line to the southern boundary line of the State of Tennessee, crossing the Tennessee river, and on to the second intersection of said river by said line; thence up said river to the mouth of Big Bear Creek; thence by a direct line to the northwest corner of Washington county, in this state, as originally formed; thence southwardly, along the line of the State of Mississippi, to the Gulf of Mexico; thence eastwardly, including all islands within six leagues of the shore, to the Perdido river; thence up the said river to the beginning; provided that the limitations and jurisdiction of this state shall extend to and include any other land and territory hereafter acquired, by contract or agreement with other states or otherwise, although such land and territory are not included within the boundaries hereinbefore designated.

This section is very specific and has, for the most part, been noncontroversial. Politically, the greatest interest in water territory was from the mid-1940s to the early 1950s when the tidelands oil issue was debated. One reason for greater support for the Republican nominee for president, Dwight D. Eisenhower, among southern elites in the 1952 election was his endorsement of states' rights to tidelands oil.

SECTION 38.

The boundaries of the several counties of this state as they now exist are hereby ratified and confirmed.

This section is unambiguous. Its contemporary significance is, along with numerous other provisions, to restrict any kind of county government reorganization in the interests of greater professionalization in the performance of public services and the achievement of economies of scale in implementing functions on a wider territorial basis.

SECTION 39.

The legislature may, by a two-thirds vote of each house thereof, arrange and designate boundaries for the several counties of this state, which boundaries shall not be altered, except by a like vote; but no new county shall be formed hereafter of less than six hundred square miles ... [Ellipses indicate obsolete and/or transitional language.]

SECTION 40.

No county shall be altered or changed, or in the event of the creation of new counties shall be established so as to run within seven miles of the county courthouse of any old county.

Sections 38–41 provide protection to county political and economic interests. This section reiterates the status quo language of Section 38 and further protects the county seat by providing that it will not face competition for trade from any town less than seven miles (a half-day's journey by horseback) away which might be the seat of a new county.

SECTION 41.

No courthouse or county site shall be removed except by a majority of the qualified electors of said county, voting at an election held for such purpose, and when an election has once been held no other election shall be held for such purpose until the expiration of four years; [specific local exception] ...

The location of courthouses was traditionally an intensely controversial matter for numerous political, economic, social, and other reasons. This section clearly specifies the procedures to be used for conducting referenda on the question of changing a county seat from one location to another. The Court early on said that, "this clause was inserted in the organic law in response to public sentiment engendered by supposed abuses by the legislature." (Marengo County v. Matkin, 32 So. 669 (1902))

SECTION 41.01.

After the ratification of this amendment, the legislature shall not establish any branch courthouse or any division or branch of any court of record to be held at

> any place other than the county seat, nor shall the legislature abolish any branch courthouse now existing, unless such proposal be first submitted to a vote of the qualified electors of the county or counties to be affected and is approved by a majority of those voting upon such proposition.

This amendment (81, 1950) was designed to defuse the at times extremely intense political controversy surrounding the location of county offices. The high court observed a few years after its approval that its objective was "to maintain the status quo" in this area "unless a majority of the qualified electors of the county first indicate their desire for a change." (Opinion of the Justices, 67 So. 2d 153 (1953))

Article III

Distribution of Powers of Government

SECTION 42.

The powers of the government of the State of Alabama shall be divided into three distinct departments, each of which shall be confided to a separate body of magistracy, to wit: Those which are legislative, to one; those which are executive, to another; and those which are judicial, to another.

This section reflects a naïve Madisonianism, making more explicit than the U.S. Constitution the desirability of a strict separation of powers.

The Court held during the height of the Progressive movement, when numerous local experiments were being tried which submerged the principle of separation of powers, that the principle did not apply to municipal government. (Wilkinson v. Lane, 181 Ala. 646 (1913)) The Court has also recognized that modern public administration may require the delegation to agencies of legislative, executive, and judicial powers. (Ex parte Darnell, 76 So. 2d 770 (1954))

This section works against an activist, "law-making" judiciary. The Court ruled over a half-century ago that judges had no authority to revise the tax laws. This was something only the legislature could do. (Champion v. McLean, 95 So. 2d 82 (1957)) Further, the legislature itself is to determine if it manages its affairs (e.g., voting) in accordance with its own rules. The Court will not get involved in matters such as this. (Birmingham-Jefferson Civic Ctr. Auth. v. City of Birmingham (912 So. 2d 204 (2005))

SECTION 43.

In the government of this state, except in the instances in this Constitution hereinafter expressly directed or permitted, the legislative department shall never exercise the executive and judicial powers, or either of them; the executive shall never exercise the legislative and judicial powers, or either of them; the judicial shall never exercise the legislative and executive powers, or either of them; to the end that it may be a government of laws and not of men.

This section takes the previous section's commitment to separation of powers a step further by stipulating that there is to be no intermingling of powers. This watertight compartmentalizing of powers would, in the eyes of the framers, help fulfill the Ciceronian ideal of "a government of laws and not of men."

Despite the obvious commingling of powers which seems clear to even the most casual observer of the contemporary governmental scene, the Court asserted in 1974 that, "The powers of the three branches of government must be kept separate and inviolate." (Aldridge v. Grund, 302 So. 2d 842) Also in the mid-1970s the Court ruled that the "Governor [could not], by executive order, appropriate public funds for education when the Legislature adjourns without passing an appropriations bill." (Wallace v. Baker, 336 So. 2d 156 (1976))

When the Court was still under Democratic control it looked like the judiciary might actually order the legislature to ensure adequacy of education funding throughout the state. However, by the turn of the century the Supreme Court, under steadily increasing Republican influence, decided that the judiciary had to forsake involvement when it came to determining the nuts and bolts of education finance, this being a legislative function. (Ex parte James, 836 So. 2d 813 (2002))

In another area involving the legislature, the Court ruled in 2010 that the state education board had not encroached on legislative authority when it forbade its members from being employed by the community colleges. This prohibition did not add to the qualifications for legislative office to be enumerated in our next section. (Hill v. Galliher, 65 So. 3d 362)

SECTION 43.01.

No order of a state court, which requires disbursement of state funds, shall be binding on the state or any state official until the order has been approved by a simple majority of both houses of the Legislature. This amendment shall not apply to orders, judgments, or decrees requiring payment of compensation for the taking of property by eminent domain or arising out of challenges to taxation or to such other orders, judgments, or decrees as may be otherwise required by statute, or settled principles of Alabama common law as decided by the Alabama appellate courts, not inconsistent with other provisions of this Constitution. Nothing herein shall be construed to preclude a court from making findings of fact or conclusions of law and orders relating thereto, that standards required by the United States Constitution, the Constitution of Alabama of 1901, laws of this state or of the United States, or rules or regulations promulgated pursuant thereto, are not being met, and from ordering the responsible entity or entities to comply with such standards.

This constitutional change (582, 1996) was designed to reinforce the new-found judicial denial of any power of its own to compel the legislature to make appropriations—whether to schools or in any other area of governmental activity. To some extent it represented constitutional overkill since, due especially to Republican membership gains, it was becoming increasingly clear that no judicial orders, such as contemplated by this section, would be issued in the future. (See, for example, Ex parte James (836 So. 2d 813 (2002)), where the Court said that the Alabama Constitution did not allow judges to have a say in how the state's public education system was funded.) Symbolically, the section also amounted to accumulated popular and legislative negative antipathy toward federal court orders—on which Amendment 582 could have no impact.

Article IV

Legislative Department

SECTION 44.

The legislative power of this state shall be vested in a legislature, which shall consist of a senate and a house of representatives.

Other than specify the bicameral division of legislative power in Alabama, the Court holds that this section affirms representative rather than direct popular government in the state. (Opinion of the Justices, 251 So. 2d 739 (1971)) Thus the Court advised the legislature that using a statewide referendum to determine whether a proposed law would go into effect or not contradicted this section.

In the American federal system, reserved powers belong to the states; those which are appropriate for exercise by government rest with the state legislatures. This article will identify which are appropriate and which are inappropriate objects of state legislation. This section also has implications for the extent to which the legislature may authorize actions by others, actions which seem to amount to the exercise of legislative powers. For example, the governor is able to prorate state funds when it is discovered that revenues will not reach the level of appropriations. This was authorized by the legislature in the Fletcher Budget Act of 1933.

In order to accommodate to the need of delegation, the Court has long made a distinction between legislative powers (which are not able to be delegated) and "quasi"-legislative powers (which under certain circumstances, can be delegated). (See Askew v. Hale County, 54 Ala.639 (1875).)

SECTION 45.

The style of the laws of this state shall be: "Be it enacted by the legislature of Alabama," which need not be repeated, but the act shall be divided into sections for convenience, according to substance, and the sections designated merely by figures. Each law shall contain but one subject, which shall be clearly expressed in its title, except general appropriation bills, general revenue bills, and bills adopting a code, digest, or revision of statutes; and no law shall be revived, amended, or the provisions thereof extended or conferred, by reference to its title only; but so much thereof as is revived, amended, extended, or conferred, shall be re-enacted and published at length.

This section is relatively clear with respect to the form bills considered for passage by the Alabama legislature should take. It antedates the 1901 Constitution, having originated in the Constitution of 1865.

It has several purposes, including reduction of logrolling by assembling unrelated sections of a bill which a majority of legislators could be induced to support because of benefits received, but which would not pass if the individual bills were separately considered. Also, by preventing a very abbreviated bill format, it seeks to minimize surprise either of legislators or the people generally regarding the subjects of legislation being considered for passage or actually passed. (See Lindsay v. U.S. Savings & Loan Co., 24 So. 171 (1898), State v. Hester, 172 So. 2d 61 (1954), and Opinion of the Justices, 319 So. 2d 682 (1975).)

The section recognizes the inability of legislators to read all bills in full (even if they were so inclined) in the requirement for a title which clearly capsulizes the bill that follows. Of course, coming up with a fully appropriate title for a bill may be difficult, and the Court will employ "liberality of construction" and avoid "all nice criticism" when reviewing a law which is challenged on this basis. (See the old case of Ex parte Pollard, 40 Ala. 77 (1866), which is quoted in Kendrick v. Boyd, 51 So. 2d 694 (1951).) Also, if a bill has a saving clause, nonpertinent sections (as related to the law's title) may be stricken, while consistent sections are permitted to remain in force. (Sweet v. Wilkinson, 40 So. 2d 427 (1949))

In 1987 the Court enumerated the purposes of this section as follows: (1) "notification of the public of the nature of the pending legislation," (2) "avoidance of fraud on the legislature by inadvertent passage of provisions not related to the title," and (3) "prevention of logrolling legislation." (Opinion of the Justices, 512 So. 2d 682 (1975))

The Court has held that this section is inapplicable to proposed constitutional amendments (Bonds v. State Department of Revenue, 49 So. 2d 280 (1950)); however, most of the sections identified as the product of amendments in this volume do relate primarily to one general subject.

SECTION 46.

Senators and representatives shall be elected by the qualified electors on the first Tuesday after the first Monday in November unless the legislature shall change the time of holding elections and in every fourth year thereafter. The terms of the senators and representatives shall commence on the day after the general election at which they are elected, and expire on the day after the general election held in the fourth year after their election, except as otherwise provided in this Constitution. [Transitional material omitted.] ... Whenever a vacancy shall occur in either house, the governor shall issue a writ of election to fill such vacancy for the remainder of the term.

In Alabama, unlike in most other states, both senators and representatives serve simultaneous four-year terms. In a majority of states, representatives serve two-year terms, senators, four. There are no term limits in Alabama.

SECTION 46.01.

The legislature may provide for the continuity of the legislature of the state of Alabama and the representation therein of each of the political subdivisions of the state in the event of an attack by an enemy of the United States, by providing for the selection of emergency interim legislators who shall be designated for temporary succession to the powers and duties but not the office of a legislator in case of such emergency. Such emergency interim legislator may serve only when the legislator in whose stead he is authorized to serve has died or is unable temporarily for physical, mental or legal reasons to exercise the powers and discharge the duties of his office, and until such time as the elected legislator is able to resume the duties of his office, or in case of a vacancy in such office a successor has been elected in accordance with section 46 of this Constitution.

This section, ratified as Amendment 159 (1961) a few months after the Berlin Wall was erected, reflects another aspect of emergency preparedness besides bomb shelters.

SECTION 47.

Senators shall be at least twenty-five years of age, and representatives twenty-one years of age at the time of their election. They shall have been citizens and residents of this state for three years and residents of their respective counties or districts for one year next before their election, if such county or district shall have been so long established, but if not, then of the county or district from which the same shall have been taken; and they shall reside in their respective counties or districts during their terms of office.

This section was written at a time when a man's life expectancy was much less than it is now. (Women didn't have the vote until 1920.) A representative's required minimum age (21) was the same as the minimum voting age in 1901; senators needed to be at least four years older. The average legislator in 2015 was in his or her mid-50s. Also, all legislators are lifetime U.S. citizens and have been residents of Alabama most of their lives. Occasionally, someone may be ineligible to run because he or she has not lived in the district for a year. However, there have been no incidents of legislators losing their seats because they moved out of their districts in the twenty-first century.

The Court has observed that the year's district residency requirement is designed to ensure that the potential legislator's constituents "could know him [her] and he [she] could learn something of their needs." (Butler v. Amos, 292 So. 2d 645 (1974)) However, this provision made more sense "when county lines defined legislative districts" instead of less fundamental boundaries used in the construction of census enumeration districts, employed in Alabama apportionment plans since the early 1970s. (Knight v. Gray, 420 So. 2d 247 (1982)) Be that as it may, "[T]he residence of the candidate must have been for at least one year at one or more successive places within the physical confines of the district the candidate wishes to serve." (Ibid. This quotation is from the argument of the Democratic Party counsel in the case.)

SECTION 48.01.

All sessions of the legislature shall be held at the capitol in the senate chamber and in the hall of the house of representatives, unless at any time it should from any cause become impossible or dangerous for the legislature to meet or remain at the capitol, or for the senate to meet or remain in the senate chamber, or for the representatives to meet or remain in the hall of the house of representatives, in which case the governor may convene the legislature, or remove it after it has convened, to some other place, or may designate some other place for the sitting of the respective houses, or either of them, as necessity may require. The legislature shall convene on the second Tuesday in January next succeeding their election and shall remain in session for not longer than ten consecutive calendar days. No business can be transacted at such sessions except the organization of the legislature, the election of officers, the appointment of standing committees of the senate and the house of representatives for the ensuing four years, which election and appointment may, however, also be made at such other times as may be necessary, the opening and publication of the returns and the ascertainment and declaration of the results of the election for governor, lieutenant-governor, attorney-general, state auditor, secretary of state, state treasurer, and commissioner of agriculture and industries, the election of such officers in the event of a tie vote, the determination of contested elections for such offices, the judging of the election returns and qualification of the members of the legislature, and the inauguration of the governor and the other elected state officers whose terms of office are concurrent with that of the governor. At the beginning of each such organization session, and at such other times as may be necessary, the senate shall elect one of its members president pro tempore thereof, to preside over its deliberations in the absence of the lieutenant-governor, and the house of representatives shall elect one of its members as speaker, to preside over its deliberations. The president of the senate and the speaker of the house of representatives shall each hold his respective office until his successor has been elected and qualified. The provisions of this Constitution in conflict herewith are hereby modified to conform to the provisions of this amendment....

This section (57, 1946) provides for the legislature's short organizational session, the certification of the election returns for the executive officials listed, and arranging for the inauguration of the governor and other executive officials whose terms are coterminous with that of the governor. While it also stipulates legislative determination of the outcomes of contested elections, legislation is now in place providing for automatic recounts when the margin of the presumed election winner is only razor-thin over that of his or her opponent. (Section 17-16-21, *Code of Alabama 1975*)

SECTION 48.02.

In the event the legislature determines it to be necessary or desirable that the Capitol be repaired, renovated, restored, constructed or reconstructed, the legislature, by resolution shall designate and provide a suitable place for the meeting of the legislature and the transacting of business of the legislative department. Such place shall be designated and known as the Alabama State House.

The Alabama legislature normally meets and does almost all of its work in the building formerly occupied by the state transportation department. This is the case despite the implication in this amendment (428, 1982) that the Alabama State House would be the legislative seat only during the restoration (long since completed) of the historic capitol. (427, 1982)

SECTION 49.01.

Section 1.

(a) The Legislature recognizes that the public trust in the legislative body is of paramount importance. The Legislature further recognizes that government transparency and accountability are vital to the preservation of the public trust. To that end, it is the purpose of this amendment to remove the power of determining legislative compensation or expenses from the hands of the Legislature itself, to validate the basis upon which legislative compensation and expenses are established in an objective manner based on measurable standards, and to allow the citizens of Alabama to vote on this issue. It is the will of the Legislature to resolve the issue of legislative compensation and expenses once and for all by providing for compensation and expenses for members of the Legislature and the President of the Senate and by providing for compensation to be paid at the same rate as the median household income in Alabama and expenses in the same amounts and manner as expenses are allowed under law for state employees generally.

(b) All laws or parts of laws in conflict with this amendment are repealed, including, but not limited to: Those portions of Amendments 39, 57, and 339 of the

Constitution of Alabama of 1901, relating to the compensation and expenses of members of the Legislature; Act 87-209, Act 90-490, Act 91-95, Act 91-108, and Act 2007-75; and Section 29-1-8, Code of Alabama 1975.

Section 2. The annual basic compensation for each member of the Legislature and the President of the Senate shall be the median annual household income in Alabama, as ascertained and adjusted each year by the State Personnel Board to take effect on the first day of January of each year.

Section 3.

(a) No member of the Legislature or the President of the Senate may receive reimbursement for any expenses except as provided in this section.

(b) Subject to approval by the President of the Senate or by the Speaker of the House for the respective members of their Houses, and except as otherwise provided in subsection (d), a member of the Legislature may be reimbursed for any of the following:

(1) Expenses incurred for travel on official business in the same amounts or at the same rates as for state employees traveling in the service of the state under state law, rules, and policies, provided that, for a member of the Legislature, the travel is to a place outside his or her district.

(2) Actual expenses other than travel expenses incurred in the performance of official duties.

(3) Expenses authorized pursuant to Act 1196 of the 1971 Regular Session for the presiding officer of each House.

(c) Reimbursement for expenses may only be made under subdivision (1) and (2) of subsection (b) after a determination of the presiding officer of the member's House that the travel or expense is in the service of the state and on submission of a signed voucher submitted in the same manner as a request for reimbursement of expenses by a state employee.

(d) Except for the expenses of transportation, no member of the Legislature who resides less than 50 miles from the seat of government may be reimbursed for any travel expenses for travel between his or her place of residence and the seat of government.

(e) In making the determination required by subsection (c), the presiding officer of either House may not determine a particular expense incurred by any member of the Legislature was not in the service of the state on any basis that discriminates between members of the Legislature.

(f) Reimbursement for expenses authorized pursuant to this section shall be paid in a timely manner that is consistent with expense reimbursement regulations jointly promulgated by the President of the Senate and the Speaker of the House pursuant to the Alabama Administrative Procedure Act. Such regulations shall, to the extent possible, mirror similar regulations applicable to state employees. The President of the Senate and the Speaker of the House may not discriminate between members of the Legislature regarding the timely reimbursement of authorized expenses.

(g) The State Personnel Board may promulgate such rules as it deems necessary to enforce its responsibilities under this amendment and, in conjunction with the Comptroller, shall provide an annual report on compensation and reimbursement of expenses to members of the Legislature.

Section 4.

(a) The compensation and reimbursement for expenses provided in Sections 2 and 3 shall constitute the total amounts payable to the presiding officers and members of the Legislature, beginning with the terms commencing immediately after the 2014 General Election.

(b) The Legislature may not increase, supplement, or otherwise enlarge the compensation or reimbursement for expenses payable to its members by this amendment.

One of the practices of the legislature that has aroused the most anger among the citizenry has been the way in which its members have raised their pay beyond the minimal amount authorized in the Constitution of 1901 originally. Typically, legislators would, during the first session of the quadrennium for which they were elected, raise their expense allowance. The author of the resolution hiking pay would generally be a member coming from a "safe" district as far as his own tenure was concerned. Sometimes the resolution would even be approved on a voice vote.

This new section (871, 2012) attempts to make a genuine reform with regard to legislative pay and to remove the question as a perennial political issue. Instead of the set amount of a few dollars, as established in the original Constitution, supplemented by generous expense allowances, henceforth legislators will "be paid at the same rate as the median household income in Alabama." Their expense reimbursements will be "in the same amounts and manner as expenses are allowed under law for state employees generally." As the reader will note, the expenses for which legislators are reimbursable are identified. Finally, legislators are not allowed to alter these constitutional provisions related to their salaries and expenses. This is possibly the most widely commended amendment added to the Constitution in many years.

SECTION 50.

The legislature shall consist of not more than thirty-five senators, and not more than one hundred and five members of the house of representatives, to be apportioned among the several districts and counties, as prescribed in this Constitution ...

This section specifies the number of members to compose each house of the legislature. It is accurate in part today thanks to federal court decisions in the 1970s which had the effect of reducing the House from 106 to 105 members. The obsolete portion of this section (not reproduced here) was its stipulation of at least one representative per county. Proper apportionment could not be attained and this provision adhered to. Thus it was jettisoned by federal judges, primarily responsible for crafting Alabama's modern legislative districting schemes. (See applicable cases below.)

SECTION 51.

The senate, at the beginning of each regular session, and at such other times as may be necessary, shall elect one of its members president pro tem, thereof, to preside over its deliberations in the absence of the lieutenant governor; and the house of representatives, at the beginning of each regular session, and at such other times as may be necessary, shall elect one of its members as speaker; and the president of the senate and the speaker of the house of representatives shall hold their offices respectively, until their successors are elected and qualified. In case of the temporary disability of said presiding officers, the house to which he belongs may elect one of its members to preside over that house and to perform all the duties of such officer during the continuance of his disability; and such temporary officer, while performing duty as such, shall receive the same compensation to which the permanent officer is entitled by law, and no other. Each house shall choose its own officers and shall be the judge of the election, returns, and qualifications of its members.

The language here is unambiguous and has provided little occasion for controversy. It should be observed, however, that while the Constitution says that "[e]ach house shall choose its own officers," until recent times it was the custom for the incoming governor to designate whom he wanted as speaker. This individual the House would then elect as soon as it went into organizational session. This practice has not prevailed since the closing years of the era of George Wallace in the 1980s.

SECTION 52.

A majority of each house shall constitute a quorum to do business; but a smaller number may adjourn from day to day and compel the attendance of absent members, in such manner and under such penalties as each house may provide.

While the Court holds that an "act must be done [at a minimum] by a majority of a quorum" (Opinion of the Justices, 152 So. 901 (1934)), it is a fact that much legislation, particularly of the local sort, passes when far fewer are actually in the House and Senate chambers.

SECTION 53.

Each house shall have power to determine the rules of its proceedings and to punish its members and other persons, for contempt or disorderly behavior in its presence; to enforce obedience to its processes, to protect its members against violence, or offers of bribes or corrupt solicitation; and with the concurrence of two-thirds of the house, to expel a member, but not a second time for the same offense; and the two houses shall have all the powers necessary for the legislature of a free state.

The Court advises that the legislature's rule-making power "is unlimited except as controlled by other provisions of [the] Constitution." (Opinion of the Justices, 179 So. 2d 155 (1965)) Absent any conflict, judges will not "look to the wisdom or folly, the advantages or disadvantages" of these rules. (Ibid.) The opinion cited here was prompted by Governor George Wallace's attempt to get the Senate to approve an amendment allowing him to succeed himself in 1965.

This section describes how the House and Senate may establish and seek to maintain an environment appropriate for the discharge of the legislative function. While a chamber does have the right to expel an erring member by a two-thirds vote, the Court holds that "the legislature must afford a member the minimal procedural due process requirements of the federal constitution." Furthermore, "a member cannot be expelled for reasons which violate the first amendment." (State v. Reed, 364 So. 2d 303 (1978))

Most recently the Court ruled that the Constitution did not compel open legislative sessions; moreover, even if it did, it would be outside the judiciary's scope of authority to compel the legislature to abide by any rule to the contrary. (Ex parte Marsh et al. (145 So. 3d 744) (2013))

SECTION 54.

A member of the legislature, expelled for corruption, shall not thereafter be eligible to either house, and punishment for contempt or disorderly behavior shall not bar an indictment for the same offense.

The language of this section is very clear. It has provoked no controversy.

SECTION 55.

Each house shall keep a journal of its proceedings and cause the same to be published immediately after its adjournment, excepting such parts as, in its judgment, may require secrecy; and the yeas and nays of the members of each house on any question shall, at the request of one-tenth of the members present, be entered on the journal. Any member of either house shall have liberty to dissent from or protest against any act or resolution which he may think injurious to the public, or to an individual, and have the reasons for his dissent entered on the journal.

The language of this section is unambiguous. Its principal constitutional significance is that it is the journal, which has been properly signed by the appropriate legislative officers and submitted as required to the secretary of state's office, that the courts will use as the decisive evidence of what went on "officially" in the legislature. (See Montgomery Beer-Bottling Works v. Gaston, 28 So. 497 (1900).) They will not probe to see if what actually happened differs from the account given in the journal.

SECTION 56.

Members of the legislature shall, in all cases, except treason, felony, violation of their oath of office, and breach of the peace, be privileged from arrest during their attendance at the session of their respective houses, and in going to and returning from the same; and for any speech or debate in either house shall not be questioned in any other place.

This section has occasionally been the subject of discussion among members of the public and in the media, especially when stories arise regarding legislators who are able to relieve themselves of penalties associated with speeding in their automobiles after being stopped by state highway troopers by explaining that they are on legislative business. A close approximation to this section has appeared in all of the Constitutions and no changes are expected.

In recent years the Court has ruled that citizens had no constitutional right to complain if legislators chose to act contrary to their own rules during conference committee meetings. To reiterate, this is an area into which the judiciary will not intrude. (Ex parte Marsh (__ So. 3d __) (2013))

SECTION 57.

The doors of each house shall be opened except on such occasions as, in the opinion of the house, may require secrecy, but no person shall be admitted to the floor of either house while the same is in session, except members of the legislature, the officers and employees of the two houses, the governor and his secretary, representatives of the press, and other persons to whom either house, by unanimous vote, may extend the privileges of its floor.

Privileges of the floor formerly were rather freely given. However, this is not the case at the present time and even media representatives must cover the legislature from within a glass-enclosed press gallery.

SECTION 58.

Neither house shall, without the consent of the other, adjourn for more than three days, nor to any other place than that in which they may be sitting except as otherwise provided in this Constitution.

This very clear section is not often questioned. However, during the administration of James E. Folsom, Sr., the governor and the legislature (particularly the Senate) had diametrically opposing views on the wisdom of calling a constitutional convention to deal with the issue of legislative reapportionment. The governor called multiple sessions in an effort to get the legislature to assemble a convention. The Senate snubbed its collective nose at the governor by adjourning shortly after it was convened. The Court advised the upper house in this historical context, however, that it could "not constitutionally adjourn sine die without the concurrence of the House of Representatives." (Opinion of the Justices, 47 So. 2d 642 (1950))

SECTION 59.

No senator or representative shall, during the term for which he shall have been elected, be appointed to any office of profit under this state, which shall have been created, or the emoluments of which shall have been increased during such term, except such offices as may be filled by election of the people.

This section, in contrast with the preceding one, is complex. It seeks to prevent legislative service from being an immediate steppingstone to appointive administrative office. Legislators can be appointed to positions the only compensation for which is the payment of expenses. This was a ruling many years ago when a war emergency council was created which included legislative members. (Opinion of the Justices, 13 So. 2d 674 (1943)) Also, if the salary of the preexisting position has not been changed, the legislator does not have a problem in vacating his or her seat and taking a different job.

SECTION 60.

No person convicted of embezzlement of the public money, bribery, perjury, or other infamous crime, shall be eligible to the legislature, or capable of holding any office of trust or profit in this state.

This section is interpreted to mean that upon sentencing for the crimes mentioned, the public office then occupied is vacated. (Stone v. State, 104 So. 894 (1925)) In 1993 the ethics conviction of Governor Guy Hunt instantly removed him from office and put the chief executive's position in the hands of Lieutenant Governor James E. Folsom, Jr. This was because of legislation which speeded up removal to occur at the moment of conviction rather than at the time of sentencing. (See the Alabama *Code*, sec. 36-9-2.)

As regards future public service, the Court held in Randolph County v. Thompson (502 So. 2d 357 (1987)) that "a pardon does not restore to one pardoned the eligibility to hold public office." An individual's ability to reclaim his or her civil and political rights would depend heavily on a favorable decision from the State Board of Pardons and Paroles.

SECTION 61.

No law shall be passed except by bill, and no bill shall be so altered or amended on its passage through either house as to change its original purpose.

There is no evidence of any bill ever being declared unconstitutional because its "purpose" had been improperly altered. Further, since the Court relies only on the journals to ascertain what the purpose of a bill was, it would be practically impossible to determine a change in purpose. The journals do not present verbatim debates on bills.

SECTION 62.

No bill shall become a law until it shall have been referred to a standing committee of each house, acted upon by such committee in session, and returned therefrom, which facts shall affirmatively appear upon the journal of each house.

As noted in the commentary on Section 55, the Court will generally not entertain protestations that what is spread upon the journal did not in fact occur. With regard to legislative rules, "compliance with them by the legislative department [will be assumed] unless the contrary is shown to be the case." (State v. Buckley, 54 Ala. 599 (1875)) No case law has developed regarding a procedure for going beyond the legislative record. The Court ruled in 1901 that "to the journals only, of the two houses . . . can we look to ascertain the nature, character, and extent of action taken by the legislative body." (Jackson v. State, 31 So. 380)

SECTION 63.

Every bill shall be read on three different days in each house, and no bill shall become a law, unless on its final passage it be read at length, and the vote be taken by yeas and nays, the names of the members voting for and against the same be entered upon the journals, and a majority of each house be recorded thereon as voting in its favor, except as otherwise provided in this Constitution.

This section is the most often disregarded in practice. Bills are seldom read aloud except as a delaying tactic. As was stated with respect to previous sections where the journal is the basis for determining compliance or noncompliance, "compliance will be presumed, nothing appearing to the contrary." (Clifton v. State, 118 So. 235) (App. 1928))

The courts will not even insist that the journals show compliance with every procedure stipulated in this and other sections for proper consideration of legislation. "If the journals do not show [the appropriate number of bill readings] the judicial department will presume that it had been read three times"; furthermore, "it is to be presumed that members knew that this had been done," that is, that correct form was followed. (Walker v. Griffith, 60 Ala. 361 (1877)) In sum, the determination of whether the legislature has acted in such a way that it followed its own rules is a nonjusticiable question not susceptible to being resolved by a court. (Birmingham-Jefferson Civic Ctr. Auth. v. City of Birmingham (912 So. 2d 204) (2005))

SECTION 64.

No amendment shall be adopted except by a majority of the house wherein the same is offered, nor unless the amendment with the names of those voting for and against the same shall be entered at length on the journal of the house in which the same is adopted, and no amendment to bills by one house shall be concurred in by the other, unless a vote be taken by yeas and nays, and the names of the members voting for and against the same be recorded at length on the journal; and no report of a committee of conference shall be adopted in either house, except upon a vote taken by yeas and nays, and entered on the journal, as herein provided for the adoption of amendments.

Showing how reluctant the Court generally has been to insist that the legislature comply with both the letter and spirit of constitutional provisions regarding how it conducts its business, it ruled in 1911 that this section, for example, called for legislative journals to indicate a vote only in favor of a proposed amendment, not a vote on the amended bill in full. (Brandon v. Askew, 54 So. 605 (1911)) Again, with this section as with others stipulating how legislative business is to be conducted, obedience is presumed. (State v. Buckley, 54 Ala. 599 (1875))

SECTION 65.

The legislature shall have no power to authorize lotteries or gift enterprises for any purposes, and shall pass laws to prohibit the sale in this state of lottery or gift enterprise tickets, or tickets in any scheme in the nature of a lottery; and all acts, or parts of acts heretofore passed by the legislature of this state, authorizing a lottery or lotteries, and all acts amendatory thereof, or supplemental thereto, are hereby avoided.

As the lottery increased in popularity in other states in the mid-twentieth century, interest grew in Alabama to rescind these constitutional proscriptions against lotteries. Nevertheless, when a lottery proposed by Governor Don Siegelman was put before the voters in October 1999, it was rejected by a margin of 54 percent to 46 percent. The Protestant culture of Alabama has traditionally looked on gambling as sinful. Alabama judicial dockets have been generously supplied with bingo cases in recent years. It has frequently been held that if a game is challenged as gambling in violation of Section 25, the defendants must be able to show that their game called for a minimum amount of skill on the part of the participants. (Opinion of the Justices (795 So. 2d 630) (2001)) In 2010 the Court held a municipal ordinance to be invalid because its definition of bingo was one which did not call for the exercise of any skill on the part of players. (Surles v. City of Ashville, 2010 Ala. LEXIS 16). Skill must be more important than mere chance if a challenged game is to be found acceptable under Section 65. (State ex. rel. Tyson v. Ted's Game Enters. (893 So. 2d 355 (2002), Civ. App.)

SECTION 66.

The presiding officer of each house shall, in the presence of the house over which he presides, sign all bills and joint resolutions passed by the legislature, after the same shall have been publicly read at length immediately before signing, and the fact of reading and signing shall be entered upon the journal; but the reading at length may be dispensed with by a two-thirds vote of a quorum present, which fact shall also be entered on the journal.

The reading of the journal is almost always dispensed with unless a minority within the chamber is trying to obstruct the progress of some unwanted piece of legislation. This section—and its general nonuse—is by no means unique to the Alabama Constitution.

SECTION 67.

The legislature shall prescribe by law the number, duties, and compensation of the officers and employes of each house, and no payment shall be made from the state treasury or be in any way authorized to any person except to an acting officer or employe elected or appointed in pursuance of law.

The secretary of the Senate and the clerk of the House are the principal legislative officers. Many years ago state legislatures were notoriously overstaffed, and this section sought to regulate the compensation of an excessive number of employees.

SECTION 68.

The legislature shall have no power to grant or authorize or require any county or municipal authority to grant, nor shall any county or municipal authority have power to grant any extra compensation, fee, or allowance to any public officer, servant, or employe, agent or contractor, after service shall have been rendered or contract made, nor to increase or decrease the fees and compensation of such officers during their terms of office, nor shall any officer of the state bind the state to the payment of any sum of money but by authority of law; provided this section shall not apply to allowances made by commissioners' courts or boards of revenue to county officers for ex officio services nor prevent the legislature from increasing or diminishing at any time the allowances to sheriffs or other officers for feeding, transferring, or guarding prisoners.

As its language makes clear, this section's primary subject of concern is compensation paid to local officials. The most important aspect of this section is the prohibition against altering (usually upward) salaries of local officials during their current term of office. Illustrating a strictness of construction, the court holds that public hospital corporations and public hospital associations are not identifiable as Alabama political subdivisions. This means that they are not circumscribed in their financial activities by the constitutional restrictions being identified here. (Alabama Hospital Association v. Dillard, 388 So. 2d 903 (1980)) (County commissions are now uniformly called this instead of boards of revenue.)

SECTION 68.01.

Any provisions of this Constitution or amendments thereto to the contrary notwithstanding, neither the legislature, nor any county of the state shall, by the imposition of new, different, and additional duties or otherwise, increase, or authorize the increase of, the salary, fees or other compensation of any officer of the state or of any county of the state, who is elected or appointed for a fixed term, during the term for which he is elected or appointed, regardless of whether such officer may be removed at the pleasure of the authority electing or appointing him or only upon impeachment; nor shall the legislature or any county of the state in any manner or by any means decrease, or authorize the decrease of, the salary, fees or other compensation of any such officer, during the term for which he is elected or appointed; nor shall the legislature or any county of the state increase or decrease, or authorize the increase or decrease of, the salary, fees or other compensation of any person filling an unexpired term in any such office during the remainder of such term, either before or after the appointment or election of such person to fill the unexpired term. As to officers who are members of any court, board, commission, or similar body whose terms do not run concurrently, any increase or decrease in the salary, fees, or other compensation of the members of any such court, board, commission, or similar body shall become effective as to all such members thereof immediately after the expiration of the term or terms of office of the member or members whose term or terms first expire.

This section (92, 1952) forbids state and county officer salary increases or decreases during the terms that those who are targeted for the increases or decreases are currently serving. A special procedure is provided for members of plural bodies serving overlapping terms. This section does not apply to rank-and-file bureaucratic employees.

SECTION 69.

All stationery, printing, paper, and fuel used in the legislative and other departments of government shall be furnished and the printing, binding, and distribution of laws, journals, department reports, and all other printing, binding, and repairing and furnishing the halls and rooms used for the meeting of the legislature and its committees, shall be performed under contract, to be given to the lowest responsible bidder below a maximum price, and under such regulations as shall be prescribed by law; no member or officer of any department of the government shall be in any way interested in such contract, and all such contracts shall be subject to the approval of the governor, auditor, and treasurer.

In the old days, state printing was one of the most lucrative plums that could be awarded to supporters of successful state candidates. This was when government did not do very much. So a constitutional provision was inserted specifying that contracts for printing (and the services mentioned) would be approved by three executive officers. Normally, they would be expected to distribute contracts in some mutually agreeable sequence among their supporters. Later, competitive bid laws were passed to more seriously depoliticize the awarding of contracts. Today this section is interpreted to necessitate contracts when private enterprise does printing work for state agencies. (Associated Industries of Alabama v. Britton, 371 So. 2d 904 (1979)) A few years after the Constitution of 1901 went into effect, historian Charles A. Beard noted, with a bit of unbelief regarding the restrictive nature of constitutions written in this period, that the legislature of Alabama "must even buy its fuel according to the rules laid down in the fundamental law of the commonwealth." (Beard, *American Government and Politics*, New York: Macmillan, 1914, p. 706)

SECTION 70.

All bills for raising revenue shall originate in the house of representatives. The governor, auditor, and attorney-general shall, before each regular session of the legislature, prepare a general revenue bill to be submitted to the legislature, for its information, and the secretary shall have printed for the use of the legislature a sufficient number of copies of the bill so prepared, which the governor shall transmit to the house of representatives as soon as organized to be used or dealt with as that house may elect. The senate may propose amendments to revenue bills. No revenue bill shall be passed during the last five days of the session.

This section follows the U.S. Constitution in requiring that revenue bills originate in the lower house, which was at the outset the only group of legislators directly elected by the people of the states. The Alabama Constitution has always provided for this as well.

The ex officio general revenue committee is no longer used. The Alabama executive branch, although still diffuse, is not quite as fragmented as this section would suggest. The governor, buttressed by the Department of Finance, is clearly the chief executive.

The ban on last-minute revenue bills is clearly evaded. The legislature considers tax bills right up to the minute of adjournment. As long ago as 1931, a new gas tax was passed at the end of the legislative session, but the Court held that it was not a "revenue bill." (See Opinion of the Justices, 136 So. 589 (1931).) An artificial distinction has been made between discrete tax items and "general revenue bills." (See Woco Pep Co. v. Butler, 142 So. 509 (1932).) The same distinction is made between a "bill for raising revenue" and a "revenue bill" in the first and last sentences of this section. (See Opinion of the Justices, 31 So. 2d 558 (1947).) Also, the section does not apply to bills designed to achieve some programmatic end but which also provide some means to finance the policy. (See Beeland Wholesale Co. v. Kaufman, 174 So. 516 (1937).) For example, the Court advised in 1987 that a bill which put environmental protection fees on motor fuels did not fall into the category of "revenue bill," because the aim of the law was not just to generate revenue but "to provide for a disposition of fees collected for returning polluted groundwater to a quality comparable to its previous state." (Opinion of the Justices, 511 So. 2d 505) Later, in 1997, the Criminal Appeals Court held that revenue-raising bills had to start in the House only if their primary purpose was to generate funds for the state treasury, not to achieve some programmatic purpose. (Finley v. State (695 So. 2d 258)) This was essentially the same ruling as made in 2010 in a case involving incarcerated felons at state penal institutions. (State Ala. Dep't of Corr. v. Merritt (2010 Ala. Civ. App. LEXIS 172)

SECTION 71.

The general appropriation bill shall embrace nothing but appropriations for the ordinary expenses of the executive, legislative, and judicial departments of the state, for interest on the public debt, and for the public schools. The salary of no officer or employe shall be increased in such bill, nor shall any appropriations be made therein for any officer or employe unless his employment and the amount of his salary have already been provided by law. All other appropriations shall be made by separate bills, each embracing but one subject.

This section had its genesis in the Constitution of 1875. This middle sentence is new to 1901. The Court is reasonably lenient regarding the "one subject" requirement, holding that it is satisfied "if [an] act has but one general subject which is contained in its title." (Opinion of the Justices, 154 So. 2d 12 (1963) It will be noted that the Constitution does not require appropriations bills to originate in a particular house. For many years the legislature has passed two basic appropriations bills annually, the general fund and the educational trust fund, the latter being by far the larger of the two. Section 71 is not violated when an appropriations bill not only makes outlays but specifies how shortfalls are to be dealt with. (See Riley v. Joint Fiscal Comm. of the Ala. Legislature (26 So. 3d 1150) (2009).)

SECTION 72.

No money shall be paid out of the treasury except upon appropriations made by law, and on warrants drawn by the proper officer in pursuance thereof; and a regular statement and account of receipts and expenditures of all public moneys shall be published annually, in such manner as may be by law directed.

Since the 1940s the Department of Finance has had the principal responsibility for preparing and issuing the State of Alabama's annual financial report.

This section came into play most notably when the legislature adjourned in 1976 without passing the educational trust fund appropriation bill. This happens on occasion when, despite the problems associated with delay and the budget isolation amendment (Section 71.01 (448, 1984)), the legislature waits until the last minute to pass one or both of the appropriations bills and time runs out before action can be completed. In 1976 the Court ruled that Governor George Wallace could not "by executive order, appropriate public funds for education when the Legislature adjourns without passing an appropriation bill." (Wallace v. Baker, 336 So. 2d 156 (1976))

SECTION 73.

No appropriation shall be made to any charitable or educational institution not under the absolute control of the state, other than normal schools established by law for the professional training of teachers for the public schools of the state, except by a vote of two-thirds of all the members elected to each house.

Appropriations have regularly been made by the legislature to nonstate institutions—for example, Tuskegee University. The only stipulation, as stated here, is that two-thirds of each house approve of the grants.

SECTION 74.

No act of the legislature shall authorize the investment of any trust fund by executors, administrators, guardians, or other trustees in the stock of any private corporation; any such acts now existing are avoided, saving investments heretofore made; provided, however, that unless otherwise provided by the legislature, any of said mentioned trust funds may be invested in corporation [sic] or institutions, investments in which are guaranteed as to principal by the United States government or insured as to principal by any instrumentality or agency thereof, provided such investments shall not exceed the amount insured by any such instrumentality or agency.

The present Section 74 is Amendment 40, ratified in 1939. The original section ended with the word "made." The language following provides needed flexibility in the investments authorized here. Absent this amendment, the supposed objects of concern would have had their interest-bearing accounts able to draw only the most paltry rates of interest—which was a good way to characterize interest rates being paid in 2015.

SECTION 75.

The power to change venue in civil and criminal causes is vested in the courts, to be exercised in such manner as shall be provided by law.

This section is clear. The legislature has not attempted to intrude upon what the Constitution here grants to the judiciary.

SECTION 76.

When the legislature shall be convened in special session, there shall be no legislation upon subjects other than those designated in the proclamation of the governor calling such session, except by a vote of two-thirds of each house. [Obsolete material.] ...

This section provides the foundation for gubernatorial dominance of the agenda of special legislative sessions and is a major component of gubernatorial strength generally. In Alabama, as in many other states, legislative sessions are typically rather short and face mandatory cut-off points. However, special sessions also occur for reasons of gubernatorial interest. The legislature is free to reject what the governor proposes, to accept it, or, more probably, make modifications as it sees fit.

SECTION 77.

No state office shall be continued or created for the inspection or measuring of merchandise, manufacture, or commodity, but any county or municipality may appoint such officers when authorized by law.

This quaint section reflects a long-standing commitment to a laissez-faire economy. It originated in the Constitution of 1875 and has no direct relationship to any section preceding or following it. The Court once said that it was so evident in meaning as to require no interpretation. (State v. McGough, 24 So.

395 (1898)) It is routinely ignored since many state employees are engaged in inspection activities today.

SECTION 78.

No act of the legislature changing the seat of government of the state shall become a law until the same shall have been submitted to the qualified electors of the state at a general election, and approved by a majority of such electors voting on the same; and such act shall specify the proposed new location.

Moving the capital from Montgomery to some other city has never been seriously considered almost from the very day it was located there. Montgomery has been Alabama's capital city since 1846. Within Montgomery, however, the meeting place of the legislature changed in 1986 from the historic Capitol to the building formerly occupied by the old Highway Department. This move was authorized by Section 48.02 (427, 1982). This structure was officially designated the State House.

SECTION 79.

A member of the legislature who shall solicit, demand, or receive, or consent to receive, directly or indirectly, for himself or for another, from any company, corporation, association, or person, any money, office, appointment, employment, reward, thing of value, or enjoyment, or of personal advantage or promise thereof, for his vote or official influence, or for withholding the same; or with an understanding expressed or implied, that his vote or official action shall be in any way influenced thereby, or who shall solicit or demand any such money or other advantage, matter, or thing aforesaid, for another as consideration for his vote, or influence, or for withholding the same; or shall give or withhold his vote or influence in consideration of the payment or promise of such advantage, matter, or thing to another, shall be guilty of bribery within the meaning of this Constitution; and shall incur the disabilities and penalties provided thereby for such offense, and such additional punishment as is or shall be provided by law.

This section defines bribery. Despite the great detail into which the section goes, it can be argued that there is, in effect, informal bribery when modern political action committees (PACs) contribute heavily to legislative and other campaign coffers, and then with great satisfaction see legislators vote in the groups' interest, even if no quid pro quo or direct link can be found between the campaign contributions and subsequent favorable legislative votes. In March 2012 an Alabama gambling entrepreneur and several legislators were acquitted of charges that they were involved in a conspiracy to fix legislative votes on a bill being considered by the House and Senate in 2010 that would have greatly expanded gambling in the state. (See Kim Chandler, "Milton McGregor, 5 Others Acquitted in Alabama Gambling Trial," www.al.com, March 8, 2012) (accessed February 9, 2015).

SECTION 80.

Any person who shall, directly or indirectly, offer, give, or promise any money, or thing of value, testimonial, privilege, or personal advantage to any executive or judicial officer or member of the legislature to influence him in the performance of any of his public or official duties, shall be guilty of bribery, and be punished in such manner as may be provided by law.

Whereas Section 79 deals with the taking of bribes, this section defines the offering of bribes. Perhaps surprisingly, given Alabama's reputation for corruption, it has not been the subject of contemporary litigation.

SECTION 81.

The offense of corrupt solicitation of members of the legislature or of public officers of this state or any municipal division thereof, and any occupation or practice of solicitation of such members or officers, to influence their official action, shall be defined by law, and shall be punished by fine and imprisonment in the penitentiary; and the legislature shall provide for the trial and punishment of the offenses enumerated in the two preceding sections, and shall require the judges to give the same specially in charge to the grand juries in all the counties of this state.

This section builds on Sections 79 and 80, providing a firm basis for statutory enactments punishing bribery in any part of state or local government. The absence of case law in this area testifies to the paltriness of efforts to identify and punish corrupt conduct in violation of the spirit of Sections 79, 80, and 81 of the Alabama Constitution.

SECTION 82.

A member of the legislature who has a personal or private interest in any measure or bill proposed or pending before the legislature, [sic] shall disclose the fact to the house of which he is a member, and shall not vote thereon.

Despite the apparent clarity of this section, there has been a continuing concern that legislators have, in fact, been advancing their personal interests through legislative service, contrary to the spirit, if not so frequently the letter, of the Constitution. Probing newspaper reports often have pointed to legislative conflicts of interest, and it is not difficult to cite numerous examples of senators and representatives promoting legislation in which they have a personal interest. The courts will apparently frown only on those actual votes on bills that favor legislators apart from their membership in identifiable economic groups outside the legislature. The Court held in 1993 that legislators are forbidden only from actions that yield them direct and personal financial advantage. (Lambert v. Wilcox County Commission, 623 So. 2d 727 (1993))

Section 82 was amplified somewhat in 1998 when the Court stated that it not only covered actual voting on bills but also any other activities designed to promote a measure's passage. (Opinion of the Justices (716 So. 2d 1149)

In mid-December 2010 the newly elected Republican legislature in special session passed a package of bills related primarily to strengthening existing ethics and campaign finance laws. (See David White, "In Alabama Legislature Ethics Sweep, Details Remain," www.al. com, December 17, 2010) (accessed February 9, 2015). With the advantage of half a decade of hindsight it can be said that the new legislation did not change the political culture of Alabama very much.

SECTION 83.

In all elections by the legislature the members shall vote viva voce, and the votes shall be entered on the journal.

An election "viva voce" is when the names of members are called and their votes are recorded. This section was a candidate for change during the legislative reform movement of the 1960s and 1970s. It was argued that, in the case of the election of the speaker of the House, representatives ought to be permitted to vote by secret ballot so they would not be subject to intimidation by the governor whose choice for speaker they would then have more freedom to oppose. However, when the governor lost the power to name the speaker, in part because of disuse, proposals to change this section were no longer made. Since 2010 the speaker has been the choice of the House Republican caucus.

SECTION 84.

It shall be the duty of the legislature to pass such laws as may be necessary and proper to decide differences by arbitrators to be appointed by the parties who may choose that mode of adjustment.

Some states have made considerable use of arbitration as an alternative to regular court settlement of disputes between private parties. Alabama has as well, especially since the appellate courts have come to be dominated by Republicans. There has been considerable litigation, but it has primarily involved constitutional language seeming to guarantee the right to a jury trial.

SECTION 85.

It shall be the duty of the legislature ... with[in] every ... period of twelve years, to make provision by law for revising, digesting, and promulgating the public statutes of this state, of a general nature, both civil and criminal.

This section provides the constitutional authorization for the *Code*. It has not been adhered to strictly. For example, following the 1940 Alabama *Code*, the next *Code* (and the current one) was issued in 1975. Compilation of a code is such a laborious and expensive task today that a mere dozen years between codes would be impractical. A similar provision has appeared in each of Alabama's six Constitutions.

SECTION 86.

The legislature shall pass such penal laws as it may deem expedient to suppress the evil practice of dueling.

The Constitution makes the moral judgment that dueling is evil and mandates legislative action to stop it. This section originated in the Constitution of 1819. However, it is one of the few subjects that are treated more briefly than in early Constitutions when dueling was a problem.

SECTION 87.

It shall be the duty of the legislature to regulate by law the cases in which deduction shall be made from the salaries or compensation of public officers for neglect of duty in their official capacities, and the amount of such deduction.

This section has been in all of the Constitutions. Prior to the adoption of the Constitution of 1901, the Court ruled that for neglect of duty to be proven, it was necessary to show not merely failure due to "carelessness" but also by "design" in spite of a "capacity to perform." (White v. State, 26 So. 343 (1899)) There is no record of this section ever having been invoked under the present Constitution. It represents a naïve notion about how to enforce high standards of administrative performance.

SECTION 88.

It shall be the duty of the legislature to require the several counties of this state to make adequate provision for the maintenance of the poor.

This section reflects the decentralized welfare "system" which prevailed in Alabama prior to the 1930s. Before that time, the basic way the county made "provision for the maintenance of the poor," though hardly adequate, was through the operation of poorhouses or poor farms to which would resort the poorest of the poor who were without family to see even to their most basic needs. Today, county welfare officials are basically subunits of the state welfare agency, which, in turn, operates primarily on the basis of federal regulations and federal funds. With respect to health care, the role of local governments continues to be minimized, most recently by the passage of the Affordable Care Act ("Obamacare") by Congress in 2009–10.

SECTION 89.

The legislature shall not have the power to authorize any municipal corporation to pass any laws inconsistent with the general laws of the state.

There is no regular, systematic review of municipal ordinances to ascertain if they are consistent with the general laws of the state. Much local legislation creates variances between policies and practices in one locality and those in another part of the state.

A slightly more detailed version of this section appeared in the Constitution of 1868. Apparently the decision of the Court in Mobile v. Yuille (3 Ala. 137 (1841)) had allowed too much local ordinance-making discretion. That decision was overruled in Huntsville v. Phelps (27 Ala. 55 (1855)). This section conforms to Dillon's rule, which holds that municipal powers issue from the state and may be regulated by the state as it sees fit, "consistent with the Constitution." (Ott v. Moody, 216 So. 2d 177 (1968)) As recently as 2002 the Civil Appeals Court held that a local ordinance relating to solid waste was inconsistent with state law and thus was unconstitutional. (Ala. Disposal Solutions-Landfill, L.L.C. v. Town of Lowndesboro (837 So. 2d 292))

SECTION 90.

In the event of the annexation of any foreign territory to this state, the legislature shall enact laws extending to the inhabitants of the acquired territory all the rights and privileges which may be required by the terms of acquisition not inconsistent with this Constitution. Should the state purchase such foreign territory, the legislature, with the approval of the governor, shall be authorized to expend any money in the treasury not otherwise appropriated, and, if necessary, to provide also for the issuance of state bonds to pay for the purchase of such foreign territory.

The possibility of acquiring foreign territory was always recognized in Alabama Constitutions. However, the 1901 Constitution, written in the heyday of American imperialism immediately following the Spanish-American War, is more detailed.

SECTION 91.

The legislature shall not tax the property, real or personal, of the state, counties, or other municipal corporations, or cemeteries; nor lots in incorporated cities and towns, or within one mile of any city or town to the extent of one acre, nor lots one mile or more distant from such cities or towns to the extent of five acres, with the buildings thereon, when same are used exclusively for religious worship, for schools, or for purposes purely charitable.

This section removes from state tax rolls any property used by a state or local governmental entity, cemetery, religious organization, school, or charity. In a Bible Belt state, this takes away a considerable amount of property from the taxable category. The exemption for business schools applies only to realty; that is, lots with buildings on them are exempted from taxes. (State v. Bridges, 21 So. 2d 316 (1945)) Property taxes are lower in Alabama than in any other state, so, if such taxes were permissible here, they would not, in most instances, amount to a substantial burden on the institutions upon whom they fell.

SECTION 92.

The legislature shall by law prescribe such rules and regulations as may be necessary to ascertain the value of real and personal property exempted from sale under legal process by this Constitution, and to secure the same to the claimant thereof as selected.

This section applies primarily to homesteads. See Article X as it relates to this very complex subject.

SECTION 93.

The state shall not engage in works of internal improvement, nor lend money or its credit in aid of such, except as may be authorized by the Constitution of Alabama or amendments thereto; nor shall the state be interested in any private or corporate enterprise, or lend money or its credit to any individual, association, or corporation, except as may be expressly authorized by the Constitution of Alabama, or amendments thereto. When authorized by laws passed by the legislature the state may appropriate funds to be applied to the construction, repair, and maintenance of public roads, highways and bridges in the state ... When authorized by laws passed by the legislature the state may engage in the construction, improvement, repairs and maintenance and operation of public airports, air landing fields and other air navigation facilities in the state of Alabama and may appropriate money or otherwise provide funds for this purpose.

This is the most amended section of the Constitution of 1901. It originated in the Constitution of 1875. (See Sheppard v. Dowling, 28 So. 791 (1900).) It reflected both the financially wrenching experiences of Reconstruction and, more distantly, the collapse of the State Bank during the 1837 Panic. Nevertheless, this section, more than any other, shows the continuing naiveté of the framers of the early-twentieth-century Alabama Constitution. Only a group of white gentlemen preoccupied with completing the removal of the possibility of blacks playing any significant role in Alabama political life could have believed that a section which originally declared, "the state shall not engage in works of internal improvement . . . or lend money or its credit to any individual, association, or corporation" would work in future years. Indeed, the very first amendment to the Constitution of 1901 was to authorize state involvement in road building, which for many years would be the number one function of Alabama state government. Numerous constitutional provisions have had to authorize public works activities despite the language of Section 93, even as amended. Amendment 53 (Section 93.12) is typical. It authorizes several programs pertaining to public hospitals and health facilities "notwithstanding section 93." The version of Section 93 that appears here is Amendment 58 (which begins with "except . . ."), ratified in 1946. The original section, as noted, embodied the extreme limited-government, low-tax mentality reflected elsewhere in the 1875 and 1901 Montgomery constitutions. It was not long, however, until the Constitution would begin to be used by more entrepreneurially minded men bent on employing it not primarily to maintain an outmoded political, social, and economic order but to improve their opportunities for amassing large amounts of capital. As recently as Amendment 451 (Section 93.14), ratified in 1985, a soil, water, and conservation program had to be authorized "notwithstanding" Section 93 (and 94). This section has necessitated more statewide amendments than any other. References will be made back to Section 93 in the explication of some of these sections. In 1996 the Court held that the state's operation of a system of liquor stores was not inconsistent with Section 93 despite the fact that elsewhere in the United States the sale of distilled spirits is generally a function of private enterprise. (Ex parte Alabama Alcoholic Bev. Control Bd. (683 So. 2d 952))

SECTION 93.01.

The legislature may hereafter, by general law, provide for the promotion of the production, distribution, improvement, marketing, use and sale of catfish. The legislature may provide for the promotion of catfish and catfish products by research, education, advertising and other methods, and the legislature is further authorized to provide means and methods for the financing of any such promotional activity by prescribing a procedure whereby producers of catfish by referendum among such producers levy upon themselves and collect assessments, fees, or charges upon the purchase of catfish feed for the financing of any such promotional program or activity in cooperation with buyers, processors, dealers, distributors of catfish feed and handlers of catfish. The legislature may make provisions for the nonpayment of assessments by catfish producers and shall make provisions for the refund of assessments to any purchaser of catfish feed who does not desire to participate in an assessment program.

The legislature shall provide for the collection, disbursement, distribution or expenditure of assessments or charges authorized hereunder and to provide penalties for failure to make collection and distribution of assessments. The legislature shall provide for the designation of a nonprofit association or organization for the promotion and betterment of catfish and catfish products to administer and carry out such promotional program which shall include the conducting of elections or referendums among producers of catfish. The legislature may provide the manner by which such referendum is held, including the procedure for application for approval to conduct the referendum, the appropriate action to be taken by the state board of agriculture and industries on such application, the requirements and eligibility of the association or organization which will conduct such referendum, the procedures for voting and eligibility to vote in such referendum, the details of the conduct of such referendum. The legislature shall further provide for the deposit, withdrawal, disbursement and expenditure by the designated association of any funds received subject to the supervision and control of the activities as authorized herein by the department of agriculture and industries and the state board of agriculture and industries. The legislature shall further provide a procedure whereby said association or organization is bonded, for the examination and auditing of said association or organization, and for reasonably necessary rules and regulations to be adopted by the state board of agriculture and industries to effectively carry out the intent and purposes herein enumerated. Assessments, fees or other charges collected as authorized by any legislative act adopted under authority hereof shall not be considered as a tax within the meaning of this constitution or any provision thereof. Any uniformity requirements of this constitution shall be satisfied by the application of the program upon catfish.

This section is almost identical with several other promotional sections. The same comments apply. It was adopted as Amendment 492 in 1988.

SECTION 93.02.

Notwithstanding any other provision of this Constitution, the legislature may hereafter, by general law, provide for the promotion of the production, distribution, marketing, use, improvement and sale of cattle. The legislature may provide for the promotion of cattle and the cattle industry by research, education, advertising and other methods, and the legislature is further authorized to provide means and methods for the financing of any such promotional activity by prescribing a procedure whereby owners of cattle may by referendum held among the owners of cattle in this state levy upon themselves and collect assessments, fees, or charges upon the sale of cattle for the financing of any promotional program or activity in cooperation with processors, dealers and handlers of cattle. The legislature shall make provisions for the nonpayment of assessments by cattle owners, and for the refund of assessments to any cattle owner dissatisfied with the assessment program. The legislature shall provide for the collection and distribution of any such assessments or charges by dealers, handlers, processors and purchasers of cattle and provide penalties for failure to make collection and distribution of such assessments. The legislature shall provide for the designation of a nonprofit association or organization organized for the promotion and betterment of cattle and beef products to administer and carry out such promotional program which shall include the conducting of elections or referendums among cattle owners. The legislature shall further provide for the deposit, withdrawal, disbursement and expenditure by the designated association of any funds received subject to the supervision and control of the activities authorized herein by the department of agriculture and industries and the state board of agriculture and industries. Assessments, fees or other charges collected as authorized by any legislative act adopted in pursuance hereof shall not be considered as a tax within the meaning of this Constitution or any provision thereof. Any uniformity requirements of this Constitution shall be satisfied by the application of the program upon cattle and beef products.

Now follow two more promotion amendments. Section 93.02 (452, 1985) represents the second cattle promotion measure. (It succeeded Amendment 201, which had been the first promotion amendment to pass, in 1962.) The first amendment became outdated because it specifically limited promotion assessments to a maximum of ten cents per head of cattle selling for more than ten dollars each. This section has enjoyed a longer life span since its framers wisely eschewed such narrow specificity.

SECTION 93.03.

Notwithstanding any other provision of this Constitution, the legislature may hereafter, by general law, provide for the eradication or control of the boll weevil in cotton. The legislature may provide for and is authorized to provide means and methods for the financing of this activity by prescribing a procedure whereby cotton growers may, by referendum held among such growers in this state, levy upon themselves and collect assessments, fees and charges, based upon the amount of acreage of cotton planted. The legislature is authorized to make provisions for the collection and distribution of assessments or charges authorized hereunder and to provide penalties for failure to pay said assessments. The legislature shall provide for the designation of a non-profit organization which has been organized for the purpose of eradicating or controlling the boll weevil in cotton; to administer and carry out said eradication or control program; to also include conducting elections or referendums among cotton growers.

The legislature shall further provide for the deposit, withdrawal, disbursement and expenditure by the designated organization of any funds received ... [See Section 93.07]. The legislature shall further provide a procedure for the examination and auditing of said organization and for reasonable rules and regulations to be adopted by the state board of agriculture and industries; to effectively carry out the intent and purposes herein enumerated. Any uniformity requirements of this Constitution shall be satisfied by the application of the program to eradicate or control the boll weevil in cotton.

As will be seen shortly, Section 93.06 (388, 1980) provided for the promotion of cotton (along with peanuts and milk). This section (449, 1984) is concerned with promotion indirectly by a program to deal more effectively with a perennial problem besetting Alabama's now vastly diminished number of cotton growers, the pesky boll weevil. This section contains a stronger admonition by authorizing penalties on the noncooperative. Despite the backing provided by the state to the private anti–boll weevil group, the assessments it collects are still declared not to be taxes within the meaning of the Constitution.

SECTION 93.04.

The legislature may hereafter, by general law, provide for the promotion of the production, distribution, improvement, marketing, use and sale of wheat and other feed grains as defined and authorized by the legislature. The legislature may provide for the promotion of wheat and other feed grains and wheat and other feed grain products by research, education, advertising and other methods. The legislature is further authorized to provide means and methods for the financing of any such promotional activity by prescribing a procedure whereby producers of wheat and other feed grains may by referendum among such producers levy upon themselves and collect assessments, fees, or charges upon the sale of wheat and other feed grains for the financing of any such promotional program or activity in cooperation with buyers, processors, dealers, and handlers of wheat and other feed grains. The legislature may make provisions for the non-payment of assessments by wheat and other feed grain producers, and shall make provisions for the refund of assessments to any wheat and other feed grain producer who does not desire to participate in an assessment program. The legislature shall provide for the collection, disbursement, distribution or expenditure of assessments or charges authorized hereunder and to provide penalties for failure to make collection and distribution of assessments.

The legislature shall provide for the designation of a nonprofit association or organization for the promotion and betterment of wheat and other feed grains and wheat and other feed grain products to administer and carry out such promotional program which shall include the conducting of elections or referendums among producers of wheat and other feed grains. [See Section 93.06.]

This section (453, 1986) was the first to promote the Alabama grain industry. The same comments made with respect to most of the previous promotion sections apply as well to this one.

SECTION 93.05.

The legislature may hereafter, by general law, provide for an indemnification program to peanut farmers for losses incurred as a result of Aspergillus flavus and freeze damage in peanuts. The legislature is further authorized to provide means and methods for the financing of any such indemnification program by prescribing a procedure whereby peanut growers may by referendum among such growers levy upon themselves and collect assessments, fees or charges upon the sale of peanuts for the financing of any such indemnification program in cooperation with buyers, processors, dealers and handlers of peanuts; provided, no assessment levied hereunder shall exceed five dollars per ton on any peanuts sold by peanut growers. The legislature shall provide for the collection and distribution of any such assessments and provide penalties for fraud in the collection or distribution of such assessments. The legislature shall provide for the designation of a nonprofit association or organization organized for the promotion and betterment of peanut production to administer and carry out such indemnification program which shall include the conducting of elections or referendums among peanut growers and to cooperate with underwriters in executing a contract or contracts to cover claims for crop damage due to Aspergillus flavus or freeze damage. Assessments, fees or other charges collected or disbursed as authorized by any legislative act adopted in pursuance hereof shall not be considered as a tax within the meaning of this Constitution or any provision thereof.

This section (approved as Amendment 383 in 1980) represents an effort by a very limited economic group, specifically peanut farmers, to use the state Constitution as a means of reimbursing themselves as a group from losses sustained as a result of disease and bad weather affecting their crop. The last sentence of the amendment is necessary because the Constitution, as we have seen, forbids the delegation of the power to tax private individuals—and this program bears strong resemblance to a tax.

SECTION 93.06.

The legislature may hereafter, by general law, provide for the promotion of the production, distribution, improvement, marketing, use, and sale of peanuts,

> milk, and cotton. The legislature may provide for the promotion of peanuts, milk, and cotton and peanut, milk, and cotton products by research, education, advertising, and other methods, and the legislature is further authorized to provide means and methods for the financing of any such promotional activity by prescribing a procedure whereby growers of peanuts, and producers of milk and cotton may by referendum among such growers and producers levy upon themselves and collect assessments, fees, or charges upon the sale of peanuts, milk, and cotton for the financing of any such promotional program or activity in cooperation with buyers, processors, dealers, and handlers of peanuts, milk, and cotton. The legislature may make provisions for the nonpayment of assessments by peanut growers and milk and cotton producers, and shall make provisions for the refund of assessments to any peanut growers and milk producers who do not desire to participate in an assessment program. The legislature shall provide for the collection, disbursement, distribution, or expenditure of assessments or charges authorized hereunder and to provide penalties for failure to make collection and distribution of assessments. The legislature shall provide for the designation of a nonprofit association or organization for the promotion and betterment of peanuts, milk, and cotton and peanut, milk, and cotton products to administer and carry out such promotional program which shall include the conducting of elections or referendums among growers of peanuts and producers of milk and cotton. The legislature may provide the manner by which such referendum is held, including the procedure for application for approval to conduct the referendum, the appropriate action to be taken by the State Board of Agriculture and Industries on such application, the requirements and eligibility of the association or organization which will conduct such referendum, the procedures for voting and eligibility to vote in such referendum, the details of the conduct of such referendum. The legislature shall further provide for the deposit, withdrawal, disbursement, and expenditure by the designated association of any funds received subject to the supervision and control of the activities as authorized herein by the Department of Agriculture and Industries and the State Board of Agriculture and Industries. The legislature shall further provide a procedure whereby the association or organization is bonded, for the examination and auditing of the association or organization, and for reasonably necessary rules and regulations to be adopted by the State Board of Agriculture and Industries to effectively carry out the intent and purposes herein enumerated.
>
> The legislature shall provide, by enabling legislation, the definition of peanut growers and milk producers.
>
> Assessments, fees or other charges collected as authorized by any legislative act adopted under authority hereof shall not be considered as a tax within the meaning of this Constitution or any provision thereof.

On July 15, 2014, the date of the Republican and Democratic primary runoffs, this revised Section 93.06 was approved. It terminated the option cotton farmers previously had of getting a refund of the money they had been assessed to promote the use of cotton products. Sponsors of the amendment recognized that voter participation in an Alabama runoff is typically very small and this would maximize the amendment's chances of being passed. Agribusiness supporters were solid in their support for it. Peanut growers and milk producers still had the option of getting their assessments returned to them. With the adoption of the new Section 93.06 the difference between an assessment and a tax for cotton producers was obliterated. The power to tax had, in effect, been delegated to private interests despite the Constitution's presumed ban on such delegations.

SECTION 93.07.

Notwithstanding any other provision of this Constitution, the legislature may hereafter, by general law, provide for the promotion of the production, distribution, marketing and use of poultry and poultry products. The legislature may provide for the promotion of poultry and poultry products and the poultry industry by research, education, advertising and other methods, and the legislature is further authorized to provide means and methods for the financing of any such promotional activity by prescribing a procedure whereby producers, owners or growers of poultry may by referendum held among such producers, owners or growers of poultry in this state levy upon themselves and collect assessments, fees, or charges upon the sale of poultry and poultry products for the financing of any such promotional program or activity in cooperation with processors, dealers, handlers and other buyers of poultry and poultry products. Provided, no assessment levied hereunder shall exceed two and one-half cents (2 ½) per hen or other domesticated fowl or any other classes of poultry sold by producers thereof. The legislature is authorized to make provisions for nonpayment and for the refund of assessments levied upon owners, producers or growers of poultry to any such person who does not desire to participate in the promotional program. The legislature shall provide for the collection and distribution of assessments or charges authorized hereunder and to provide penalties for failure to make such collection and distribution of assessments. The legislature shall provide for the designation of a nonprofit association or organization organized for the promotion and betterment of poultry and poultry products in Alabama to administer and carry out such promotional program which shall include conducting elections or referendums among producers, owners or growers of poultry. The legislature shall further provide for the deposit, withdrawal, disbursement and expenditure by the designated association of any funds received subject to the supervision and control of the activities authorized herein by the department of agriculture and industries and the state board of agriculture and industries. Assessments, fees or other charges collected as authorized by any legislative act adopted under authority hereof shall not be considered as a tax within the meaning of this Constitution or any provision thereof. Any uniformity requirements of this Constitution shall be satisfied by the application of the program upon poultry and poultry products.

This section (428, 1982) is the ninth of eleven currently operable amendments which have been added to the Constitution since the original cattle amendment in 1962. This section succeeds the first poultry amendment in 1963. The mention of a specific assessment amount assures that, when this sum becomes outdated, another amendment will be required.

SECTION 93.08.

The legislature may hereafter, by general law, provide for the promotion of the production, distribution, improvement, marketing, use and sale of soybeans. The legislature may provide for the promotion of soybeans and soybean products by research, education, advertising and other methods, and the legislature is further authorized to provide means and methods for the financing of any such promotional activity by prescribing a procedure whereby by producers of soybeans may by referendum among such producers levy upon themselves and collect assessments, fees, or charges upon the sale of soybeans for the financing of any such promotional program or activity in cooperation with buyers, processors, dealers, and handlers of soybeans. The legislature may make provisions for the nonpayment of assessments by soybean producers, and shall make provisions for the refund of assessments to any soybean producer who does not desire to participate in an assessment program. The legislature shall provide for the collection, disbursement, distribution or expenditure of assessments or charges authorized hereunder and to provide penalties for failure to make collection and distribution of assessments. The legislature shall provide for the designation of a nonprofit association or organization for the promotion and betterment of soybeans and soybean products to administer and carry out such promotional program which shall include the conducting of elections or referendums among producers of soybeans. [etc., see Section 93.06] ... Assessments, fees or other charges collected as authorized by any legislative act adopted under authority hereof shall not be considered as a tax within the meaning of this Constitution or any provision thereof. Any uniformity requirements of this Constitution shall be satisfied by the application of the program upon soybeans.

Instead of a general constitutional amendment authorizing agriculturists producing all types of crops and livestock to assess themselves in order to promote their economic interests, the Alabama constitutional pattern is typically to enact a separate provision as here with soybeans (401, 1982). This section permits those associated with soybeans to do the things indicated and to collect revenues to finance the authorized activities without violating the constitutional injunction against private taxation.

SECTION 93.09.

Notwithstanding any other provision of this Constitution, the legislature may hereafter, by general law, provide for the promotion of, the production, research, distribution, marketing, use, improvement and sale of swine and swine products. The legislature may provide for the promotion of swine and the swine industry by research, education, advertising and other methods, and the legislature is further authorized to provide means and methods for the financing of any such promotional activity by prescribing a procedure whereby producers of swine may by referendum held among the swine producers in this state levy upon themselves and collect assessments, fees, or charges upon the sale of swine for the financing of any promotional program or activity in cooperation with processors, dealers and handlers, of swine and swine products. The legislature may make provisions for the nonpayment of assessments by swine producers and shall make provisions for the refund of assessments to any swine producer dissatisfied with the assessment program. The legislature shall provide for the collection and distribution of any such assessments or charges by dealers, handlers, processors and purchasers of swine and swine products and provide penalties for failure to make collection and distribution of such assessments. The legislature shall provide for the designation of a nonprofit association or organization organized for the promotion and betterment of swine and swine products to administer and carry out such promotional program which shall include the conducting of elections or referendums among swine producers. The legislature may provide the manner by which such referendum is held, including the procedure for application for approval to conduct the referendum, the appropriate action to be taken by the state board of agriculture and industries on such application, the requirements and eligibility of the association or organization which will conduct such referendum, the procedures for voting and eligibility to vote in such referendum and the details of the conduct of such referendum. The legislature shall further provide for the deposit, withdrawal, disbursement and expenditure by the designated association of any funds received subject to the supervision and control of the activities as authorized herein by the department of agriculture and industries and the state board of agriculture and industries. The legislature shall further provide a procedure whereby said association or organization is bonded, for the examination and auditing of said association or organization, and for reasonably necessary rules and regulations to be adopted by the state board of agriculture and industries to effectively carry out the intent and purposes herein enumerated. Assessments, fees or other charges collected as authorized by any legislative act adopted in pursuance hereof shall not be considered as a tax within the meaning of this Constitution or any provision thereof. Any uniformity requirements of this Constitution shall be satisfied by the application of the program upon swine and swine products.

This section succeeded the original swine promotion amendment (Amendment 327) adopted in 1973. (That amendment is not reproduced in this volume.) This section (400, 1982) removes the five-cent maximum promotional assessment on market hogs and the three-cent assessment on feeder pigs.

SECTION 93.10.

The Legislature, by general law, may provide for the promotion of the production, distribution, improvement, marketing, use, and sale of sheep or goats. The Legislature may provide for the promotion of sheep and goats and their products by research, education, advertising, and other methods. The Legislature may provide means and methods for the financing of any promotional activity by prescribing a procedure whereby producers of sheep and goats may levy upon themselves and collect assessments, fees, or charges upon the sale of sheep and goats for the financing of any promotional program or activity in cooperation with buyers, processors, dealers, distributors, and handlers of sheep and goats. The Legislature may make provisions for the nonpayment of assessments by sheep and goat producers and shall make provisions for the refund of assessments to any producer of sheep or goats who does not desire to participate in an assessment program. The Legislature shall provide for the collection, disbursement, distribution, or expenditure of assessments or charges authorized by this amendment and provide penalties for failure to make the collection and distribution of assessments. The Legislature shall provide for the designation of a nonprofit association or organization for the promotion and betterment of sheep and goats and their products to administer and carry out any promotional program which shall include the conducting of elections or referendums among producers of sheep and goats. The Legislature may provide the manner by which a referendum is held, including the procedure for application for approval to conduct the referendum, the appropriate action to be taken by the State Board of Agriculture and Industries on an application, the requirements and eligibility of the association or organization which will conduct the referendum, the procedures for voting and eligibility to vote in the referendum, and the details of the conduct of the referendum. The Legislature shall further provide for the deposit, withdrawal, disbursement, and expenditure by the designated association of any funds received subject to the supervision and control of the activities as authorized by the Department of Agriculture and Industries and the State Board of Agriculture and Industries. The Legislature shall further provide a procedure for the association or organization to be bonded, for the examination and auditing of the association or organization, and for reasonably necessary rules and regulations to be adopted by the State Board of Agriculture and Industries to effectively carry out the intent and purposes of this amendment. Assessments, fees, or other charges collected as authorized by a legislative act adopted under authority of this amendment are not to be considered a tax within the meaning of this constitution or any other provisions. Any uniformity requirements of this constitution shall be satisfied by the application of the program upon the sheep and goat industry.

This is the tenth of the Alabama Constitution's "promotion amendments," the beneficiaries of this one being participants in the sheep and goat industry. Its provisions are very similar to the agribusiness measures that preceded it. (See, for example, the immediately preceding Section 93.09 (715, 2002).)

SECTION 93.11.

Section 1. The legislature may form or provide for the formation of drainage districts for establishing and maintaining drainage systems; and provide for the assessment of the whole or part of the cost of such improvements against the lands and property in such district to the extent of the increased value thereof by reason of special benefits derived from such improvements and may provide for the issuance of bonds for such districts with or without an election.

Section 2. This amendment shall be retroactive and retrospective and shall operate to ratify, confirm and validate the act of the legislature of Alabama, which act provided for the drainage of farm, wet, swamp and overflow lands in the state of Alabama and authorized the organization of drainage districts, conferred the right of eminent domain to the extent necessary to carry out the purpose of said act and provided for raising of revenues by bond issue or otherwise to pay the cost and expense of installing and maintaining drainage systems so as to promote the public health and general welfare and, [sic] which act was approved March 4, 1915; and this amendment shall operate to confirm and validate all corporate organizations under authority of such law, all procedure had [sic], all acts done, all bonds issued, contracts entered into and assessments made by such corporations under authority of law.

This section was passed as Amendment 22 in 1928. It is very comprehensive in its authorization for drainage districts, going so far as to approve retroactively legislation that would have been invalid without it.

SECTION 93.12.

The state, notwithstanding section 93 of the Constitution as amended and section 94 of the Constitution, may acquire, build, establish, own, operate and maintain hospitals, health centers, sanatoria and other health facilities.

The legislature for such purposes may appropriate public funds and may authorize counties, municipalities and other political subdivisions to appropriate their funds and may designate or create an agency or agencies to accept and administer funds appropriated or donated for such purposes by the United States government to the state upon such terms and conditions as may be imposed by the United States government.

This is one of many additions to the Alabama Constitution required to circumvent the original and amended Sections 93 and 94. This section (53, 1946) was ratified in the same year that the Hill-Burton Act, making federal grants for the purposes identified here, was passed. Its co-sponsor was Alabama Senator Lister Hill, and it was one of an increasing number of programs of cooperative federalism begun in this period. Unfortunately, from the perspective of the unwieldy length of the Alabama Constitution, several more constitutional amendments on the same subject would be needed during the ensuing fifteen years. One illustration of the narrow interpretation given this amendment came in 1957 when the Court advised that the legislature could not permit counties to use part of the proceeds from special hospital taxes to cover the hospital bills of indigent patients. (Opinion of the Justices, 95 So. 2d (1957))

SECTION 93.13.

The legislature may by general, special or local laws authorize the formation of a body corporate for the development of one or more irrigation districts for the purposes of providing irrigation and water conservation in the state of Alabama, and may authorize the counties and municipalities lying within the boundaries of such district or districts to contribute public funds to such body corporate, and may authorize such body corporate to enter into contract with the government of the United States or any agency thereof, and with other states or political subdivisions thereof, and with other bodies corporate organized within this or other states for the development of one or more irrigation districts in the state of Alabama, and may authorize such body corporate to issue revenue bonds payable solely out of revenues accruing to such body corporate, and may authorize such body corporate to do and perform all other such acts necessary and proper for the full development of said Alabama irrigation district or districts provided, however, nothing herein shall authorize any such public corporation to engage in or finance, directly or indirectly, the production, transmission or sale of electric power.

This section (227, 1965) authorizes federal-local intergovernmental cooperation in the areas of water resource utilization and conservation. The strength of private power companies, determined to prevent another Tennessee Valley Authority or miniature versions thereof, is manifested in the last sentence of the section.

SECTION 93.14.

The legislature may by general law provide for the creation and organization of a commission charged with the responsibility of improving soil and water conservation and forestry practices within the state, and in order to further the carrying out of that responsibility the legislature may appropriate moneys to such commission for the purpose of meeting the expenses of the commission and to allow the commission to share, through a cost-sharing award or grant program, the costs of soil conservation projects and practices, water quality improvements, reforestation projects and improved forestry practices on or with respect to agricultural or timber land in the state owned or operated by individuals or other types of persons specified by the legislature, Sections 93 and 94 of this Constitution, as amended, to the contrary notwithstanding. In any law enacted by the legislature respecting soil and water conservation cost-sharing grants as contemplated hereby, the legislature shall provide for the powers of the commission and for the receipt, withdrawal, disbursement and expenditure by such commission of any appropriated moneys and other funds received by the commission to fund its expenses and cost-sharing programs.The legislature shall provide that such commission shall consist of such citizens of the state [as] may be designated by law by the legislature, provided that [the] legislature may designate as ex officio members of the commission persons who are holders of other public offices or officers of such private organizations and associations as the legislature may designate that are interested in agricultural or timber property and soil and water conservation practices related thereto. Moneys appropriated to such commission for cost-sharing grants to be made pursuant to criteria provided by the legislature or promulgated by the commission pursuant to legislative delegation of the power to do so, shall be invested by the commission at its direction, or retained in the state treasury as the commission shall determine, until expended at the direction of the commission, provided that none of such appropriated moneys shall revert to the fund or funds from which they were appropriated in the event such moneys remain undisbursed or unencumbered on the last day of the fiscal year of the state in which they were appropriated to the commission, but rather shall remain available for disbursement by the commission in its programs in subsequent fiscal years.

The language here is clear and requires little interpretation. It will be recalled that the original Sections 93 and 94 referred to here were written to severely restrict state and local involvement in cooperative entrepreneurial endeavors with private interests, which are specifically authorized here with respect to soil, water, and forest resources through the use of a soil and water commission.

SECTION 93.16.

Section 1. The legislature may provide for the formation of water management districts for the establishment of works of improvement for the drainage of wet, swamp, and overflowed lands of the state, and for flood prevention or the conservation, development, utilization, and disposal of water within the state, confer the right of eminent domain for such purposes, provide for the taxing of the whole or part of the cost of such improvements against the lands and property in such district to the extent of the increased value thereof by reason of special benefits derived from such improvements; and provide for the issuance of bonds for such districts with or without an election; provided, however, that nothing herein shall authorize any such water management districts to engage in or finance, directly or indirectly, the production, transmission or sale of electric power.

Section 2. The provisions of this amendment are cumulative and shall not be construed to repeal amendment XV (15) or amendment XXII (22).

Since Section 93.13 (227, 1965) was so restrictive, providing only for districts with responsibilities related to water conservation, it was necessary only one year later to ratify this section (257, 1966) pertaining to water resources. This is another example of over-specificity contributing to the proliferation of constitutional amendments.

SECTION 93.17.

The Legislature, by general law, may provide for the promotion of the production, distribution, improvement, marketing, use, and sale of shrimp and seafood. The Legislature may provide for the promotion of shrimp and seafood products by research, education, advertising, and other methods, and the Legislature is further authorized to provide the means and methods for the financing of any promotional activity by prescribing a procedure whereby producers of shrimp and seafood by referendum among such producers levy upon themselves and collect assessments, fees, or charges upon the sale of shrimp and seafood for the financing of any promotional program or activity in cooperation with buyers, processors, dealers, distributors, and handlers of shrimp and seafood. The Legislature may make provisions for the nonpayment of assessments by shrimp and seafood producers and shall make provisions for the refund of assessments to any handler of shrimp and seafood who does not desire to participate in an assessment program.

The Legislature shall provide for the collection, disbursement, distribution, or expenditure of assessments or charges authorized hereunder and provide penalties for failure to make collection and distribution of assessments.

The Legislature shall provide for the designation of a nonprofit association or organization for the promotion and betterment of shrimp and seafood products to administer and carry out such promotional program which shall include the conducting of elections or referendums among producers of shrimp and seafood.

The Legislature may provide the manner by which the referendum is held, including the procedure for application for approval to conduct the referendum, the appropriate action to be taken by the State Board of Agriculture and Industries on an application, and the requirements and eligibility of the association or organization which will conduct the referendum. The Legislature shall further provide for the deposit, withdrawal, disbursement, and expenditure by the designated association of any funds received subject to the supervision and control of the activities as authorized herein by the Department of Agriculture and Industries. The Legislature shall further provide a procedure whereby the association or organization is bonded, for the examination and auditing of the association or organization, and for reasonably necessary rules and regulations to be adopted by the State Board of Agriculture and Industries to effectively carry out the intent and purposes herein enumerated. Assessments, fees, or other charges collected as authorized by any legislative act adopted under authority hereof shall not be considered as a tax within the meaning of this constitution and shall be satisfied by the application of the program upon shrimp and seafood.

This section was, before its incorporation into the body of the Constitution, Amendment 766 (2004). Its provisions do not differ materially from that of its immediate predecessor, Section 93.10 (715, 2002).

SECTION 94.

(a) The Legislature shall not have power to authorize any county, city, town, or other subdivision of this state to lend its credit, or to grant public money or thing of value in aid of, or to any individual, association, or corporation whatsoever, or to become a stockholder in any corporation, association, or company, by issuing bonds or otherwise. The Legislature may enact general, special, or local laws authorizing political subdivisions and public bodies to alienate, with or without a valuable consideration, public parks and playgrounds, or other public recreational facilities and public housing projects, conditional upon the approval of a majority of the duly qualified electors of the county, city, town, or other subdivision affected thereby, voting at an election held for that purposes.

(b) Notwithstanding the provisions of subsection (a), local school boards of education may expend public funds for the recognition of significant contributions to education in Alabama and to promote educational excellence by students, faculty, staff, and the public. Recognitions shall be in the form of trophies, plaques, academic banquets, and other honors that promote academic excellence in the public schools of Alabama and recognize special deeds that strengthen public education in Alabama.

The original Constitution of 1901 did not forbid counties and municipalities from engaging in works of internal improvement. Indeed, in the horse-and-buggy thinking of the delegates to the Montgomery convention, it was naively anticipated that counties could continue to engage in this type of public activity without state involvement. The original Section 94 was first replaced in the era of massive resistance (1956), when Amendment 112 substituted new language beginning with, "It is . . ." It allowed local governments to divest themselves of the facilities mentioned which were under orders to let black citizens in. Like Section 93, this section has to be referred to directly or indirectly when constitutional amendments are passed legitimizing some local activity not originally authorized. The third iteration of Section 94 simply authorized local school boards to use public funds to recognize outstanding academic accomplishments by the education constituents mentioned in paragraph (b).

SECTION 94.01.

(a) The governing body of any county, and the governing body of any municipality located therein, for which a local constitutional amendment has not been adopted authorizing any of the following, shall have full and continuing power to do any of the following:

(1) Use public funds to purchase, lease, or otherwise acquire real property, buildings, plants, factories, facilities, machinery, and equipment of any kind, or to utilize the properties heretofore purchased or otherwise acquired and improve and develop the properties for use as sites for industry of any kind or as industrial park projects, including, but not limited to, grading and the construction of roads, drainage, sewers, sewage and waste disposal systems, parking areas, and utilities to serve the sites or projects.

(2) Lease, sell, grant, exchange, or otherwise convey, on terms approved by the governing body of the county or the municipality, as applicable, all or any part of any real property, buildings, plants, factories, facilities, machinery, and equipment of any kind or industrial park project to any individual, firm, corporation, or other business entity, public or private, including any industrial development board or other public corporation or authority heretofore or hereafter created by the county or the municipality, for the purpose of constructing, developing, equipping, and operating industrial, commercial, research, or service facilities of any kind.

(3) Lend its credit to or grant public funds and things of value in aid of or to any individual, firm, corporation, or other business entity, public or private, for the purpose of promoting the economic and industrial development of the county or the municipality.

(4) Become indebted and issue bonds, warrants which may be payable from funds to be realized in future years, notes, or other obligations, or evidences of indebtedness to a principal amount not exceeding 50 percent of the assessed value of taxable property located therein as determined for state taxation, in order to secure funds for the purchase, construction, lease, or acquisition of any of the property described in subdivision (1) or to be used in furtherance of any of the other powers or authorities granted in this amendment. The obligations or evidences of indebtedness may be issued upon the full faith and credit of the county or any municipality or may be limited as to the source of their payment.

The recital in any bonds, warrants, notes, or other obligations or evidences of indebtedness that they were issued pursuant to this amendment or that they were issued to provide funds to be used in furtherance of any power or authority herein authorized shall be conclusive, and no purchaser or holder thereof need inquire further. The bonds, warrants, notes, or other obligations or evidences of indebtedness issued hereunder shall not be considered an indebtedness of the county or any municipality for the purpose of determining the borrowing capacity of the county or municipality under this Constitution.

(b) In carrying out the purpose of this amendment, neither the county nor any municipality located therein shall be subject to Section 93 or 94 of the Constitution. Each public corporation heretofore created by the county or by any municipality located therein including specifically any industrial development board incorporated under Article 4 of Chapter 54 of Title 11 of the Code of Alabama 1975, and any industrial development authority incorporated or reincorporated under Chapter 92A of Title 11 of the Code of Alabama 1975, and the

Shoals Economic Development Authority enacted under Act No. 95-512, 1995 Regular Session, are validated and the powers granted to the board or authority under its respective enabling legislation are validated notwithstanding any other provision of this Constitution. The powers granted by this amendment may be exercised as an alternative to, or cumulative with, and in no way restrictive of, powers granted by law to the county, or to any municipality, or to any agency, board, or authority created pursuant to the laws of this state.

(c) Neither the county nor any municipality located therein shall lend its credit to or grant any public funds or thing of value to or in aid of any private entity under the authority of this amendment unless prior thereto both of the following are satisfied:

(1) The action proposed to be taken by the county or municipality is approved at a public meeting of the governing body of the county or municipality, as the case may be, by a resolution containing a determination by the governing body that the expenditure of public funds for the purpose specified will serve a valid and sufficient public purpose, notwithstanding any incidental benefit accruing to any private entity or entities.

(2) At least seven days prior to the public meeting a notice is published in the newspaper having the largest circulation in the county or municipality, as the case may be, describing in reasonable detail the action proposed to be taken, a description of the public benefits sought to be achieved by the action, and identifying each individual, firm, corporation, or other business entity to whom or for whose benefit the county or the municipality proposes to lend its credit or grant public funds or thing of value.

For purposes of the foregoing, any sale, lease, or other disposition of property for a price equal to the fair market value thereof shall not constitute the lending of credit or a grant of public funds or thing of value in aid of a private entity.

Nothing in this amendment shall authorize the county commission to own or operate a cable television system.

(d) This amendment shall have prospective application only. Any local constitutional amendments previously adopted and any local law enacted pursuant to such amendment shall remain in full force and effect.

This section (772, 2004) represents an alternative approach to county economic development. Instead of passing a separate amendment for each county (local amendments aren't presented in this volume) all counties not already authorized by a separate amendment to engage in the activities mentioned here now have the power to do so. The accelerated growth of the uniquely huge Alabama Constitution would have been slowed somewhat if the same approach had been followed with respect to the numerous agribusinesses mentioned in the Constitution's eleven promotional amendments.

SECTION 94.02.

Any other provision of the Constitution heretofore adopted to the contrary notwithstanding, the legislature is hereby authorized to enact legislation permitting municipalities and counties to establish tax increment districts, as may be defined in such legislation; to authorize the payment to any such municipality or county of the increase in ad valorem taxes resulting from the redevelopment or revitalization of any such district except to the extent that any such payment would jeopardize the payment of any bonded indebtedness secured by any tax applicable in the proposed district; and subject to the mutual agreement of the municipality and county affected thereby to provide that all such increases in ad valorem taxes shall be payable to such municipality or county until the indebtedness or costs incurred for any project have been paid in full; to provide that public moneys, including the proceeds of obligations issued by the municipality or county for such purposes, may be expended for the acquisition of property and the redevelopment, rehabilitation or conservation thereof which may be disposed of to or for the benefit of private interests for compensation established by the governing body of [sic] county or municipality, as the case may be [sic] which established such district, but for not less than the fair market value thereof determined by one or more independent appraisals of such property; and to provide that any such obligations shall not be chargeable against the constitutional debt limit of the issuer unless such obligations shall be general obligations of the issuer in addition to being payable from such increases in property taxes. Any legislation passed at the same session of the legislature at which this amendment is proposed, which shall be in furtherance of or in implementation of the authority hereby granted [sic] is hereby validated and confirmed.

This section (475, 1988) gives cities and counties operating through redevelopment authorities permission to purchase and rehabilitate property and then relinquish it to private business for a price at least equal to the fair market value. The section represents a positive approach to urban redevelopment.

SECTION 95.

There can be no law of this state impairing the obligation of contract by destroying or impairing the remedy for their enforcement; and the legislature shall have no power to revive any right or remedy which may have become barred by lapse of time, or by any statute of this state.

After suit has been commenced or any cause of action, the legislature shall have no power to take away such cause of action, or destroy any existing defense to such suit.

This is the state's version of the obligation of contracts clause as contained in the U.S. Constitution. As would be expected, the state provision is more detailed. This section was probably unnecessary because Section 22 also forbids passage of laws impairing contractual obligations. In construing this section, the Court has been careful to exclude the state as an entity against whom claims can be enforced by means of suit. (See Ballinger Construction Co. v. State Board of Adjustment, 175 So. 387 (1937).) Showing the use of this section in defense of business interests in the 1980s was Tyson v. Johns-Manville Sales Corp. (399 So. 2d 263 (1981)). Here the Court held that the legislature offended the last part of this section by authorizing more time to file suits claiming health impairment due to exposure to asbestos. More recently the Court held that a change in a law lowering damages for debtors who had been assessed excess finance charges could not be brought into an action that was already in progress when the change was made. (United Cos. Lending Corp. v. Autrey, 723 So. 2d 617 (1998))

SECTION 96.

The legislature shall not enact any law not applicable to all the counties in the state, regulating costs and charges of courts, or fees, commissions or allowances of public officers.

A comparison of the actual facts with the language of this section shows how frequently the Constitution is evaded. Perhaps the extreme length of the Constitution contributes to its evasion since supposed commandments are lost in constitutional minutiae. In 2015 court costs varied widely among Alabama's counties. The Court said that the framers' purpose in inserting this section was "to secure uniformity throughout the state as to costs and charges of court, fees, commissions, percentages and allowances of public officers." (Morgan County v. Edmondson, 192 So. 2d 274 (1939)) This goal has definitely not been achieved. Of course, when the Constitution of 1901 was approved, the norm was to pay public officials, including court personnel, by means of fees, costs, and court charges they collected. (See Green v. Austin, 425 So. 2d 411 (1982).) Now, however, the modern bureaucratic norm of payment through salaries is generally followed. This section is another of the major causes of the proliferation of constitutional amendments.

SECTION 96.01.

The legislature may, from time to time, by general or local law applicable to the various counties of this state, establish the salaries, fees, commissions or allowances to be charged or received by the tax assessors, tax collectors, license commissioners, revenue commissioners or other officials charged with the assessing and collecting of ad valorem taxes in the various counties of this state, including changing the method and basis of their compensation; and may place any or all of such officials on a salary and further provide for disposition of the fees, commissions, allowances or other compensation theretofore paid to such officials; and may provide that the salaries of such officials may be paid from the ad valorem taxes assessed and collected by them on a pro rata basis from the various funds receiving such ad valorem taxes ... The legislature may by local act provide for the abolishment, combination or other alteration of the offices of tax assessor, tax collector or license commissioner with approval of a majority of voters in the county affected.

In the event this amendment is approved and subsequently ratified by the qualified electors of this state who vote thereon when it is submitted, then any law theretofore passed by the legislature addressing the subject matter covered by this amendment shall become effective according to the provisions of said law.

This section (411, 1982), one of forty-one state and local amendments ratified in the year 1982 alone, is more salutary than its contemporaries because it provides a general legislative authorization to systematize the compensation of all county revenue-related officials rather than continuing to do this on a piecemeal, county-by-county basis. The expectation was that those still not being paid on the preferred basis of a salary but according to the old fee system would be converted to salaries soon. Also desirable from a public administration perspective is the legislative authorization to combine or otherwise alter the key county revenue offices.

SECTION 97.

The legislature shall not authorize payment to any person of the salary of a deceased officer beyond the date of his death.

The only significant litigation regarding this section turned on who is a public officer. In Cobb v. Home Insurance Co. (91 So. 627 (App. 1921)), the Court held that a firefighter was not. Thus payment of a pension to his descendants was not unconstitutional.

SECTION 98.

The legislature shall not retire any officer on pay, or part pay, or make any grant to such retiring officer; however, the legislature shall have the authority to provide that superintendents of education shall be eligible to participate in the Teachers' Retirement System of Alabama as the legislature may see fit.

The original Section 98 was amended by Amendment 513 (1990), the language of which appears here. The new language begins with "however." This section reflects the low-cost government philosophy which prevailed for such a long span of Alabama history. In the legislature in recent years, as legislative service has become more of a new career than a steppingstone or an act of noblesse oblige on the part of the landed gentry, some legislators have sought pensions. These members are envious of the fact that state government has been used so successfully to promote a comfortable retirement for other public occupational groups. In 1989 the Court ruled that the duties of a public officer were generally discharged more independently than employees who worked mostly under the direction of hierarchical superiors. The former could not be pensioned without an amendment to the Constitution excepting the office from the language of this section. (Edmonds v. Bronner, 547 So. 2d 1172) Ex-governors have sometimes been given the honorific title of governor's counsellor in order to provide a constitutional basis for paying them a stipend during their final years. Most recently, the Court ruled that former sheriffs who participated in a supernumerary program were not in violation of Section 98 because they did not have a vested interest in this quasi-retirement system. (Cleburne County Comm'n v. Norton (979 So. 2d 766) (2007))

SECTION 99.

Lands belonging to or under the control of the state shall never be donated, directly or indirectly, to private corporations, associations, or individuals, or railroad companies; nor shall such lands be sold to corporations or associations for a less price than that for which they are subject to sale to individuals; provided, that nothing contained in this section shall prevent the legislature from granting a right of way, not exceeding one hundred and twenty-five feet in width, as a mere easement, for railroads or telegraph or telephone lines across state land, and the legislature shall never dispose of the land covered by such right of way except subject to such easement.

This section emerged out of an environment in which corrupt legislators sometimes did, in fact, make land grants to private corporations, most notably to railroads, for little consideration. The exact type of problem addressed here, however, has not returned in recent times, so this section has not been a controverted one. Other favors extended to corporate power have been both more numerous and more important.

SECTION 100.

No obligation or liability of any person, association, or corporation held or owned by this state, or by any county or other municipality thereof, shall ever be remitted, released, or postponed, or in any way diminished by the legislature; nor shall such liability or obligation be exchanged or transferred except upon payment thereof; nor shall such liability or obligation be exchanged or transferred except upon payment of its face value; provided, that this section shall not prevent the legislature from providing by general law for the compromise of doubtful claims.

Section 95 dealt primarily with the contractual obligations of private parties. This section deals with obligations to the state which are also, according to its terms, to be strictly adhered to. This section was original with the Constitution of 1901. The Court has interpreted the section realistically. The state is allowed to compromise a state claim if the debtor is unable to pay the full amount of his or her obligation to the state. The state must pursue its interests, however, to the fullest extent possible. (See State v. Brooks, 53 So. 2d 329 (1951).) Most significantly, the Court holds that liability for taxes levied by the state comes under the stringent terms of this section and, as such, "cannot be remitted, released, or postponed, or in any way diminished by the Legislature, nor can such obligation or liability be extinguished except by payment." (Alabama Education Association v. Grayston, 382 So. 2d 501 (1980))

SECTION 101.

No state or county official shall, at any time during his term of office, accept, either directly or indirectly, any fee, money, office, appointment, employment, reward or thing of value, or of personal advantage, or the promise thereof, to lobby for or against any measure pending before the legislature, or to give or withhold his influence to secure the passage or defeat of any such measure.

This section represents another attempt to prevent corruption of the democratic process through the acceptance of official favors which amounts to taking a bribe. Perhaps surprisingly, this section has produced no noteworthy litigation. This may be because in Alabama's traditional political culture there is no strong support for prosecution of conflicts of interest which could reasonably be construed to fall within the prohibitions of this section.

SECTION 103.

The legislature shall provide by law for the regulation, prohibition, or reasonable restraint of common carriers, partnerships, associations, trusts, monopolies, and combinations of capital, so as to prevent them or any of them from making scarce articles of necessity, trade, or commerce, or from increasing unreasonably the cost thereof to the consumer, or preventing reasonable competition in any calling, trade or business.

This section reflects agrarian antipathy toward big business in whatever form that it takes to oppress the consumer of goods and services of the industrious entrepreneur. Thus, while there is much stodgy conservatism in the Constitution, there is also language, as here, inserted to protect the public interests against the abusive actions of organized corporate power. The Court observed in 1885 that monopolies were illegal under common law and so would be illegal in this common law state even if they were not proscribed by the Constitution. (Birmingham, etc. Railway v. Birmingham Street Railway, 79 Ala. 465) In 1909 the federal court, interpreting this section, made a distinction between "reasonable" and "unreasonable" business alliances. It is only the latter, the court held, that the Constitution forbids. "Combinations of capital" which do not "unreasonably" increase consumer financial burdens are not prohibited. (Citizens' Light, Heat & Power Co. v. Montgomery Light and Water Power Co., 171 F. 553 (M.D. Ala.)) The "dominant purpose" of Section 103 is to promote "reasonable competition." Sometimes legislative actions may cost consumers but supposedly encourage more sellers in the marketplace. In 1987 the Court ruled that the legislature could forbid retailers to sell below their cost if to do so would hurt their competitors. (State v. Mapco Petroleum, Inc., 519 So. 2d 1275) The reasoning behind preventing consumers from getting bargains in these situations is that below-cost selling would ultimately harm the public through monopolies and higher prices.

SECTION 104.

The legislature shall not pass a special, private, or local law in any of the following cases:

This section is the most all-encompassing effort of the Constitution to protect against what were regarded as the "evils" of local, private, and special legislation. In many instances they trace back to abuses, for which state-dominated legislatures were notorious, in the nineteenth century. The categories are mixed in this enumeration. The comprehensiveness of the list here reflects the pervasive distrust of the legislature which had grown throughout the nineteenth century.

The problem of local legislation was one the framers were determined to solve once and for all. They tried valiantly, but failed. The legislature ingenuously circumvented many of these provisions for most of the twentieth century. The Court found in 1934 that the "dominating purpose" of Section 104 "was to destroy the practice of 'legislative courtesy'" which facilitated the adoption of disparate local laws "and to compel the enactment of general laws covering these subjects, providing a uniform system applicable to the state as a whole." (Bridges v. McWilliams, 152 So. 457) This objective, if this observation is true, was hopelessly naïve. In 2002 the Court issued the opinion that the legislature could not "regulate" liquor traffic (by allowing its sale) where there had been none before the legislature acted. The Court said that "regulate" meant to change the conditions under which an activity was then being conducted. It is impossible to regulate something that legally does not exist. (Opinion of the Justices, 825 So. 33 2d 109 (2002))

(1) Granting a divorce;

The first iteration of this subsection goes back to the Constitution of 1861. The Constitution of 1819 had specifically provided that divorces would not be final without legislative approval.

(2) Relieving any minor of the disabilities of nonage;

This clause is self-explanatory and has not provoked controversy.

(3) Changing the name of any corporation, association, or individual;

The only judicial clarification required for this clause was the ruling, in 1879, that the corporations contemplated are private, not municipal. (Ex parte City Council, 64 Ala. 463 (1879))

(4) Providing for the adoption or legitimizing of any child;

This clause is self-explanatory. These matters are handled bureaucratically in the modern administrative state.

(5) Incorporating a city, town, or village;

In early Alabama municipal corporations came into existence by virtue of a special legislative act. In time, general laws were passed under which local citizens could, by following proper procedures, incorporate themselves. This clause made the general law route the only constitutionally valid one. (See

Cooper v. Valley Head, 101 So. 874 (1924); also State v. Harris, 67 So. 2d 26 (1953).) While the Court ruled, soon after the Constitution went into effect, that the legislature could terminate a municipal corporation by special act, this would not be possible today without a thorough examination by the U.S. Justice Department to ensure that African-American voting rights were not adversely affected. (The early case referred to is Ensley v. Simpson, 166 Ala. 366 (1909).)

(6) Granting a charter to any corporation, association, or individual;

In contrast to clause (3), this clause is interpreted as applying to both public and private corporations. (Opinion of the Justices, 319 So. 2d 699 (1975)) Positively, the legislature has broad power to set up corporations to act in behalf of state interests. (State v. Harris, 1941 So. 2d 175 (1961))

(7) Establishing rules of descent or distribution;

The legislature could not provide that the estate of a named deceased person would be divided among the heirs in specified ways.

(8) Regulating the time within which a civil or criminal action may be begun;

General statutes of limitations, not special laws, determine the time boundaries for the trying of civil and criminal cases.

(9) Exempting any individual, private corporation, or association from the operation of any general law;

This clause has been more subject to evasion than those immediately preceding it. And, the Court has been prone to acquiesce as, for example, when the legislature substituted the office of commissioner of public schools for that of superintendent of education, a mere name change but which the Court held did not contravene this clause calling for dealing with individual matters through general laws, not through perhaps arbitrary local legislation. (See Opinion of the Justices, 66 So. 2d 779 (1953).)

(10) Providing for the sale of the property of any individual or estate;

In 1977 a local law that authorized forfeiting to the state of motor vehicles, guns, rifles, ammunition, etc., used in illegal nighttime deer hunting was thrown out as inconsistent with this clause. (State v. Dorough, 342 So. 2d 781)

(11) Changing or locating a county seat;

As noted earlier, proposed changes in county seats were among the most bitterly contested issues in local politics. The legislature is instructed here not to do this.

(12) Providing a change of venue in any case;

Changes of venue are to be made by judges based on their determination as to the possibility of a fair trial being conducted in the area where a wrong was alleged to have been committed.

(13) Regulating the rate of interest;

The legislature can and does regulate rates of interest charged in the state as a whole but such action is forbidden at the substate level. Most recently the legislature has been urged to curb rates charged by payday lenders, which have proliferated in recent years, coinciding with the influx of low-income Hispanics, many of whom have been victimized by their usurious practices.

(14) Fixing the punishment of a crime;

Punishments for particular crimes are decided upon in the courts where their alleged perpetrators are being tried. In 1963 the Court held that a law, the scope of which would be confined to Jefferson County, punishing those who contributed to the delinquency of minors, violated this clause. (Thompson v. State, 149 So. 2d 916) In 1985 the Court advised that a proposal to pass a purely local law to curb nighttime hunting was also inconsistent with this clause. (Opinion of the Justices, 468 So. 2d 881)

(15) Regulating either the assessment or collection of taxes ...

The goal of this clause was tax law immunity (State v. Bowles, 116 So. 662 (1928)), a goal that has certainly not been achieved. Its lack of achievement is reflected in the numerous local tax amendments which must be passed to overcome constitutional obstacles to local responsiveness to local problems such as this one. The Court said in 1971 that the clause was "not aimed at the exercise of the sovereign legislative power to levy taxes for lawful purposes by local or special laws." (Mobile v. Salter, 255 So. 2d 5, quoting Sisk v. Cargile, 35 So. 114 (1903)) Thus a law giving a named county the right to enact its own license tax and registration fee on motor vehicles was permissible. (Opinion of the Justices, 96 So. 2d 634 (1957))

(16) Giving effect to an invalid will, deed, or other instrument;

The language of this clause is clear. It has not been the subject of constitutional controversy.

(17) Authorizing any county, city, town, village, district, or other political subdivision of a county, to issue bonds or other securities unless the issuance of said bonds or other securities shall have been authorized before the enactment of such local or special law, by a vote of the duly qualified electors of such county, township, city, town, village, district, or other political subdivision of a county, at an election held for such purpose, in the manner that may be prescribed by law ...

The clause reiterates the framers' determination to make the encumbering of new financial obligations a very tedious process. All bonds must be issued pursuant to a popular referendum unless some other constitutional provision authorizes such action. One modern method of circumventing this constitutional provision is for a municipality to issue what are termed certificates of participation (COPs) to finance the purchase of such items as furniture and equipment without having to secure voter approval for bonds. Technically, the buyers of the COPs own the articles until they are paid off on a short- to intermediate-term basis. The COPs do not count against the jurisdiction's normal debt limit.

(18) Amending, confirming, or extending the charter of any private or municipal corporation, or remitting the forfeiture thereof; provided, this should not prohibit the legislature from altering or rearranging the boundaries of the city, town, or village;

In the mid-1990s, when the City of Tuscaloosa was in negotiations to bring a Mercedes-Benz plant to west Alabama, the Court ruled that legislative annexation of territory for Tuscaloosa adjacent to the town of Vance did not conflict with this subsection because it clearly authorized state alteration or rearrangement of municipal boundaries. (Town of Vance v. City of Tuscaloosa (661 So. 2d 739) (1995))

(19) Creating, extending, or impairing any lien;

Liens or mortgages are created in ordinary commercial intercourse. The legislature is forbidden to interfere through special laws in the ways mentioned here.

(20) Chartering or licensing any ferry, road, or bridge;

As of 2015 ferries are practically extinct. Roads and bridges are usually built and maintained with monies from grants, taxes, and bond proceeds. This was frequently not the case in the nineteenth century.

(21) Increasing the ... fees of constables;

Fees of constables, a very unimportant position the abolition of which is frequently advocated, are regulated now by Section 160, Article VI.

(22) Establishing separate school districts;

This clause requires school districts to be established on the basis of general laws. In 1934 an act that sought to create defined school districts in a particular county was voided based on this clause. (Kyle v. Wiggins, 102 So., 145) In 2015 there were 67 county systems and 106 others, a number which includes mostly city districts but also special schools such as the Alabama School of Fine Arts in Birmingham. The city systems have been established on the basis of local initiative under the terms of general laws.

(23) Establishing separate stock districts;

A stock district is a district perhaps coterminous with county boundaries, perhaps less—within which livestock are not allowed to run at large. In 1922 an abused county classification law applicable to counties within a very narrow 30,900–30,975 population range) was voided pursuant to this section. (State v. Williams, 93 S. 381 (App.))

(24) Creating, increasing, or decreasing fees, percents, or allowances of public officers;

As previously noted most public officers (including all judges) are paid on the basis of salaries, not fees. This clause also has been the subject of numerous local amendments excepting particular counties from its terms. With the decline of compensatory fees, this clause is less relevant today than previously. The goal of this clause was "to secure uniformity throughout the State as to costs and charges of court, fees, commissions, percentages and allowances of public officers." (Morgan County v. Edmondson, 192 So. 274 (1939)) It was not achieved. This was reiterated as a constitutional mandate in 1982, but it is still frequently evaded. (The case referred to is Green v. Austin, 425 So. 2d 411 (1982).)

(25) Exempting property from taxation or from levy or sale;

A great deal of property is exempted from taxation, but this is through general law.

(26) Exempting any person from jury, road, or other civil duty;

Grand or petit jury service represents the only regularly compelled form of state service today. Rather than attempting to exempt from service, the trend in recent years has been to remove most such exemptions with the goal of having venires which are more actively reflective of the areas within which trials will be held and which will, to a greater degree, assure to those on trial a judgment by their peers.

(27) Donating any lands owned by or under control of the state to any person or corporation;

The language of this clause is clear. While it may sometimes be felt that the state provides too many favors to affluent private interests, outright donation of land has not recently been one of them.

(28) Remitting fines, penalties, or forfeitures;

The legislature has not transgressed this clause. Subjects of fines, penalties, or forfeitures should not expect to find relief through a special act of the legislature.

(29) Providing for the conduct of elections or designating places of voting, or changing the boundaries of wards, precincts, or districts, except in the event of the organization of new counties, or changing of the lines of old counties;

As noted previously, the most important provisions governing election administration today are federal, not state. The key source to the validity for the kinds of actions mentioned here is not the Alabama Constitution but the Voting Rights Act of 1965 passed pursuant to the Reconstruction Amendments (Thirteenth, Fourteenth, and Fifteenth) of the U.S. Constitution. In 1987 the Alabama Supreme Court declared unconstitutional the distribution of campaign materials near polling places in part on the basis of this clause. (Kiel v. Purvis, 51 So. 2d 190)

(30) Restoring the right to vote to persons convicted of infamous crimes, or crimes involving moral turpitude;

There has been no local law relating to the restoration of the right to vote. There has, however, been much concern that too many persons previously convicted of felonies but who are no longer in confinement have lost their right to vote and that the process through which they must go to get it restored is too tedious. This burden has fallen mostly on young African Americans. The now-dominant Republican Party resists liberalizing existing laws in this area in expectation that ex-felons would, in all likelihood vote Democratic were their names to be placed on the voter rolls.

(31) Declaring who shall be liners between precincts or between counties.

In the situations where people live on the boundaries of precincts and counties, the legislature is to specify the precinct and county in which they are properly to vote.

The legislature shall pass general laws for the cases enumerated in this section, provided that nothing in this section shall affect the right of the legislature to enact local laws regulating or prohibiting the liquor traffic; but no such local law shall be enacted unless notice shall have been given as required in section 106 of this Constitution.

Following clause 31, this last sentence gives the legislature the positive mandate to pass general laws dealing with the foregoing subjects. However, the increasing prohibition sentiment of the times found expression in the encouragement to the legislature to pass specific local laws curbing traffic in alcoholic beverages. The Court gave the opinion in 2002 that this concluding sentence should not be interpreted to mean that the legislature could authorize the sale of alcoholic beverages where they were not already being legally sold. (Opinion of the Justices (825 So. 2d 109)) Numerous other cases have arisen under other subsections of Section 104 relating to alcoholic beverages, noted earlier as, with the exception of race relations, the most contentious issue in the long history of Alabama politics. (See, for example, Gibson v. City of Alexander City, 779 So. 2d 1153 (2000).)

SECTION 105.

No special, private, or local law, except a law fixing the time of holding courts, shall be enacted in any case which is provided for by a general law, or when the relief sought can be given by any court of this state; and the courts, and not the legislature, shall judge as to whether the relief sought can be given by any court; nor shall the legislature indirectly enact any such special, private, or local law by the partial repeal of a general law.

This section further illustrates the framers' determination to curb local legislation passed under the guise of local policy. The framers generally felt that the legislature had enjoyed too much discretion under the then-operative Constitution of 1875 with regard to the passage of local legislation. Thus they inserted this new section into the Constitution they were drafting, providing "an additional constitutional proscription upon the type or kind of legislation the legislature is allowed to enact." (Green v. Austin, 425 So. 2d 411 (1982)) The framers "prohibited the enactment of a local act when the subject is already subsumed by [a] general statute." (Ibid., quoting from Peddycoart v. Birmingham, 354 So. 2d 808 (1978))

By 1905 the Court had already conceded to the legislature the power to legislate in terms of illogical classifications of localities so long as they were constructed for ostensibly sensible reasons. (State v. Thompson, 38 So. 679) However, the Court declared a closed-ended classification void in Kearley v. Hamilton, 137 So. 424 (1931). The Peddycoart decision mentioned earlier resulted in the legislature establishing an open-ended classification system. (Peddycoart v. Birmingham, 354 So. 2d 808 (1978))

SECTION 106.

No special, private, or local law shall be passed on any subject not enumerated in Section 104 of this Constitution, except in reference to fixing the time of holding courts, unless notice of the intention to apply therefor shall have been published, without cost to the state, in the county or counties where the matter or thing to be affected may be situated, which notice shall state the substance of the proposed law and be published at least once a week for four consecutive weeks in some newspaper published in such county or counties, or if there is no newspaper published therein, then by posting the said notice for two consecutive weeks at five different places in the county or counties prior to the introduction of the bill; and the legislature through a certification by the clerk of the house or secretary of the senate that notice and proof was attached to the original copy of the subject bill and shall be filed in the department of archives and history where it shall constitute a public record. The courts shall pronounce void every special, private, or local law which the journals do not affirmatively show was passed in accordance with the provisions of this section.

This section, dating from 1976, indicates a possible subject for local laws (excluding those not heretofore delegated to the legislature) and specifies the exact procedure to be followed to validly enact a policy applying to less than the state as a whole. When considering local bills, normally a very perfunctory process, the legislature (in effect, the delegation of legislators from the area to be affected) can change the bill, though not "materially." (Wilkins v. Woolf, 208 So. 74 (1968)) Amendment 341 modestly simplified the process of introducing local bills. As recently as 2011, however, the Court threw out a proposed Jefferson County (Birmingham) tax because voters had not been informed to the extent the Constitution requires as far as local legislation is concerned. (Jefferson County v. Weissman (69 So. 3d 827))

It should be noted that this amendment's legal advertising requirement is very attractive to small newspapers in the state. The view is held in some quarters that the de facto newspaper subsidy contributes to a general lack of critical reporting into the merits and demerits of the proposed local legislation being advertised in the local papers.

SECTION 106.01.

Any statute that was otherwise valid and constitutional that was enacted before January 13, 1978, by the legislature of this state and was a general act of local application on a population basis, that applied only to a certain county or counties or a municipality or municipalities of this state, shall not be declared invalid or unconstitutional by any court of this state because it was not properly advertised in compliance with section 106 of this Constitution.

All such population based acts shall forever apply only to the county or counties or municipality or municipalities to which they applied on January 13, 1978, and no other, despite changes in population.

The population based acts referred to above shall only be amended by acts which are properly advertised and passed by the legislature in accordance with the provisions of this Constitution.

This section (389, 1980) was necessary to prevent problems created as a result of the Alabama Supreme Court's ruling in the Peddycoart case (354 So. 2d 808 (1978)), declaring the previous approach to passing much local legislation (without advertising) by making it appear to be statewide (frequently through some sort of very narrow population classification) to be constitutionally invalid. This section gives retroactive approval to such legislation, provided that it was otherwise acceptable.

SECTION 107.

The legislature shall not, by a special, private, or local law, repeal or modify any special, private, or local law except upon notice being given and shown as provided in the last preceding section.

This section requires repealers to go through the same process specified for special, private, and local laws stipulated in Section 106.

SECTION 108.

The operation of a general law shall not be suspended for the benefit of any individual, private corporation or association; nor shall any individual, private corporation or association be exempted from the operation of a general law except as in this article otherwise provided.

The language of this section is reasonably clear. However, it is quite true that efforts are sometimes made to exempt a select group of people (e.g., legislators) from the requirements imposed by law on other citizens similarly situated. An example was to excuse legislators from the continuing education requirements for being licensed to sell real estate. It did not succeed. However, the Court has mostly upheld legislation when challenged as being in violation of this section. (See, for example, Dobbs v. Shelby County Econ. & Indus. Dev. Auth., 749 So. 2d 425 (1999).)

SECTION 109.

The legislature shall pass laws under which local and private interests shall be provided for and protected.

After much prohibitory language regarding local and private legislation, this section instructs the legislature again to focus on general laws instead. The constitutional advice frequently has gone unheeded. The Court early on gave the legislature the go-ahead to pass narrowly drawn laws where prior general laws had not addressed the interests that were now being responded to. (Sisk v. Cargile, 35 So. 114 (1903))

SECTION 110.

A general law is a law which in its terms and effect applies either to the whole state, or to one or more municipalities of the state less than the whole in a class. A general law applicable to such a class of municipalities shall define the class on the basis of criteria reasonably related to the purpose of the law, provided the legislature may also enact and change from time to time a general schedule of not more than eight classes of municipalities based on population according to any designated federal decennial census, and general laws for any purpose may thereafter be enacted for any such class. Any law heretofore enacted which complies with the provisions of this section shall be considered a general law.

No general law which at the time of its enactment applies to only one municipality of the state shall be enacted unless notice of the intention to apply therefor shall have been given and shown as provided in Section 106 of the Constitution for special, private or local laws, provided, that such notice shall not be deemed to constitute such law a local law.

A special or private law is one which applies to an individual, association or corporation. A local law is a law which is not a general law or a special or private law.

Act No. 79-263 (House Bill No. 68) entitled "An Act to establish eight classes of municipalities, by population, based on the 1970 Federal decennial census" approved June 28, 1979, and each and every Act of the legislature thereafter enacted referred or relating to a class of municipalities as established in said Act No. 79-263 are hereby in all things ratified, approved, validated and confirmed as of the date of their enactment, any provision or provisions of the Constitution of Alabama, as amended to the contrary notwithstanding.

The language reprinted here is from Amendment 397, ratified in 1982. It reflects the stipulations as most recently responded to by the legislature regarding increased judicial scrutiny of supposed general laws with only a local application (sometimes nicknamed GBLAs, general bills of local application). It gives retroactive approval to local legislation passed pursuant to a 1979 response to the problem of local legislation. In that year the Supreme Court had given the opinion that, pursuant to Section 110 as written at that time, general laws could divide Alabama municipalities into no more than eight population-based categories. (Opinion of the Justices, 373 So. 2d 1051 (1979))

SECTION 111.

No bill introduced as a general law in either house of the legislature shall be so amended on its passage to become a special, private or local law.

This section concludes the Alabama Constitution's approach, original and revised, to the dilemma particularly of local legislation. Its goal is to prevent surprises for local residents who, had local publication requirements been complied with, would have known early on what state legislation was being contemplated for them. (Mitchell v. Mobile County, 313 So. 2d 172 (1975))

SECTION 111.01.

The legislature shall not hereafter by general, special or local law authorize the state highway department or any other agency of the state of Alabama, other than a court of county commissioners, board of revenue or like county governing body, to assume responsibility for the construction, repair or maintenance of all county roads or bridges within a county unless the assumption of such responsibility by the state highway department or other agency shall be approved by a vote of the duly qualified electors of the county in which such roads lie at an election held for such purpose, in the manner that may be prescribed by law. Provided, the state highway department, or other state agency may engage in the construction, repair or maintenance of a county road or bridge upon written agreement signed by the director and a majority of the members of the county governing body; and provided further that the legislature is not prohibited from authorizing the highway director or other state agency to designate certain routes or roads within a county as a part of the state highway system.

This provision's objective was to end the practice by which some legislators had secured the passage of local laws placing responsibilities pertaining to roads under the jurisdiction of what is now designated the Department of Transportation, making them "captive counties" in popular parlance. Now the state will not accept such jurisdiction no matter what county voters desire, and there are no "captive counties." (Amendment 142, 1957)

SECTION 111.02.

The legislature may pass laws to provide for the termination of alimony upon the remarriage of the spouse receiving the alimony or upon such spouse living openly or cohabiting with a member of the opposite sex. Such laws may be made to apply retroactively.

In this section (390, 1980) the Constitution authorizes the legislature "to limit the discretion of the court by directing that an award of alimony in a prior decree be terminated by the court upon proof that the receiving spouse has remarried." (Oliver v. Oliver, 431 So. 2d 1271 (Civ. App. 1983)) This the legislature did, and the Court upheld the action based on this section. (Ibid.) With the advent of same-sex marriage, fairness would seem to require adding cohabitation with a member of either sex to the interpretation of this section relating to the termination of alimony.

SECTION 111.03.

No law, whether general, special or local, whose purpose or effect is to provide for a new or increased expenditure of county funds held or disbursed by the county governing body shall become effective as to any county of this state until the first day of the fiscal year next following the passage of such law. The foregoing notwithstanding, a law, whether general, special or local, whose purpose or effect is to provide for a new or increased expenditure of county funds held or disbursed by the county governing body, shall become effective according to its own terms as any other law if: (1) such law is approved by a resolution duly adopted by and spread upon the minutes of the county governing body of the county affected thereby; or (2) such law (or other law or laws which specifically refer to such law) provides the respective county governing bodies with new or additional revenues sufficient to fund such new or increased expenditures.

One of the most objectionable practices of the state, from the county perspective, has been for the legislature to mandate some new or augmented expenditure on the part of the county without providing the increased revenues needed to pay the bill. This section, added in 1988 (Amendment 474), seeks to protect counties from this practice in the ways clearly identified in the text.

SECTION 111.04.

[This section is exactly like Section 111.03 except that "municipal" or "municipality" is substituted for county. The same comments apply. (491, 1988)]

SECTION 111.05.

(a) No general law, or state executive order whose purpose or effect is to require a new or increased expenditure of funds held or disbursed by the governing body of a municipality or county, or an instrumentality thereof, shall become effective as to any municipality or county, or an instrumentality thereof, until approved by an ordinance enacted, or a resolution adopted, by the governing authority of the affected municipality, county, or instrumentality or until, and only as long as, the Legislature appropriates funds for the purpose to the affected municipality, county, or instrumentality and only to the extent and amount that the funds are provided, or until a law provides for a local source of revenue within the municipality, county, or instrumentality for the stated purpose and the affected municipality, county, or instrumentality is authorized by ordinance or resolution to levy and collect the revenue and only to the extent and amount of the revenue.

(b) This [section] shall not apply to:

(1) A local law as defined in Article IV, Section 110, Constitution of Alabama 1901.

(2) An act defining a new crime or amending the definition of an existing crime.

(3) An act, statute, [or] executive order enacted, promulgated, or adopted and effective prior to January 6, 1999, which by its provisions requires expenditures by the county or municipality at any time after that date.

(4) An act enacted, or state executive order promulgated or adopted to comply with a federal mandate, only to the extent of the federal mandate.

(5) An act adopted or enacted by two-thirds of those voting in each house of the Legislature and any rule or regulation adopted pursuant to implement that act or adopted pursuant thereto.

This section (621, 1999) has not yet been subject to any litigation that has reached the appellate levels of the Alabama judiciary.

SECTION 111.06.

No moneys derived from any fees, excises, or license taxes, levied by the state, relating to registration, operation, or use of vehicles upon the public highways except a vehicle-use tax imposed in lieu of a sales tax, and no moneys derived from any fees, excises, or license taxes, levied by the state, relating to fuels used for propelling such vehicles except pump taxes, shall be expended for other than the cost of administering such laws, statutory refunds and adjustments allowed therein, cost of construction, reconstruction, maintenance and repair of public highways and bridges, costs of highway rights-of-way, payment of highway obligations, the cost of traffic regulation, and the expense of enforcing state traffic and motor vehicle laws. The provisions of this amendment shall not apply to any such fees, excises, or license taxes now levied by the state for school purposes for this whole state or for any county or city board of education therein; and the legislature may provide for the manufacture, distribution and use on private passenger or pleasure motor vehicles of personalized license plates or tags, bearing some special letters, figures, mark or badge of distinction or personal

> prestige in lieu of the regular license plates or tags, and if it does so, the legislature must also require that such tags may be procured only by payment of a fee or charge, in addition to the regular fee, excise or license tax for the registration, operation or use of such motor vehicles upon the highways. The moneys derived from the additional charge made for such special or distinctive license plates or tags, in excess of the cost of the manufacture and distribution of such plates or tags, may be used in such manner as the legislature prescribes.

The new language of the section (354, 1976), which differentiates it from the now superseded Amendment 93, begins with, ". . . and the legislature may provide." Showing the degradation of the "fundamental" concept of American state constitutional law, this section merely authorizes "vanity" vehicle tags and the disposition of the profits therefrom.

Article V

Executive Department

SECTION 112.

The executive department shall consist of a governor, lieutenant governor, attorney-general, state auditor, secretary of state, state treasurer, superintendent of education, commissioner of agriculture and industries, and a sheriff for each county.

The components of Alabama's constitutionally plural executive are enumerated. In terms of actual power, the department heads with constitutional status are not necessarily the most influential. It is surprising to find the county sheriff identified as a member of the state executive branch. All of these are elective except the superintendent of education who, under Section 262 (284, 1969), is appointed by a popularly chosen board of education.

SECTION 113.

The supreme executive power of this state shall be vested in a chief magistrate, who shall be styled "The Governor of the State of Alabama."

Despite the plurality of the state executive, the Constitution makes clear who is officially supreme within this sphere, even though some of its other provisions make the governor's actual supremacy problematic.

SECTION 114.

The governor, lieutenant governor, attorney-general, state auditor, secretary of state, state treasurer, and commissioner of agriculture and industries shall be elected by the qualified electors of the state at the same time and places appointed for the election of members of the legislature in the year nineteen hundred and two, and in every fourth year thereafter.

In an arrangement which should promote more responsible government, the governor and all legislators are elected at the same time for the same term. However, in the absence of a viable two-party system—once overwhelmingly Democratic and now Republican-dominant—this electoral arrangement has frequently failed to produce coordinated executive and legislative action. During much of the twentieth century, the typically Democratic governor did enjoy a considerable amount of legislative influence, but this was more due to his patronage powers than to the fact that he and they were elected on a clearly identified ticket.

SECTION 115.

The returns of every election for governor, lieutenant governor, attorney-general, state auditor, secretary of state, state treasurer, and commissioner of agriculture and industries shall be sealed up and transmitted by the returning officers to the seat of government, directed to the speaker of the house of representatives, who shall, during the first week of the session to which such returns shall be made, open and publish them in the presence of both houses of the legislature in joint convention; but the speaker's duty and the duty of the joint convention shall be purely ministerial. The result of the election shall be ascertained and declared by the speaker from the face of the returns without delay. The person having the highest number of votes for any one of said offices shall be declared duly elected; but if two or more persons shall have an equal and the highest number of votes for the same office, the legislature by joint vote, without delay, shall choose one of said persons for said office. Contested elections for governor, lieutenant governor, attorney-general, state auditor, secretary of state, state treasurer, and commissioner of agriculture and industries shall be determined by both houses of the legislature in such manner as may be prescribed by law.

For most of the twentieth century, it was known after the Democratic primary elections (first primary and probable run-off) who would be Alabama's next governor (and other executive officers). At present it is the Republican primary which is most important since Republicans occupy all statewide elective positions. There has never been a need to resort to the extraordinary procedures identified in this section.

SECTION 116.

The governor, lieutenant governor, attorney general, secretary of state, state treasurer, and commissioner of agriculture and industries, shall hold their respective offices for the term of four years from the first Monday after the second Tuesday in January next succeeding their election and until their successors shall be elected and qualified. Each of said officers shall be eligible to succeed himself in office, but no person shall be eligible to succeed himself for more than one additional term.

Amendment 282, ratified in 1968, is substituted for the original section. This amendment was approved following the unsuccessful legislative effort of Governor George Wallace to win the right to succeed himself in 1965 and the subsequent election of his wife, Lurleen Wallace, as governor in 1966.

SECTION 117.

The governor and lieutenant governor shall each be at least thirty years of age when elected, and shall have been citizens of the United States ten years and resident citizens of this state at least seven years next before the date of their election. The lieutenant governor shall be ex officio president of the senate, but shall have no right to vote except in the event of a tie.

Alabama's traditional political culture typically is not friendly to newcomers seeking any elective office. Most Alabama governors recently have been lifelong Alabamians, men of middle age or somewhat older. (Lurleen Burns Wallace is the state's only woman governor to date.)

SECTION 118.

The governor, lieutenant governor, attorney-general, state auditor, secretary of state, state treasurer, and commissioner of agriculture and industries, [sic] shall receive compensation to be fixed by law, which shall not be increased or diminished during the term for which they shall have been elected, and shall, except the lieutenant governor, reside at the state capital during the time they continue in office, except during epidemics. The compensation of the lieutenant governor shall be the same as that received by the speaker of the house, except while serving as governor, during which time his compensation shall be the same as that allowed the governor.

The 2014 annual salaries of the officials named were as follows: governor, $120,000; lieutenant governor, $69,000; attorney general, $168,000; and secretary of state, state treasurer, state auditor, and commissioner of agriculture and industries, $85,000. (Figures have been rounded to the nearest thousand dollars. A 1969 act makes the attorney general's salary comparable to that of an associate justice of the Supreme Court.) While campaigning for governor in 2010, Dr. Robert Bentley promised voters that he would not accept a salary until Alabama reached full employment, which is identified as 5.2 percent. He was elected to a second term in 2014 and was still not drawing a salary. (In mid-2015 the seasonally adjusted state unemployment rate was 6.1 percent.) The Supreme Court ruled in the Depression year of 1934 that all salaries were exempt from the proration which has been such a regular part of Alabama financial management. (See Abramson v. Hard, 155 So. 590.)

SECTION 120.

The governor shall take care that the laws be faithfully executed.

This is the equivalent of Article II, Section 3, of the U.S. Constitution.

SECTION 121.

The governor may require information in writing, under oath, from the officers of the executive department, named in this article, or created by statute, on any subject, relating to the duties of their respective offices, and may at any time require information in writing, under oath, from all officers and managers of state institutions, upon any subject relating to the condition, management and expenses of their respective offices and institutions. Any such officer or manager who makes a willfully false report or fails without sufficient excuse to make the required report on demand, is guilty of an impeachable offense.

This section is the state version of Article III, Section 3, of the U.S. Constitution. The Alabama constitutional language regarding communications to the chief executive is much more explicit, however—another cause of the extreme length of many state constitutions.

SECTION 122.

The governor may, by proclamation, on extraordinary occasions, convene the legislature at the seat of government, or at a different place if, since their last adjournment, that shall have become dangerous from an enemy, insurrection, or other lawless outbreak, or from any infectious or contagious disease; and he shall state specifically in such proclamation each matter concerning which the action of that body is deemed necessary.

This section provides the basis for identifying the governor as chief legislator, namely, his or her power to call special sessions and to specify the agenda for such sessions. (See Section 76 with reference to the legislature's authorization to consider measures not included in the governor's special session call.)

SECTION 123.

The governor shall, from time to time, give to the legislature information of the state of the government, and recommend for its consideration such measures as he may deem expedient; and at the commencement of each regular session of the legislature, and at the close of his term of office, he shall give information by written message of the condition of the state; and he shall account to the legislature, as may be prescribed by law, for all moneys received and paid out by him or by his order, and at the commencement of each regular session he shall present to the legislature estimates of the amount of money required to be raised by taxation for all purposes.

The first part of this section is the equivalent of Article II, Section 2, of the U.S. Constitution. The specifically finance-related reports discussed in the rest of the section have no federal constitutional equivalent.

SECTION 124.

The governor shall have power to grant reprieves and commutations to persons under sentence of death. The legislature shall have power to provide for and to regulate the administration of pardons, paroles, remission of fines and forfeitures, and may authorize the courts having criminal jurisdiction to suspend sentence and to order probation. No pardon shall relieve from civil and political disabilities unless specifically expressed in the pardon.

The language here is that of Amendment 38, ratified in 1939. It provides the basis for a more bureaucratically and professionally oriented system of pardons and paroles than the ex officio board stipulated in the Constitution originally.

SECTION 125.

Every bill which shall have passed both houses of the legislature, except as otherwise provided in this Constitution, shall be presented to the governor; if he approve, he shall sign it; but if not, he shall return it with his objections to the house in which it originated, which shall enter the objections at large upon the journal and proceed to reconsider it. If the governor's message proposes no amendment which would remove his objections to the bill, the house in which the bill originated may proceed to reconsider it, and if a majority of the whole number elected to that house vote for the passage of the bill, it shall be sent to the other house, which shall in like manner reconsider, and if a majority of the whole number elected to that house vote for the passage of the bill, the same shall become a law, notwithstanding the governor's veto. If the governor's message proposes amendment, which would remove his objections, the house to which it is sent may so amend the bill and send it with the governor's message to the other house, which may adopt, but cannot amend, said amendment; and both houses concurring in the amendment, the bill shall again be sent to the governor and acted on by him as other bills. If the house to which the bill is returned refuses to make such amendment, it shall proceed to reconsider it; and if a majority of the whole number elected to that house shall vote for the passage of the bill, it shall be sent with the objections to the other house by which it shall likewise be reconsidered, and if approved by a majority of the whole number elected to that house, it shall become a law. If the house to which the bill is returned makes the amendment, and the other house declines to pass the same, that house shall proceed to reconsider it, as though the bill had originated therein, and such proceedings shall be taken thereon as above provided. In every such case the vote of both houses shall be determined by yeas and nays, and the names of the members voting for or against the bill shall be entered upon the journals of each house, respectively. If any bill shall not be returned by the governor within six days, Sunday excepted, after it shall have been presented, the same shall become a law in like manner as if he had signed it, unless the legislature, by its adjournment, prevent return, in which case it shall not be a law; but when return is prevented by recess, such bill must be returned to the house in which it originated within two days after the reassembling, otherwise it shall become a law, but bills presented to the governor within five days before the final adjournment of the legislature may be approved by the governor at any time within ten days after such adjournment, and if approved and deposited with the secretary of state within that time shall become law. Every vote, order, or resolution to which concurrence of both houses may be necessary, except on questions of adjournment and the bringing on of elections by the two houses, and amending this Constitution, shall be presented to the governor; and, before the same shall take effect, be approved by him; or, being disapproved, shall be repassed by both houses according to the rules and limitations prescribed in the case of a bill.

This is a very long section, but it requires little interpretation. It provides very specifically for the governor's role in the legislative process in the following contingencies: (a) ordinary passage of a bill, (b) gubernatorial veto without executive amendment, (c) gubernatorial veto with executive amendment, (d) passage of a bill without action by the governor at the conclusion of the period for signing or vetoing it, (e) gubernatorial pocket veto (by implication) at the end of the period specified for gubernatorial action during which time the legislature has adjourned, and (f) applicability of the foregoing procedures to subjects of legislative action not classifiable as ordinary bills. Contrasts with the president are most evident with respect to the governor's power of executive amendment, the legislative vote necessary to override an executive veto (a majority of the membership instead of two-thirds of a quorum), and the number of days the executive has to act on legislatively passed bills (six days instead of ten when the legislature is in session). The governor must act on bills passed at the close of a legislative session within ten days of the assembly's adjournment.

SECTION 126.

The governor shall have power to approve or disapprove any item or items of any appropriation bill embracing distinct items, and the part or the parts of the bill approved shall be the law, and the item or items disapproved shall be void, unless repassed according to the rules and limitations prescribed for the passage of bills over the executive veto; and he shall in writing state specifically the item or items he disapproves, setting the same out in full in his message, but in such a case the enrolled bill shall not be returned with the governor's objection.

This section provides the basis for the governor's item veto power with respect to appropriation bills. This is a power the governor of Alabama possesses in common with the governor of forty-five other states and which several recent presidents have asked for but not received. The last clause means that only the item or items in dispute are sent back to the legislature. The rest of the approved bill which was passed by the legislature and approved by the governor is filed as required with the secretary of state.

SECTION 127.

In case of the governor's removal from office, death or resignation, the lieutenant governor shall become governor. If both the governor and lieutenant governor be removed from office, die or resign more than sixty days prior to the next general election, at which any state officers are to be elected a governor and lieutenant governor shall be elected at such election for the unexpired term, and in the event of a vacancy in the office, caused by the removal from office, death or resignation of the governor and lieutenant governor, pending such a vacancy and until their successors shall be elected and qualified, the office of governor shall be held and administered by either the president pro tem of the senate, speaker of the house of representatives, attorney-general, state auditor, secretary of state, or state treasurer. If any of these officers be under any of the disabilities herein specified, the office of governor shall be administered in the order named by such of these officers as may be free from such disability. If the governor shall be absent from the state over twenty days, the secretary of state shall notify the lieutenant governor, who shall enter upon the duties of governor; if both the governor and the lieutenant governor shall be absent from the state over twenty days, the secretary of state shall notify the president pro tem. of the senate, who shall enter upon the duties or governor, and so on, in case such absence [sic] he shall notify each of the other officers named in their order, who shall discharge the duties of the office until the governor or other officer entitled to administer the office in succession to the governor returns. If the governor-elect fail or refuse from any cause to qualify, the president pro tem. of the senate, the speaker of the house of representatives, the attorney-general, state auditor, secretary of state, and state treasurer, shall, in like manner, in the order named, administer the office until the governor-elect or lieutenant governor-elect qualifies.

This is another long section, providing for the filling of vacancies in the gubernatorial office. It was used in April 1993, when Guy Hunt was convicted of violating the state's ethics law and James E. Folsom, Jr., immediately became governor in his stead. The only aspects of Section 127 to have been used are the succession to the governorship and the lieutenant governor becoming acting governor in the wake of the governor's absence from the state for more than twenty days (for example, Jere Beasley for George C. Wallace while he was hospitalized in Maryland due to an assassination attempt). Since the office of lieutenant governor was reinstituted in the 1901 Constitution, lieutenant governors have served as acting governor on four separate occasions.

SECTION 128.

If the governor or other officer administering the office shall appear to be of unsound mind, it shall be the duty of the supreme court of Alabama, at any regular term, or at any special term, which it is hereby authorized to call for the purpose, upon request in writing, verified by their affidavits, of any two of the officers named in section 127 of this Constitution, not next in succession to the office of governor, to ascertain the mental condition of the governor or other officer administering the office, and if he is adjudged to be of unsound mind, to so decree, a copy of which decree, duly certified, shall be filed in the office of the secretary of state; and in the event of such adjudication, it shall be the duty of the officer next in succession to perform the duties of the office until the governor or other officer administering the office is restored to his mind. If the incumbent denies that the governor or other person entitled to administer the office has been restored to his mind, the supreme court, at the instance of any officer named in section 127 of this Constitution, shall ascertain the truth concerning the same, and if the officer has been restored to his mind, shall so state; and in the event of such adjudication, the office shall be restored to him. The supreme court shall prescribe the method of taking testimony and the rules of practice in such proceedings, which rules shall include a provision for the service of notice of such proceedings on the governor or person acting as governor.

This section provides for the exercise of the office of governor in the case of the mental illness of the incumbent. The proceedings for determining the severity of such illness and the safeguards for preventing irresponsible, arbitrary actions have never been employed.

SECTION 129.

The lieutenant governor, president pro tem. of the senate, speaker of the house, attorney-general, state auditor, secretary of state, or state treasurer, while administering the office of governor, shall receive like compensation as the prescribed by law for the governor, and no other.

This section has been called into play historically on four different occasions.

SECTION 130.

No person shall, at the same time, hold the office of governor and any other office, civil or military, under this state or the United States, or any other state or government, except as otherwise provided in this Constitution.

This section has not been controversial. The occupants of these offices have not attempted what the Constitution here clearly forbids.

SECTION 131.

The governor shall be commander-in-chief of the militia and volunteer forces of this state, except when they shall be called into the service of the United States, and he may call out the same to execute the laws, suppress insurrection, and repel invasion, but need not command in person unless directed to do so by resolutions of the legislature; and when acting in the service of the United States, he shall appoint his staff, and the legislature shall fix his rank.

Probably the most famous use of the National Guard by the governor came in 1954 when Governor Gordon Persons declared martial law in Phenix City following the assassination of Attorney General–nominate Albert L. Patterson there. The most spectacular instance of the president "federalizing" the Guard, calling it "into the service of the United States," occurred in June 1963 when

President John F. Kennedy took its control from Governor George Wallace to assure the peaceful integration of the University of Alabama. Most recently members of the National Guard participated in the activities of the task force used by Governor Bob Riley near the end of his second term to combat what he considered to be illegal gambling operations.

SECTION 132.

No person shall be eligible to the office of attorney-general, state auditor, secretary of state, state treasurer, or commissioner of agriculture and industries unless he shall have been a citizen of the United States at least seven years, and shall have resided in this state at least five years next preceding his election and shall be at least twenty-five years old when elected.

This section states the minimal legal qualifications for elective offices besides the governor. Again, Alabama's traditional political culture is not hospitable to outsiders seeking elective office, so winners are typically lifelong state residents.

SECTION 133.

There shall be a seal of the state, which shall be used officially by the governor, and the seal now in use shall continue to be used until another shall have been adopted by the legislature. The seal shall be called "The Great Seal of the State of Alabama."

There has been no recent change in the seal of the state. The present seal was adopted in 1939. At that time the legislature revived the "map" representation for the seal which had been employed during Alabama's first half-century of statehood. Prior to 1939 (and since Reconstruction), the "eagle on union shield" was employed.

SECTION 134.

The secretary of state shall be the custodian of the great seal of the state, and shall authenticate therewith all official acts of the governor, except his approval of laws, resolutions, appointments to office, and administrative orders. He shall keep a register of the official acts of the governor, and when necessary shall attest them, and lay copies of the same together with copies of all papers relative thereto, before either house of the legislature, when required to do so, and shall perform such other duties as may be prescribed by law.

The office of secretary of state has become increasingly important in recent years, especially as the federal government has taken initiatives to increase voter turnout (e.g., Help America Vote Act, or HAVA). In addition, whenever there is a doubt about where to assign a new duty or function, the inclination is to give it to the secretary of state. The Constitution itself assigns ten responsibilities to the secretary. In addition, twenty-eight different sections in the Alabama *Code* specify more than one thousand tasks he or she is expected to perform.

SECTION 135.

All grants and commissions shall be issued in the name and by the authority of the state of Alabama, sealed with the great seal of the state, signed by the governor and countersigned by the secretary of state.

This section is self-explanatory.

SECTION 136.

Should the office of attorney-general, state auditor, secretary of state, state treasurer, or commissioner of agriculture and industries become vacant from any cause, the governor shall fill such vacancy until the disability is removed or a successor elected and qualified. In case any of said officers shall become of unsound mind, such unsoundness shall be ascertained by the supreme court upon the suggestion of the governor.

Filling vacancies in the named executive offices on either a temporary or permanent basis is provided for. The first time a woman held a state elective executive office was when Governor Chauncey Sparks in 1944 appointed Sybil Pool to a vacancy in the secretary of state position. She was elected in her own right in 1946. (As will be recalled, under Amendment 284, the superintendent of education is appointed by the elective board.)

SECTION 137.

The attorney general, state auditor, secretary of state, state treasurer, and commissioner of agriculture and industries shall perform such duties as may be prescribed by law. The state treasurer and state auditor shall, every year, at a time fixed by the legislature, make a full and complete report to the governor, showing the receipts and disbursements of every character, all claims audited and paid out, by items, and all taxes and revenues collected and paid into the treasury, and the sources thereof. They shall make reports oftener upon any matters pertaining to their offices if required by the governor or the legislature. The attorney general, state auditor, secretary of state, state treasurer, and commissioner of agriculture and industries shall not receive to their use any fees, costs, perquisites of office or other compensation than the salaries prescribed by law, and all fees that may be payable for any services performed by such officers shall be at once paid into the state treasury. The legislature may require the attorney general to defend any or all suits brought against the state, or any subdivision thereof, or against any state school board or board of education, or against like boards or commissions by whatever name designated, or against any members, officers or employees of any such boards, or against any school official or employee throughout Alabama.

The language reproduced is that of Amendment 111 (1956), which added the last sentence, now moot, authorizing the attorney general during the era of massive resistance to defend school authorities in their efforts to preserve segregated public education in Alabama. Before this added language, some of the duties of the treasurer and auditor were identified, and permission was given to the legislature to prescribe other duties as well as job activities for the other state executive officials mentioned. It should be noted that, since the reforms of the Frank Dixon administration (1939–43), the most critical finance-related functions have been performed by the Department of Finance, not the auditor or treasurer. This illustrates growing professionalization, bureaucratization, and full-time attention to governmental business mostly by merit-appointed employees. Compensation of these officers is to be by the modern basis of salary rather than fees.

SECTION 138.

A sheriff shall be elected in each county by the qualified electors thereof who shall hold office for a term of four years unless sooner removed, and he shall be eligible to such office as his own successor. Whenever any prisoner is taken from jail, or from the custody of any sheriff or his deputy, and put to death, or suffers grievous bodily harm, owing to the neglect, connivance, cowardice, or other grave fault of the sheriff, such sheriff may be impeached, under section 174 of this Constitution. If the sheriff be impeached, and thereupon convicted, he shall not be eligible to hold any office in this state during the time for which he had been elected or appointed to serve as sheriff.

This last section of Article V deals with the most unrelated of the officials of the state executive branch, the county sheriff. The language reproduced here is that of Amendment 35 (1938), which authorized self-succession, originally forbidden to the sheriff as well as to the other executive officials. Most of the section constitutes a stern warning to sheriffs not to allow lynch mobs to take prisoners from their custody and the possible consequences if they do. This language originated in the Constitution of 1901 and amounts to one of the few examples of enlightened racial attitudes in this document.

SECTION 138.01.

A. Appointments and promotions in the civil service of this state shall be made according to merit, fitness and efficiency, to be determined, so far as practicable, by examination which, so far as practicable, shall be competitive under such laws as the legislature may enact.

B. It shall be the duty of the legislature to maintain laws necessary to implement, and to provide adequate financial support for a positive program of personnel management in the state service.

C. All state personnel laws now in effect that are not in conflict with this article shall continue in effect until they are amended or repealed as provided by law...

This is more nearly an "appropriate" constitutional provision (88, 1951) than many of the others which have been added as amendments to the Alabama Constitution of 1901. For the most part it is left to the legislature to implement "a positive program of personnel management in the state service."

SECTION 138.03.

All of the assets, proceeds or income of the teachers', employees', state police, public and judicial retirement systems of Alabama, or any successor systems thereto, and all contributions and payments made to such systems to provide for retirement and related benefits thereunder, shall be held, invested as authorized by law, or disbursed as in trust for the exclusive purpose of providing for such benefits, refunds, and administrative expenses under the management of the boards of control of the aforementioned retirement systems; and, [sic] none of such assets, proceeds, income, contributions or payments shall be used, loaned, encumbered or diverted to or for any other purpose whatsoever.

When the state has been in straitened financial circumstances, which has been frequently, it was tempting for political leaders to suggest drawing on a short-term basis from retirement system assets to meet emergency needs. This amendment removed this as an option. More recently, assets of the offshore resources fund have been drawn upon. Of course, Alabama's financial problems are compounded by the fact that the heavy preponderance of revenues is earmarked for a particular functional area when they are enacted. This heightens the feast-or-famine phenomenon.

SECTION 138.04.

All of the assets, proceeds, and income of the Alabama Retired State Employees' Health Care Trust Fund and the Alabama Retired Education Employees' Health Care Trust Fund, or any successor or assignee of the trust, and all contributions and payments made to the trustees of the trusts, shall be held, invested as authorized by law, and disbursed for the exclusive purposes of providing for administrative expenses of the respective trust and health care benefits under the management of the trustees of the respective trust in accordance with the terms of its trust agreement. None of the assets, proceeds, income, contributions, or payments shall be used, loaned, encumbered, or diverted to or for any other purposes whatsoever, except that (a) a trust may be terminated, if the State has no obligation to provide post-employment health care benefits for which the trust was established to such persons, and, in that event, the remaining assets of the trust shall revert to the State Treasury to and for the credit of the State Employees' Insurance Board, the Public Education Employees' Health Insurance Board, or its successor or assignee, as the case as may be, related to the terminated trust, or (b) if in response to a petition of the trustees of a trust requiring that the respective trust agreement be amended, a court of competent jurisdiction determines that the amendment proposed by the trustees is necessary or otherwise advisable to accomplish one or more purposes of the act authorizing and directing the creation of the trusts.

This section (798, 2007) seeks to prevent what has happened with the larger Alabama trust fund—"borrowing" from it during the frequent times of fiscal stress in state government. It stipulates that the retiree trust funds are to be used exclusively for the payment of pensions (and administrative expenses) except under circumstances which would be highly unusual.

Article VI

Judicial Department

Article VI of the Constitution of 1901 was completely repealed by Amendment 328, ratified in 1973. It is the text of this amendment, together with the interpretations which have been made since it went into effect, which are presented here.

SECTION 139.

(a) Except as otherwise provided in this Constitution, the judicial power of the state shall be vested exclusively in a unified judicial system which shall consist of a supreme court, a court of criminal appeals, a court of civil appeals, a trial court of general jurisdiction known as the circuit court, a trial court of limited jurisdiction known as the district court, a probate court and such municipal courts as may be provided by law.

(b) The legislature may create judicial officers with authority to issue warrants and may vest in administrative agencies established by law such judicial powers as may be reasonably necessary as an incident to the accomplishment of the purposes for which the agencies are created.

The expression "as provided by law" facilitates the making of needed statutory changes pertaining to the judiciary without the necessity to resort to constitutional amendment. This article promises much of the flexibility that is absent elsewhere.

SECTION 140.

(a) The supreme court shall be the highest court of the state and shall consist of one chief justice and such number of associate justices as may be prescribed by law.

(b) The supreme court shall have original jurisdiction (1) of cases and controversies as provided by this Constitution, (2) to issue such remedial writs or orders as may be necessary to give it general supervision and control of courts of inferior jurisdiction, and (3) to answer questions of state law certified by a court of the United States.

(c) The supreme court shall have such appellate jurisdiction as may be provided by law.

Section 140(c) provides for the Supreme Court's hierarchical supervision of all other Alabama courts through the exercise of its authority to hear appeals and to grant supervisory writs. (Brogden v. Employees' Retirement System, 336 So. 2d 137 (Civ. App. 1976))

SECTION 141.

(a) The court of criminal appeals shall consist of such number of judges as may be provided by law and shall exercise appellate jurisdiction under such terms and conditions as shall be provided by law and by rules of the supreme court.

(b) The court of civil appeals shall consist of such number of judges as may be provided by law and shall exercise appellate jurisdiction under such terms and conditions as shall be provided by law and by rules of the supreme court.

(c) The court of criminal appeals and the court of civil appeals shall have no original jurisdiction except the power to issue all writs necessary or appropriate in aid of appellate jurisdiction of the courts of appeals.

(d) The court of criminal appeals shall have and exercise original jurisdiction in the issuance and determination of writs of quo warranto and mandamus in relation to matters in which said court has appellate jurisdiction. Said court shall have authority to issue writs of injunction, habeas corpus and other remedial and original writs as are necessary to give it a general superintendence and control of jurisdiction inferior to it and in matters over which it has exclusive appellate jurisdiction; to punish for contempts by the infliction of a fine as high as one hundred dollars, and imprisonment not exceeding ten days, one or both, and to exercise such other powers as may be given to said court by law.

The flexible phrase "as may be provided by law," or its equivalent, occurs five times in this section. The most specific language in the section relates to the power of the Court of Criminal Appeals to punish for contempt. The contempt-punishing power of judges would be most subject to potential abuse. The Supreme Court ruled in 2007 that both the civil and criminal appeals courts were authorized to exercise a general superintendence over courts inferior to them in those areas where they possessed exclusive jurisdiction. (C.D.S. v. K.S.S. (978 So. 2d 782)) If there is a dispute as to which of the appeals courts below the Supreme Court should handle a particular case, the Supreme Court will resolve the matter.

(Ex parte State (985 So. 2d 446) (2007)) In the case of the circuit courts' jurisdiction, the Court will look to the legislature to resolve any questions regarding the kinds of cases they may decide. (Henderson v. State, 616 So. 2d (1993))

SECTION 142.

(a) The state shall be divided into judicial circuits. For each circuit, there shall be one circuit court having such divisions and consisting of such number of judges as shall be provided by law.

(b) The circuit court shall exercise general jurisdiction in all cases except as may otherwise be provided by law. The circuit court may be authorized by law to review decisions of state administrative agencies and decisions of inferior courts. It shall have authority to issue such writs as may be necessary or appropriate to effectuate its powers, and shall have such other powers as may be provided by law.

This section provides for a unified circuit (trial) court. Judges may specialize in criminal or civil cases, or more specifically, for example, in family or juvenile law, but each of these divisions will be a part of the same circuit court.

SECTION 143.

The district court shall be a court of limited jurisdiction and shall exercise uniform original jurisdiction in such cases, and within such geographical boundaries, as shall be prescribed by law, provided that the district court shall hold court in each county seat and at such other places as prescribed by law. The district court shall have jurisdiction of all cases arising under ordinances of municipalities in which there is no municipal court and shall hold court in each incorporated municipality of a population of 1,000 or more where there is no municipal court at places prescribed by law.

This was a new court for the Alabama judicial system. It replaced a hodgepodge of inferior courts within the county and all municipal courts wherein the municipality decided to forego having its own separate court.

SECTION 144.

There shall be a probate court in each county which shall have general jurisdiction of orphans' business, and of adoptions, and with power to grant letters testamentary, and of administration, and of guardianships, and shall have such further jurisdiction as may be provided by law, provided that whenever the circuit court has taken jurisdiction of the settlement of any estate, it shall have power to do all things necessary for the settlement of such estate, including the appointment and removal of administrators, executors, guardians, and trustees and including action upon the resignation of either of them.

The probate court is unique among courts because its judge is not required to be a lawyer, and because in thirteen of the sixty-seven counties he or she also presides over the county commission, the principal county governing body. Because of this dual role, it was impractical to require the probate judge to have a law degree. The original statement of the judicial reform article was replaced in 1977. It reflected the clout of probate judges by fixing their jurisdiction in the Constitution as indicated, subject to the provision in the last clause of the section. The original section had not elaborated on the powers of the probate courts but merely said that they would "have such jurisdiction as may be provided by law."

SECTION 145.

All municipal courts shall have uniform original jurisdiction limited to cases arising under municipal ordinances as prescribed by law. Judges of municipal courts shall be licensed to practice law in the state and have such other qualifications as the legislature may prescribe. A municipal judge may serve as a judge of more than one municipal court. Expenses of municipal courts and compensation of municipal judges shall be paid in a manner prescribed by law notwithstanding the provisions of section 148 of this article. Municipal judges shall be appointed and vacancies filled by the governing body of the municipality, in accordance with uniform terms, conditions and procedures as may be provided by law, notwithstanding the provisions of sections 152, 153, and 154 of this article. The prohibited activities of section 147 (a) and (b) shall not be applicable to a judge of a municipal court.

The governing body of a municipality shall have the right to elect at any time to abolish the municipal court within its limits. If such election is exercised, the jurisdiction of the court abolished shall be transferred to the district court of the district in which the municipality is located. The governing body of a municipality may, at its election, re-establish a municipal court after appropriate notice.

The framers of the new judicial article originally intended to merge all municipal courts into the new, unified state judicial system, but the political power of the municipalities was too great to permit this as the reform amendment made its tortuous way through the legislature. To the more committed reformers' chagrin, municipalities also won exclusion from several sections applicable to the personnel of other courts.

SECTION 146.

Judges of the supreme court, courts of appeals, circuit court and district court shall be licensed to practice law in this state and have such other qualifications as the legislature may prescribe. Judges of the probate court shall have such qualifications as may be provided by law.

This section shows the nearly complete movement of the state away from the old amateur justice of the peace (JP) courts of another era. All judges except probate judges must possess a license to practice law.

SECTION 147.

(a) No judge of any court of this state shall, during his continuance in office, engage in the practice of law or receive any remuneration for his judicial service except the salary and allowances authorized by law.

(b) No judge, except a judge of a probate court, shall seek or accept any nonjudicial elective office, or hold any other office of public trust, excepting service in the military forces of the state or federal governments.

(c) The supreme court shall adopt rules of conduct and canons of ethics, not inconsistent with the provisions of this Constitution, for the judges of all courts of this State.

This section reflects the desire of the reformers to professionalize and depoliticize the corps of judges insofar as this was politically feasible. In the past, a judgeship, particularly a circuit judgeship, was an important state political launching pad. This was most notably the case for circuit judge George C. Wallace.

SECTION 148.

(a) A judicial compensation commission is hereby created which shall recommend the salary and expense allowances to be paid from the state treasury for all the judges of this state except for judges of the probate court. The commission shall consist of five members: one shall be appointed by the governor, one by the president of the senate, one by the speaker of the house, and two by the governing body of the Alabama state bar.

(b) Members of the judicial compensation commission shall serve for terms of four years. Any vacancy on the commission shall be filled in the same manner in which such position was originally filled. The legislature shall appropriate sufficient funds for the expenses of the commission.

(c) No member of the commission shall hold any other public office, or office in any political party, and no member of the commission shall be eligible for appointment to a state judicial office so long as he is a member of the commission and for two years thereafter.

(d) The commission may submit a report to the legislature at any time within the first five calendar days of any session. The recommendations of the commission shall become law upon confirmation by a joint resolution or such recommendations may be altered by an act of the legislature at the session to which the report is submitted. The compensation of a judge shall not be diminished during his official term.

This section reflects a desire of the judicial elite to determine their own salaries insofar as possible. Section 148 dates only from 1982 and Amendment 426. It replaces the original section, which provided that the compensation commission's salary recommendations would go into effect unless the legislature vetoed them. Now the assembly must give positive assent to the proposals.

SECTION 149.

The chief justice of the supreme court shall be the administrative head of the judicial system. He shall appoint an administrative director of courts and other needed personnel to assist him with his administrative tasks. The chief justice may assign appellate justices and judges to any appellate court for temporary service and trial judges, supernumerary justices and judges, and retired trial judges and retired appellate judges for temporary service in any court. Adequate and reasonable financing for the entire unified judicial system shall be provided. Adequate and reasonable appropriations shall be made by the legislature for the entire unified judicial system, exclusive of probate courts and municipal courts.

The legislature shall receive recommendations for appropriations for the trial courts from the administrative director of courts and for the appellate courts from each such court.

This is perhaps the heart of the reformed judicial article with its declaration that the chief justice is the administrative head of the judicial system, a position that carries with it several important supervisory powers and responsibilities. Early on, the court was bold enough to say that it was within the judges' prerogative to decide "if the [legislative] appropriations made are 'adequate and reasonable' for the unified judicial system," but so far confrontations between the judiciary and the legislative and executive on this subject have not reached crisis proportions. (quoted from Sparks v. Parker, 368 So. 2d 528 (1979)) In a highly contentious area, that of church-state relations, the Court ruled in 1998 that its chief justice exercised solely administrative supervision over lower courts and therefore lacked the power to involve himself or herself in controversies related to prayers by jurors or religious displays in the courtrooms where trials were taking place. (State ex rel. James v. ACLU (711 So. 2d 952))

SECTION 150.

The supreme court shall make and promulgate rules governing the administration of all courts and rules governing practice and procedure in all courts; provided, however, that such rules shall not abridge, enlarge or modify the substantive right of any party nor affect the jurisdiction of circuit and district courts or venue of actions therein; and provided, further, that the right of trial by jury as at common law and declared by section 11 of the Constitution of Alabama 1901 shall be preserved to the parties inviolate. These rules may be changed by a general act of statewide application.

This section applies to municipal courts as well as the others. To some extent the ideal of uniform rules of procedure throughout all courts is being eroded because of the latitude granted the legislature in the last sentence of this section. The reformers' goal was to end and/or prevent the return of "a haphazard crazy quilt of varying procedures from one circuit to the next, or even from one courtroom to the next." (quoted from Ward v. State, 540 So. 2d 1350 (1988)) The Supreme Court recognized in Ex parte Gunn that while it could put into effect procedural rules, none of its rules could change a court's jurisdiction—especially that of a circuit court. (993 So. 2d 433 (2007)) Also, Court rules pertaining to any other judicial matter can be supplanted by a general legislative act. (M.L.H. v. State (99 So. 3rd 894) (2011))

SECTION 151.

(a) The supreme court shall establish criteria for determining the number and boundaries of judicial circuits and districts, and the number of judges needed in each circuit and district. If the supreme court finds that a need exists for increasing or decreasing the number of circuit or district judges, or for changing the boundaries of judicial circuits or districts, it shall, at the beginning of any session of the legislature, certify its findings and recommendations to the legislature.

(b) If a bill is introduced at any session of the legislature to increase or decrease the number of circuit or district judges, or to change the boundaries of any judicial circuit or district, the supreme court must, within three weeks, report to the legislature its recommendations on the proposed change. No change shall be made in the number of circuit or district judges, or the boundaries of any judicial circuit or district unless authorized by an act adopted after the recommendation of the supreme court on such proposal has been filed with the legislature.

(c) An act decreasing in the number of circuit or district judges shall not affect the right of any judge to hold his office for his full term.

As in other areas, this section seeks to maximize judicial influence in the determination of judicial personnel needs and the territories over which judges preside. However, the legislature is free, in the final analysis, to ignore judicial guidance and use whatever political considerations it deems appropriate in the making of decisions in these areas.

SECTION 152.

All judges shall be elected by vote of the electors within the territorial jurisdiction of their respective courts.

The most zealous judicial reformers would have preferred to have instituted some type of statewide Missouri plan for the selection of judges in Alabama. When this plan is used, the governor appoints a judge from a group of nominees put forward by a commission composed of both lawyers and non-lawyers. After serving a probationary period the judge may run in a retention election on the basis of his or her record on the bench. If voters approve of the record, the judge serves a full term. If they disapprove, the appointment process begins anew. That this plan was politically unrealistic in Alabama is evidenced by the language of Section 152.

SECTION 153.

The office of a judge shall be vacant if he dies, resigns, retires, or is removed. Vacancies in any judicial office shall be filled by appointment of the governor

... [local exceptions]. A judge, other than a probate judge, appointed to fill a vacancy, shall serve an initial term lasting until the first Monday after the second Tuesday in January following the next general election held after he has completed one year in office. At such election such judicial office shall be filled for a full term of office beginning at the end of the appointed term.

While gubernatorial filling of judicial vacancies is still the prevailing norm, sixteen counties provide for a semi-merit-type plan for the filling of judicial vacancies within their jurisdiction.

SECTION 154.

(a) The term of office of each judge of a court of the judicial system of this state shall be six years.

(b) A law reducing the number of judges of the supreme court or of a court of appeals shall be without prejudice to the right of judges affected to seek retention in office. The reduction shall become effective when a vacancy in the affected court occurs.

This section represents no change from previous practice.

SECTION 155.

The legislature shall provide by law for the retirement of judges, including supernumerary judges, with such conditions, retirement benefits, and pensions for them and their dependents as it may prescribe. No person shall be elected or appointed to a judicial office after reaching the age of seventy years, provided that a judge over the age of seventy may be appointed to the office of supernumerary judge if he is not eligible to receive state judicial retirement benefits.

The stated mandatory retirement age is new, and the Court has resisted efforts to modify it. (See McAfee v. Milan, 331 So. 2d 254 (1976).) Making judges less resistant to stepping down is the fact that they enjoy highly remunerative, constitutionally authorized benefits without having to go through the ruse of a supernumerary appointment.

SECTION 156.

(a) A judicial inquiry commission is created consisting of seven members. The supreme court shall appoint one appellate justice or judge and the circuit judges' association shall appoint two judges of the circuit court as members of the commission. The governor shall appoint two persons who are not lawyers and the governing body of the Alabama state bar shall appoint two members of the state bar to serve as members of the commission. The commission shall select its own chairman. The terms of the members of the commission shall be four years. A vacancy on the commission shall be filled for a full term in the manner the original appointment was made.

(b) The commission shall be convened permanently with authority to conduct investigations, receive or initiate complaints concerning any judge of a court of the judicial system of this state. The commission shall file a complaint with the court of the judiciary in the event that a majority of the members of the commission decide that a reasonable basis exists, (1) to charge a judge with violation of any canon of judicial ethics, misconduct in office, failure to perform his duties, or (2) to charge that a judge is physically or mentally unable to perform his duties. All proceedings of the commission shall be confidential except the filing of a complaint with the court of the judiciary. The commission shall prosecute the complaints.

(c) The supreme court shall adopt rules governing the procedures of the commission.

(d) The commission shall have subpoena power and authority to appoint and direct its staff. Members of the commission who are not judges shall receive per diem compensation and necessary expenses; members who are judges shall receive necessary expenses only. The legislature shall appropriate funds for the operation of the commission.

This section provides an alternative means of removing erring or incapable incumbent judges from office besides the cumbersome process of impeachment or the necessity of so serious an occurrence as the conviction of a judge on a felony charge.

SECTION 157.

(a) The court of the judiciary is created consisting of one judge of an appellate court, who shall be selected by the supreme court and shall serve as chief judge of the court of the judiciary, two judges of the circuit courts, who shall be selected by the circuit judges' association, and two members of the state bar, who shall be selected by the governing body of the Alabama state bar. The court shall be convened to hear complaints filed by the judicial inquiry commission. The court shall have authority, after notice and public hearing, (1) to remove from office, suspend without pay, or censure a judge, or apply such other sanctions as may be prescribed by law, for violation of a canon of judicial ethics, misconduct in office, failure to perform his duties, or (2) to suspend with or without pay, or to retire a judge who is physically or mentally unable to perform his duties.

(b) A judge aggrieved by a decision of the court of the judiciary may appeal to the supreme court. The supreme court shall review the record of the proceedings on the law and the facts.

(c) The supreme court shall adopt rules governing the procedures of the court of the judiciary.

(d) The court of the judiciary shall have power to issue subpoenas. The legislature shall provide by law for the expenses of the court.

As the judicial inquiry commission is the accusatory body in the alternate judicial removal plan, so the court of the judiciary is the body with the responsibility to decide whether the charge(s) brought against the judge warrant his or her removal from office or a lesser sanction. Sections 156 and 157 replace a short-lived judicial commission set up under the now-repealed Amendment 317, which was on the books only for 1972–73. So powerful is the court of the judiciary that, although the Supreme Court has the authority to review proceedings before that body, it cannot decrease or throw out its sanctions if its records show that the offending judge was undoubtedly guilty as charged. (Boggan v. Judiciary Inquiry Comm'n, 759 So. 2d 550 (1999))

SECTION 158.

In addition to the authority conferred on the court of the judiciary in Section 157, the provisions for impeachment in Article VII, Section 173, shall also apply to justices of the Supreme Court and judges of the courts of appeals. No proceeding for impeachment under Article VII, Section 173, may proceed or be initiated against a judge while the same charge or subject matter is under consideration by the judicial inquiry commission or the court of the judiciary. A finding of lack of probable cause or a termination of proceeding [sic] without a finding of wrongdoing by either the judicial inquiry commission or the court of the judiciary shall constitute a complete defense to proceedings of impeachment under Article VII, Section 173, and shall bar all further proceedings of impeachment as to the same charge or subject matter. No justice or judge who has been tried before the court of the judiciary shall be subject to impeachment on the same charge or subject matter.... No proceeding in impeachment under this section may be initiated without the verification, under oath, of at least 12 members of the House of Representatives as to the factual basis of the charge under which the article of impeachment is preferred. No article of impeachment shall be passed upon less than two-thirds majority of the House of Representatives and no conviction of impeachment shall be had upon less than two-third majority of the Senate under this section. Dissatisfaction with the ruling of a judge or justice shall not be a ground upon which impeachment under this section may proceed.

This section (580, 1996) brings the legislature back into the removal process for erring judges by stipulating that all appellate judges are also subject to impeachment proceedings if action has not been taken against them by the judicial inquiry commission or the court of the judiciary. If either of these bodies has exonerated a judge, he or she is not subject to impeachment (the processes associated with which are identified in this section). It is specifically stated that the unpopularity of a judicial ruling is never to be a basis for impeachment.

SECTION 159.

A judge shall be disqualified from acting as a judge, without loss of salary, while there is pending (1) an indictment or an information charging him in the United States with a crime punishable as a felony under a state or federal law, or (2) a complaint against him filed by the judicial inquiry commission with the court of the judiciary.

This unambiguous section has required little interpretation. The most notable case involving the section was Moore v. Judiciary Inquiry Comm'n (891 So. 2d 848 (2004)), where the ouster of Chief Justice Roy Moore was affirmed because clear and convincing evidence showed that he had indeed refused to remove the Ten Commandments monument he had installed in the judicial building despite a federal court order that he do so.

SECTION 160.

(a) A district attorney for each judicial circuit shall be elected by the qualified electors of those counties in such circuit. Such district attorney shall be licensed to practice law in this state and shall, at the time of his election and during his continuance in office, reside in his circuit. His term of office shall be six years and he shall receive such compensation as provided by law. Vacancies in the office of district attorney and in his staff shall be filled as provided by law.

(b) Clerks of the circuit courts shall be elected by the qualified electors in each county for a term of six years.... Vacancies in the office of clerk of the circuit court shall be filled by the judge or judges of the circuit court who have jurisdiction over the county in which the office of clerk of the circuit court is located.

(c) Persons elected to the position of constable to assist the courts of the state as provided by law shall be subject to the same restrictions, rights and limitations as are specified in section 280 of the Constitution of 1901, and no law shall prohibit the receipt of fees for the performance of official duties of said position while holding any other elected or appointed office.

(d)The revenue from fines, forfeitures and court costs produced in district courts from the exercise of jurisdiction under municipal ordinances shall be apportioned between the municipality and the state as shall be provided by law.

The reformed judicial article as proposed by the Alabama Constitutional Commission did not intend to give fixed constitutional status to the officers of the court mentioned here. However, their political power was such as to win for them the constitutional dignity provided in this section. In 1982 the Court of Criminal Appeals noted that the district attorney, for example, was not even a judicial officer or included within the judicial branch of government. The D.A. is an executive officer. (Dickerson v. State, 414 So. 2d 998 (Crim. App.)) He or she was "only an officer of the court to the extent that all attorneys are officers of the court." (Ibid.) Also, the court went so far in another case as to deny that the mention here of the constable gave this lowly officer constitutional status. (In re Ingram, 356 So. 2d 618 (1978)) Finally, finding an opportunity to put the circuit clerks in their proper place, a federal court declared that the office of circuit clerk was not a policy-making position despite its inclusion in this section. (Stegmaier v. Trammell, 597 F. 2d 1027 (1979))

SECTION 161.

...

(d) All judges of any court in this state, excepting the supreme court, court of criminal appeals, court of civil appeals, circuit courts, probate courts, and city courts, whose salaries or compensation are paid by their respective counties, who are qualified under the provisions of this article, and who are holding office

> at the time of the approval of this constitutional amendment by the legislature and on the date of the establishment of the district court, shall be commissioned judges of the district court. Each such judge, accepting a commission as a district judge, shall serve an initial term lasting until the first Monday after the second Tuesday in January following the next general election after he has completed three years in office as a district judge. At such election said judicial office shall be filled for a full term of office, beginning at the end of the term for which such judge was commissioned.
>
> (e) In the event a city ceases to have a city or municipal court, all judges of any city court in this state in cities which have more than one such judge at the time of approval of this constitutional amendment by the legislature and on the date of the establishment of the district court, if otherwise qualified under the provisions of this article, shall be commissioned judges of the district court. Each such judge accepting commission as a district judge shall serve an initial term lasting until the first Monday after the second Tuesday in January following the next general election after he has completed three years in office as a district judge. At such election said judicial office shall be filled for a full term of office beginning at the end of the terms for which such judge was commissioned....
>
> (h) Except to the extent inconsistent with the provisions of this article, all provisions of law and rules of court in force on the effective date of this article shall continue in effect until superseded in the manner authorized by the Constitution.

The original judicial reform article did not propose to provide the elaborate amount of incumbent protection furnished in this section. Most of this transitional language is omitted here since all incumbents have been out of office now for close to forty years. Many are deceased. The original section would have authorized only a three-year grace period for courts not mentioned in the new article. However, each of the groups of judges affected—supreme, criminal appeals, civil appeals, circuit, city—was able to guarantee its immediate continuance in office, as were district attorneys and circuit clerks. Probate judges were sufficiently confident of their political clout not to require the type of specific mention that was accorded other judges at this time.

Article VII

Impeachments

SECTION 173.

The governor, lieutenant-governor, attorney general, state auditor, secretary of state, state treasurer, [and] commissioner of agriculture and industries ... may be removed from office for willful neglect of duty, corruption in office, incompetency, or intemperance in the use of intoxicating liquors or narcotics to such an extent, in view of the dignity of the office and importance of its duties, as unfits the officer for the discharge of such duties, or for any offense involving moral turpitude while in office, or committed under color thereof, or connected therewith, by the senate sitting as a court of impeachment, under oath or affirmation, on articles or charges preferred by the house of representatives. When the governor or lieutenant-governor is impeached, the chief justice, or if he be absent or disqualified, then one of the associate justices of the supreme court, to be selected by it, shall preside over the senate when sitting as a court of impeachment. If at any time when the legislature is not in session, a majority of all the members elected to the house of representatives shall certify in writing to the secretary of state their desire to meet to consider the impeachment of the governor, lieutenant-governor, or other officer administering the office of governor, it shall be the duty of the secretary of state immediately to notify the speaker of the house, who shall, within ten days after receipt of such notice, summon the members of the house, by publication in some newspaper published at the capitol [sic], to assemble at the capitol on a day to be fixed by the speaker, not later than fifteen days after the receipt of the notice to him from the secretary of state, to consider the impeachment of the governor, lieutenant-governor, or other officer administering the office of governor. If the house of representatives prefer articles of impeachment, the speaker of the house shall forthwith notify the lieutenant-governor, unless he be the officer impeached, in which event he shall notify the secretary of state, who shall summon, in the manner herein above provided for, the members of the senate to assemble at the capitol on a day to be named in said summons, not later than ten days after receipt of the notice from the speaker of the house, for the purpose of organizing as a court of impeachment. The senate, when thus organized, shall hear and try such articles of impeachment against the governor, lieutenant-governor or other officer administering the office of governor, as may be preferred by the house of representatives.

Provision has always been made in Alabama's Constitutions for impeachments. However, this section is much more detailed than any of its predecessors. It identifies state officials subject to impeachment, the grounds on which they may be removed, and the procedures to be used in impeachment situations. "Moral turpitude" refers to "a crime involving grave infringement of the moral sentiment of the community as distinguished from statutory mal prohibita." (Lewis v. State, 387 So. 2d 795 (1980), quoting from People v. Ferguson, 55 Misc. 2d 711 (1967))

Officials are also removed from office when convicted of a felony, as Governor Guy Hunt was in April 1993. Statutes (36-9-2 of the current Alabama *Code*) provide that as soon as a guilty verdict is read against an accused public official, his or her office is vacant. These provisions make the use of impeachment processes even less likely. Looking to the future, the Constitution (Section 60 and this section) provide "that persons convicted of infamous crimes shall be ineligible to hold state office." When pardoned, as Hunt was on grounds of innocence, eligibility is restored.

SECTION 175.

The clerks of the circuit courts, or courts of like jurisdiction, and of criminal courts, tax collectors, tax assessors, county treasurers, county superintendents of education, ... coroners, ... , notaries public, constables, and all other county officers, mayors, intendants, and all other officers of incorporated cities and towns in this state, may be removed from office for any of the causes specified in section 173 of this Constitution, by the circuit or other courts of like jurisdiction of a criminal court of the county in which such officers hold their office, under such regulations as may be prescribed by law; provided, that the right to trial by jury and appeal in such cases shall be secured.

This section provides a locally expeditious method for removing the substate officials listed. Section 168, herein referred to, was in the original judicial article. A close approximation to this section originated in the Constitution of 1875. "Intendants" are public managers.

SECTION 176.

The penalties in cases arising under the ... preceding sections shall not extend beyond removal from office, and disqualifications from holding office, under the authority of this state, for the term for which the officer was elected or appointed; but the accused shall be liable to indictment and punishment as prescribed by law.

As is necessary, impeachment can carry no other punishment than removal from office, since impeachment proceedings do not provide all of the safeguards of regular court trials. Such trials are not precluded following impeachment. This section originated in the Constitution of 1875.

Article VIII

Suffrage and Elections

This section was adopted as Amendment 579 in 1996. It represented formal recognition of the complete collapse of the old white supremacist effort to deny African Americans their federally granted right to vote. The main controversy relating to the right of franchise in recent years has involved the degree to which prior conviction of a felony should disqualify a person from voting.

SECTION 177.

(a) Every citizen of the United States who has attained the age of eighteen years and has resided in this state and in a county thereof for the time provided by law, if registered as provided by law, shall have the right to vote in the county of his or her residence. The Legislature may prescribe reasonable and nondiscriminatory requirements as prerequisites to registration for voting. The Legislature shall, by statute, prescribe a procedure by which eligible citizens can register to vote.

(b) No person convicted of a felony involving moral turpitude, or who is mentally incompetent, shall be qualified to vote until restoration of civil and political rights or removal of disability.

(c) The Legislature shall by law provide for the registration of voters, absentee voting, secrecy in voting, the administration of elections, and the nomination of candidates.

(d) The right of individuals to vote by secret ballot is fundamental. Where state or federal law requires elections for public office or public votes on referenda, or

> designations or authorizations of employee representation, the right of individuals to vote by secret ballot shall be guaranteed.

The language of Section (d) is taken from Amendment 865, ratified in 2012. It basically represents the fears of business elites that the Taft-Hartley Act was going to be amended to provide that an organization's employees could indicate their support for union representation through a check-off system instead of the present secret ballot arrangement. As of the fall of 2015, however, the secret ballot remained the standard procedure for determining whether workers in an organization would be represented by a union.

Article IX

Representation

SECTION 197.

The whole number of senators shall be not less than one-fourth or more than one-third of the whole number of representatives.

At present, the number of senators is exactly one-third of the number of representatives. In 1972 the federal judicial reapportionment plan based on the 1970 census reduced the House from 106 to 105. Each Senate district formerly consisted of three House districts, but this is no longer true. When districts are constructed the main goal is to maximize the number of districts which will ultimately be won by the majority party while satisfying federal judicial requirements relative to population equity.

SECTION 198.

The house of representatives shall consist of not more than one hundred and five members, unless new counties shall be created ...

[The remainder of the section is obsolete. Ellipses indicate obsolete/unconstitutional/repealed material.]

The membership of the House increased from 105 to 106 with the creation of Houston County in 1903. No change was made in legislative reapportionment arrangements in Alabama until after the U.S. Supreme Court's ruling in Baker v. Carr in 1962 (369 U.S. 186).

SECTION 199.

It shall be the duty of the legislature ... after each ... decennial census ... to fix by law the number of representatives and apportion them among the several counties of the state, according to the number of inhabitants in them, respectively ...

This section deals specifically with reapportionment of the House of Representatives. The legislature did not heed this constitutional mandate. After the reapportionment revolution began, however, most of the time federal courts reallocated the House and Senate seats. In the most notable instance of this happening, in 1972, the court rescinded the requirement that each county have at least one representative. It used census enumeration districts which frequently crisscrossed county lines in the creation of 140 single-member districts, 35 for the Senate and 105 for the House. Multimember districts frequently employed with the original apportionment plan were held to be more likely to discriminate against black voters. It was impossible to satisfy the equal protection clause of the Fourteenth Amendment and at the same time provide each county with at least one representative unless the number of representatives was greatly expanded. (Sims v. Amos, 336 F. Supp. 924 (M.D. Ala.))

Federal intervention in this "political thicket" had come after state judges repeatedly denied requests that they provide relief. In 1950, for example, the Court declined to accept the argument "that the legislature could make no law nor do any act since it ha[d] not complied with section 199." (Bonds v. State Department of Revenue, 149 So. 2d 280) Also, in 1955 the Alabama Court said that a board of reapportionment could not be set up to relieve incumbent legislators of this apparently impossible task since this would amount to a constitutionally unacceptable delegation of a power here specifically conferred on the legislature. (Opinion of the Justices, 181 So. 2d 697)

SECTION 200.

It shall be the duty of the legislature in its first session after taking of [sic] the decennial census of the United States ... to fix by law the number of senators, and to divide the state into as many senatorial districts as there are senators, which districts shall be as nearly equal to each other in the number of inhabitants as may be, and each shall be entitled to one senator, and no more; and such districts, when formed, shall not be changed until the next apportioning session of the legislature, after the next decennial census of the United States shall have been taken; provided, that counties created after the next preceding apportioning session of the legislature may be attached to senatorial districts ...

This section deals specifically with reapportionment of the Senate. Single-member districts were called for from the beginning. Starting with the 1972 federal court–ordered apportionment plan, senatorial districts have frequently included parts of some counties that were not individually contiguous with each other, contrary to original constitutional intentions. However, to so conform would prevent proper adherence to the "one person, one vote" concept. (Reynolds v. Sims, 377 U.S. 533 (1964) Even though this concept is closely adhered to in new districting plans constructed following decennial censuses, the party that sees itself as weakened by the new lines is likely to challenge them (usually unsuccessfully) in federal court. (See Gustafson v. Johns, 434 F. Supp. 2d 1246 (2006).)

SECTION 201.

Should any decennial census of the United States not be taken, or if when taken, the same, as to this state, be not full and satisfactory, the legislature shall have the power at its first session after the time shall have elapsed for the taking of said census, to provide for an enumeration of all the inhabitants of this state, upon which it shall be the duty of the legislature to make the apportionment of representatives and senators as provided for in this article.

The legislature has never found the federal census unsatisfactory. Neither did it so find its increasingly malapportioned districts for more than sixty years after the Constitution went into effect.

Article X

Exemptions

SECTION 204.

The personal property of any resident of this state to the value of one thousand dollars, to be selected by such resident, shall be exempt from sale or execution, or other process of any court, issued for the collection of any debt contracted since the thirteenth day of July, eighteen hundred and sixty-eight or after the ratification of this Constitution.

Due to conflicting judicial decisions and statutory changes that supplemented but did not supplant the constitutional language, Sections 204–205, 206, 207, 208, and 210 are not susceptible to being accurately analyzed. The clearest judicial expositions stress that the legislature may furnish a greater homestead exemption than the Constitution authorizes, but may not diminish it. (See In re Quinlan, 12 Bankr. 824 (M.D. Ala. 1981) and Brewer and Cole, *Alabama Constitutional Law*, pp. 646–47.)

SECTION 205.

Every homestead not exceeding eighty acres, and the dwelling and appurtenances thereon, to be selected by the owner thereof, and not in any city, town, or village, or in lieu thereof, at the option of the owner, any lot in a city, town, or village, with the dwelling and appurtenances thereon owned and occupied by any resident of this state, and not exceeding the value of two thousand dollars, shall be exempt from sale on execution or any other process from a court; for any debt contracted since the thirteenth day of July, eighteen hundred and sixty-eight, or after the ratification of this Constitution. Such exemption, however, shall not extend to any mortgage lawfully obtained, but such mortgage or other alienation of said homestead by the owner thereof, if a married man, shall not be valid without the voluntary signature and assent of the wife of the same.

A bankruptcy court has held that mortgagees waive the homestead exemption provided in this section, it being subordinate to the mortgager's lien on their property. Had they been able to claim the homestead exemption it would have resulted in a monetary loss to the bank issuing their mortgages. (In re Laird, Bankr. M.D. Ala., Apr. 22, 2010))

SECTION 206.

The homestead of a family, after the death of the owner thereof, shall be exempt from the payment of any debts contracted since the thirteenth day of July, eighteen hundred and sixty-eight, or after the ratification of this Constitution, in all cases during the minority of the children.

SECTION 207.

The provisions of sections 204 and 205 of this Constitution shall not be so construed as to prevent a laborers' lien for work done and performed for the person claiming such exemption, or a mechanics' lien for work done on the premises.

SECTION 208.

If the owner of a homestead die, leaving a widow, but no children, such homestead shall be exempt, and the rents and profits thereof shall inure to her benefit.

SECTION 209.

The real and personal property of any female in this state, acquired before marriage, and all property, real and personal, to which she may afterwards be entitled by gift, grant, inheritance, or devise, shall be and remain the separate estate and property of such female, and shall not be liable for any debts, obligations, or engagements of her husband, and may be devised or bequeathed by her, the same as if she were a femme sole.

These sections give even more recognition to the rights of married women to acquire and enjoy property separate and apart from their husbands whose debts they have no general obligation to help pay out of their separate estates. This section originated in the Constitution of 1868. Under common law, the husband had the right to the personal or real property of his wife. Section 209 confirms the cessation of that right. (See Holt v. Agnew, 67 Ala. 360 (1880).)

SECTION 210.

The right of exemption hereinbefore secured may be waived by an instrument in writing, and when such waiver relates to realty, the instrument must be signed by both the husband and the wife, and attested by one witness.

Article XI

Taxation and Finance

SECTION 211.

All taxes levied on property in this state shall be assessed in exact proportion to the value of such property, but no tax shall be assessed upon any debt for rent or hire of real or personal property, while owned by the landlord or hirer during the current year of such rental or hire, if such real or personal property be assessed at its full value.

This section is based on one originally contained in the first, 1819 Constitution. The language regarding rentals was new to 1901. The Court observed in 1934 that it "was designed to secure uniformity and equality by the enforcement of an ad valorem system of taxation and to prohibit arbitrary or capricious modes of taxation without regard to value." (Pullman Car & Manufacturing Corp. v. Hamilton (155 So. 616), quoting Phoenix Carpet Co. v. State (22 So. 627 (1897)) The goal of the section began to be approximated, however, only with the intervention of the federal courts and, even today, the state's system of property taxes is roundly condemned as unfair. As we will see in this part of the book, it has continued to be challenged in federal court.

This section and other provisions of the 1901 Constitution originally identified only one class of property for tax purposes. Because the state had made the determination that all property in the state would be assessed at a uniform ratio, the federal court found that the "substantial disparit[ies] in taxation resulting from the failure of state officers to properly administer the state's tax laws [did] offend the due process and equal protection clauses of the fourteenth amendment" of the U.S. Constitution, as dissatisfied Alabama taxpayers argued when they brought suit in federal court. A system of ratios is provided in Section 217. (Weissinger v. Boswell, 350 F. Supp. 615 (M.D. Ala. 1971))

SECTION 211.01.

The legislature shall have the power to levy and collect taxes for state purposes on net incomes from whatever source derived within this state, including the incomes derived from salaries, fees and compensation paid from the state, county, municipality, and any agency or creature thereof, for the calendar year, 1933, and thereafter and to designate and define the incomes to be taxed and to fix the rates of taxes, provided that the rate shall not exceed 5 percent nor 3 percent on corporations. Income shall not be deemed property for purposes of ad valorem taxes. From net income an exemption of not less than fifteen hundred dollars ($1,500.00) shall be allowed to unmarried persons and an exemption of not less than three thousand dollars ($3,000.00) shall be allowed to the head of a family, provided that only one exemption shall be allowed to husband and wife where they are living together and make separate returns for income tax. An exemption of not less than three hundred dollars ($300.00) shall be allowed for each dependent member of the family of an income taxpayer under the age of 18 years. The legislature shall reduce the ad valorem tax from time to time when and to such an amount as the revenue derived from the income tax will justify. In the event the legislature levies an income tax, such tax must be levied upon the salaries, income, fees, or other compensation of state, county and municipal officers and employees, on the same basis as such income taxes are levied upon other persons. All income derived from such tax shall be ... used exclusively for the reduction of state ad valorem taxes.

The reader will note the specificity regarding tax rates and the radical differences generally between this section (25, 1933) and the Sixteenth Amendment of the U.S. Constitution ratified exactly two decades previously. Prior to this amendment a poorly drafted statute-based income tax (e.g., rates and exemptions not clear) had been declared unconstitutional. (Eliasburg Bros. Mercantile Co. v. Grimes, 188 So. 56 (1920))

Since this section anticipated only opposite-sex couples, such tax laws as Section 211.01 will need to be reinterpreted to ensure fairness to married couples of the same gender. The Alabama legislature would not make formal changes to accommodate same-sex unions.

The next section continues to define the use of Alabama's major growth source of revenue—the income tax. Like most other taxes, its chief beneficiaries are identified very clearly.

SECTION 211.02.

Section A. [Transitional material.]

Section B. Beginning October 1, 1947, and thereafter, all net proceeds of such tax [income tax], plus the earnings from investment of the trust funds, must be used only in the manner and in the order following: (1) To replace the revenue lost to the several funds of the state by reason of the exemption of homesteads from the state ad valorem tax. All homesteads in Alabama are hereby declared to be exempt from all state ad valorem tax to the extent of at least $2,000.00 in assessed value and a sufficient amount is hereby appropriated from the proceeds of the income tax in each fiscal year to replace the revenue lost to the several funds of the state by reason of the homestead exemption herein declared; (2) The residue shall be placed in the state treasury to the credit of the Alabama special education trust fund to be used for the payment of public school teachers salaries only.

Section C. This amendment supersedes the provisions of amendment [25, Section 211.01] relating to the disposition of the income tax proceeds insofar as the same are in conflict herewith.

All laws relating to the income tax, not in conflict herewith and valid on the date of the ratification of this amendment, are hereby validated and confirmed. The provisions hereof with respect to the creation of funds and the use thereof are declared to be self-executing.

This section (61, 1947) provided for a revision of the formula for the distribution of state income tax proceeds specified in Amendment 25 (1933, Section 211.01). It signaled the beginning of education supremacy among the functions of Alabama state government.

SECTION 211.03.

The legislature shall have power to levy and provide for the collection of taxes for state purposes on net income of corporations, from whatever source derived, for the calendar year 1963, or for any fiscal year beginning in the calendar year 1963, and each year thereafter, at a rate not exceeding five percent. However, all federal income taxes paid or accrued within the taxable year by corporations shall always be deductible in computing net income taxable under the income tax laws of this state, provided that in the case of foreign corporations the amount of federal income tax deductible shall be in proportion to income derived from sources within Alabama, to be determined in accordance with such laws as the legislature may enact.

As noted with regard to previous amendments (now incorporated as sections), this amendment is easily distinguishable from the Sixteenth Amendment to the U.S. Constitution authorizing federal income taxes. As is the Alabama constitutional pattern, it (1) relates only to corporate income taxes, (2) specifies the maximum rate, and (3) fixes a very generous deduction (i.e., federal income tax payments "shall always be deductible").

SECTION 211.04.

In computing net income for state income tax purposes for the calendar year 1965 and each year thereafter, a resident individual taxpayer shall be allowed to deduct from his gross income the amount of federal income tax paid or accrued within the taxable year. A nonresident individual income taxpayer shall be allowed to deduct only that amount of federal income tax paid or accrued in the taxable year on income received from sources within the state.

This section (225, 1965) authorizes for individual taxpayers the same federal income tax deduction previously noted as being provided for corporations in Section 211.03 (212, 1963).

SECTION 212.

The power to levy taxes shall not be delegated to individuals or corporations.

This section expresses an obvious principle of fair taxation. However, through multiple amendments, a quasi-power of taxation has been delegated to private groups (e.g., hog producers) by means of promotional amendments providing for assessments on stock or crops to increase their consumption in larger quantities or to deal with other issues (e.g., boll weevils). Also, the Court held in 1999 that Section 212 was not a barrier to the legislature's delegation to public industrial authorities of the authority to abate taxes as an encouragement to the location of new or the expansion of existing industries in their locales. (Dobbs v. Shelby County Econ. & Indus. Dev. Auth., 749 So. 2d 425 (1999))

SECTION 213.

After the ratification of this Constitution, no new debt shall be created or incurred by the state, or its authority except to repel invasion or suppress insurrection, and then only by a concurrence of two-thirds of the members of each house of the legislature, and the vote shall be taken by yeas and nays, and entered on the journals; provided, the governor may be authorized to negotiate temporary loans never to exceed three hundred thousand dollars to meet the deficiencies in the treasury, and until the same is paid no new loan shall be negotiated; ... provided, further, that this section shall not be so construed as to prevent the issuance of bonds for the purpose of refunding the existing bonded indebtedness of the state.

[The language omitted relates to indebtedness now paid and to a retired bond issue.] To prevent further deficits in the state treasury, it shall be unlawful from and after the adoption of this amendment for the state comptroller of the state of Alabama to draw any warrant or other order for the payment of money belonging to, or administered by, the state of Alabama upon the state treasurer, unless there is in the hand of such treasurer money appropriated and available for the full payment of the same. In case there is at the end of any fiscal year, insufficient money in the state treasury for the payment of all proper claims presented to the state comptroller for the issuance of warrants, the comptroller shall issue warrants for that proportion of each such claim which the money available for the payment of all said claims bears to the whole, and such warrants for such prorated sums shall thereupon be paid by the state treasurer. At the end of each fiscal year all unpaid appropriations which exceed the amount of money in the state treasury subject to the payment of the same after the proration above provided for, [sic] shall thereupon become null and void to the extent of such excess.

Any person violating any of the provisions of this amendment shall, on conviction, be punished by a fine of not exceeding five thousand dollars, or by imprisonment in the penitentiary for not more than two years, one or both, at the discretion of the jury trying the same, and the violation of any provisions of this amendment shall also be grounds for impeachment.

The language here is from Amendment 26, ratified in 1933. The strong opposition to debt possessed by the framers of the 1901 Constitution is apparent throughout the document, and especially in this section. It is one of those sections that has been most responsible for the proliferation of constitutional amendments. At least thirty-three were needed because of this section in either its original or amended form. That aspect of Amendment 26 which is of greatest significance is its call for "proration" in the event of revenue shortfalls. The proration contemplated relates primarily to bills the state owes. It was in the same period as Amendment 26 that the Fletcher Budget Act was also passed calling for proration of budgets by the governor in the same financial bind.

SECTION 213.12.

Bonds or other securities issued by or on behalf of the Alabama state docks department shall not constitute a debt of the state within the meaning of Section 213 of this Constitution, as heretofore or hereafter amended, or any similar provision of this Constitution supplemental to, or superseding, said Section 213, as so amended, if by their terms such bonds or securities do not constitute a charge on the general credit or tax revenues of the state, but are payable solely from any or all of the revenues from any or all of the state docks facilities, whereby situated (whether of [or] not such facilities were in existence or owned by or on behalf of the state at the time such bonds or securities were issued) or from sources other than state taxes, licenses or appropriations; provided, however, that the proceeds of any fee, tariff or charge (regardless of how denominated or calculated) collected by the Alabama state docks department in connection with the operation of the state docks facilities whereby situated shall be considered revenues from such facilities within the meaning of this amendment.

This section (446, 1984) gives the state docks agency the power to go further into debt since its revenue bonds hereafter were not to be construed as state debts.

SECTION 213.18.

Revenue bonds and other securities at any time issued by or on behalf of any state university, college or institution of learning for the purpose of acquiring, constructing and equipping any new building or facility or for the purpose of enlarging, extending or improving any existing building or facility shall not be deemed to constitute debt of the state within the meaning of section 213, as amended, of the Constitution, if by their terms such bonds or other securities are not made a charge on the general credit or tax revenues of the state but are made payable solely out of revenues derived from the operation of any existing building or buildings or facility or facilities as well as from the new building or facility to be acquired or constructed with the proceeds thereof or from the enlargements, extensions or improvements to any existing building or facility to be acquired or constructed with the proceeds thereof.

This section (160, 1961) provides debt flexibility for higher education institutions by allowing them to issue revenue bonds, the indebtedness incurred thereby not to be construed as state debt.

SECTION 213.37.

Notwithstanding any other provision of law, the Legislature may appropriate the revenue and other funds received or collected pursuant to any cellular radio telecommunication service tax to pay the principal and any interest due on the outstanding bonds issued by the Alabama Revolving Loan Fund Authority or its successor authority.

Prior to the time that the "no new taxes" mantra came to be so powerful, Alabama was able to levy a new cell phone tax (616, 1999). Currently, the combined state-local wireless rate is 9.28 percent. The last half of the section indicates what the proceeds are to be used for.

Section 215 originated in the Constitution of 1875. Counties had to be constitutionally authorized to levy any taxes at all. They were not deemed to have any inherent power to do so. (Phoenix Carpet Co. v. State, 22 So. 627 (1897))

SECTION 215.

No county in this state shall be authorized to levy a greater rate of taxation in any one year on the value of the taxable property therein than one-half of one per centum; ... [transitional material] provided, further, that to pay any debt or liability now existing against any county, incurred for the erection, construction, or maintenance of the necessary public buildings or bridges, or that may hereafter be created for the erection of necessary public buildings, bridges, or roads (a) any county may levy and collect such special taxes, not to exceed one-fourth of one per centum, as may have been or may hereafter be authorized by law.The proceeds of taxes levied under said proviso (a) for public building, road, or bridge purposes in excess of amounts payable on bonds, warrants, or other securities issued by the county may be spent for general county purposes, in such manner as the court of county commissioners, board of revenue, or other like county governing body may determine.

The language reproduced here is that of Amendment 208, ratified in 1962. The amendment added the last sentence, which gives financially restricted county officials the authority to spend funds not needed to pay off-road building debts for other pressing county needs.

The main thrust of the section is to restrain local government spending as state spending was also being hemmed in by all kinds of limitations discussed here and elsewhere in this volume. When the original section was written in 1901, some carpetbag debt remained, but, after that was liquidated, the framers wanted extreme frugality to be the prevailing norm.

Like other provisions mentioned here (especially Sections 214 and 216), plaintiffs who challenged them were not able to show to a federal court that they had a present-day effect on student choice in public education that was prohibited under the U.S. Constitution's Fourteenth Amendment. (Knight v. Alabama, 458 F. Supp. 2d (2004) and Lynch v. State, 568 F. Supp. 2d 1329 (2008)).

The following sections point to increasing national, state, and local concern with improved health care in the post–World War II period.

SECTION 215.01.

The governing body of any county in the state of Alabama except Mobile and Montgomery county must levy and collect or cause to be collected for use in the acquisition by purchase, lease or otherwise, or for the construction, operation, equipment and maintenance of a county hospital, in addition to all other taxes now authorized by law, a tax, not in excess of ten mills on each one hundred dollars, on all property in the county as assessed for state taxation, provided such tax is authorized by a majority of the qualified electors of the county voting upon such proposition at an election called at any time by the governing body of any county in the state, and said governing body must call such election upon a petition being filed with the chairman or any member of said governing body requesting that such an election be called or held when said petition is signed by not less than one hundred qualified electors of the county in which said election is to be held.

Said election shall be held and conducted and the results canvassed as now provided by law for holding and conducting and canvassing the returns of an election. The proceeds of the tax hereby authorized must be used exclusively for the purpose of acquiring by purchase, lease, or otherwise, or the construction, equipment, maintenance and operating of said county hospital and shall be expended for said purposes by and under the direction, supervision and control of the county governing body.

This section (59, 1946), adopted at the same time as Section 93.12 (53, 1946), differs from it in that whereas Section 93.12 was permissive regarding the authority of local governments to participate in federal programs subsidizing health facilities generally, this section specifically requires all but two counties to levy an additional property tax to support a county hospital if the tax is approved in a popular referendum.

SECTION 215.02.

If the tax is authorized by vote of a majority of the qualified electors of the county who participate in any election called for that purpose, the governing body of every county except Mobile, Montgomery and Jefferson counties must levy and collect, in addition to all other taxes authorized by law, a special county tax, not exceeding four mills on each dollar of taxable property in the county to be used solely for acquiring, by purchase, lease, or otherwise, constructing, operating, equipping, or maintaining county hospitals, or other public hospitals, non-profit hospitals and public health facilities. An election may be called at any time by the governing body of the county, and must be called within three months of receipt of a petition, signed by not less than five percent of the qualified electors of the county, requesting that the election be called. The election shall be conducted in the manner which the governing body of the county prescribes.

Whereas Section 215.01 (59, 1946) authorized a ten-mill property tax for county hospital purposes, this section (76, 1949) authorizes four more mills in sixty-four counties, again given voter consent, for hospitals and other public health facilities. The three largest counties, which generally already had better health care, were exempted from the amendment. Health care agencies supported by the new tax would be subject to continuing supervision by county authorities.

SECTION 215.03.

This [section] shall apply in all counties except Mobile and Jefferson counties. The term "public hospital purposes" as used in this amendment shall be construed to include the acquisition by purchase, lease, or otherwise, and the construction, equipment, operation, and maintenance of public hospital facilities. The term "public hospital" as used in this amendment shall be construed to include public hospitals, public clinics, public health centers, nurses' homes and training facilities, and related public health facilities of any kind.

If a majority of the qualified electors of any county in the state, except Mobile and Jefferson counties, who participate in an election held therein pursuant to the provisions of any amendment to the Constitution heretofore adopted shall vote at such election in favor of the levy and collection of a special county tax, within the limitations provided in such amendment, for public hospital purposes, the proceeds derived from the tax authorized at such election may be applied for any one or more of the purposes for which said tax may be so voted. Whenever the tax shall be voted the governing body of the county may anticipate the proceeds therefrom for any one or more of the purposes for which the tax shall be voted by issuing, without further election, interest bearing tax anticipation bonds, warrants, or certificates of indebtedness of said county payable solely from and secured by a pledge of not exceeding 75% of the annual proceeds from said tax received by the county.

The governing body of each county in which the said tax may be voted shall have the further power to designate as the agency of the county to acquire, construct, equip, operate and maintain public hospital facilities any public corporation heretofore or hereafter organized for hospital purposes in the county under any general law heretofore or hereafter enacted by the legislature. When a public corporation shall be so designated, the proceeds of said tax thereafter collected shall be paid over to it and shall be used by it for any one or more of the purposes for which the tax shall have been voted; provided, that payment of the proceeds of said tax to said public corporation shall be made only to such extent as will not result in the impairment of the obligation of any contract theretofore made with respect to said tax. Said public corporation may anticipate the proceeds from said tax so required to be paid to it by issuing, for any one or more of the purposes for which the tax shall have been voted, the bonds, warrants, or certificates of indebtedness of said public corporation, and may pledge for the payment of the principal thereof and interest thereon not exceeding 75% of the annual proceeds from said tax paid to it.

Each county in which the tax shall be voted, and in the event a public corporation shall have been designated as the agency of such county pursuant to the provisions hereof then said public corporation, [sic] shall have the power to contract with any other county or similar public corporation with respect to the acquisition by purchase, lease, or otherwise, and the construction, equipment, operation, and maintenance of public hospital facilities outside of the county and within any zone or region of which the county may be a part, and which may have heretofore been established or may hereafter be established for public hospital purposes by the legislature or by an agency designated by it, the obligations of such contract to be payable solely out of the proceeds of said tax; provided, that the proceeds of said tax shall not be used outside of the county for any purpose for which the proceeds could not be used in the county, and shall not be used with respect to public hospital facilities located outside of the county if the tax is voted specifically for public hospital facilities located in the county.

No securities issued or contracts made by a county under the authority of this amendment, which are payable solely out of the proceeds of said tax, and no securities issued or contracts made by any such public corporation, whether or not issued or made under the authority of this amendment, shall be construed to be the bonds of the county or of a political subdivision thereof within the meaning of Section 222 of the Constitution, or construed to create an indebtedness within the meaning of Section 224 of the Constitution. Said securities shall be construed to be negotiable instruments notwithstanding the fact that they may be payable solely from a limited source. All pledges of said tax and all contracts made with respect thereto pursuant to this amendment shall take precedence in the order in which they are made and shall create a charge on the proceeds of said tax prior to the expenses of operating and maintaining any public hospital facilities.

In each instance in which a special county tax for any one or more of the purposes included within the meaning of the term "public hospital purposes" has heretofore been authorized at an election held in a county pursuant to the provisions of any amendment to the Constitution heretofore adopted, all provisions of this amendment shall be applicable in said county to the same extent as if said election had been held after the adoption of this amendment.

This amendment shall be self-executing.

This section (76, 1949) was adopted only one year after Section 215.02 (72, 1948). It provides most counties additional flexibility in securing better public health facilities by, among other things, (1) giving discretion as to what type of tax they would levy to fund these facilities, (2) allowing them to issue bonds in anticipation of tax proceeds to move more quickly to upgrade facilities, (3) granting more freedom for intergovernmental cooperation in this public policy area, and (4) giving greater public debt flexibility by not charging new bonded indebtedness against constitutional debt limits.

SECTION 215.04.

The legislature may authorize the use of any portion of the proceeds of any portion of the proceeds of any special county tax levied for the purpose of acquiring, constructing, equipping, operating, and maintaining public hospitals, public clinics, public health centers, and related public health facilities of any kind, or for any one or more of the purposes included within the meaning of the term "public hospital purposes," for the purpose of providing hospital care and treatment for indigent residents of the county, or for the purpose of matching any state or federal funds made available for use in providing hospital care and treatment for indigent residents of the county, any provision of the Constitution to the contrary notwithstanding. Provided, however, that if any portion of the proceeds of such tax shall have been pledged to the payment of any bonds, warrants, notes, or other obligations or evidences of indebtedness, such portion of the proceeds of the tax as shall have been so pledged shall not be used for any purpose except in payment of such bonds, warrants, notes, or other obligations or evidences of indebtedness.

This section (125, 1957) was needed because of the need to use tax funds to help provide care for indigent patients. Previously adopted sections had authorized multiple health-related public expenditures, but not this one.

The next new area of Alabama public expenditures—especially as far as counties were concerned—was that of libraries. In a poor state like Alabama, with a low median educational level, a library was seen as a luxury that would be obtainable only by philanthropic gift as were the Carnegie libraries.

SECTION 215.05.

In addition to all taxes now or hereafter authorized by the Constitution of Alabama, any county or any incorporated municipality within the state which supports, jointly supports, or proposes to support a public library is hereby authorized to levy and collect a special tax not exceeding five one hundredths of one per centum on the value of the taxable property within such county or municipality as assessed for state taxation, the proceeds of which shall be used exclusively for public library purposes; provided, that the rate of such tax, the time it is to continue and the purpose thereof shall have been first submitted to the vote of the qualified electors of the county or municipality and voted for by a majority of those voting at such election. Elections under this amendment shall be called, held and conducted in the same way as elections on special school district tax levies.

This section (269, 1967) expands the taxing authority of all counties and municipalities in the state, but only by a very small amount and only for the specific purpose of supporting a public library. And, as is almost invariably the case with property taxes, voters who turn out for the referendum have the final say in the matter.

At this point municipalities in the state are authorized to hold referenda to approve slightly increased property taxes to be used for functions not previously provided for specifically.

SECTION 216.04.

Each municipal corporation in this state whose annual ad valorem tax rate is otherwise limited by the Constitution or any amendment thereto [to] less than one and one-fourth per centum (1 and ¼%) of the value of the property situated therein as assessed for state taxation during the preceding year shall have, in addition, to the power to levy and collect such ad valorem tax each year at the rate authorized immediately prior to the adoption of this amendment, the further power to levy and collect each year an additional tax or taxes to such extent that the total ad valorem tax rate of such municipal corporation shall not exceed one and one-fourth per centum (1 ¼%) in any one year on the property situated therein based on the valuation of such property as assessed for state taxation during the preceding year; provided, that before any such additional tax may be so levied and collected a majority of the qualified electors of any such municipal corporation voting at an election called for that purpose shall vote in favor of the levy thereof; provided further, that the total ad valorem tax or taxes to be levied and collected by any such municipal corporation shall not exceed one and one-fourth per centum (1 ¼%) in any one year; and provided further, that the adoption of this amendment shall in no wise affect, limit, modify, abridge or impair the power, authority or right of any such municipal corporation to levy and collect the special school taxes now or hereafter vested or conferred upon them, or any of them, under the Constitution or any amendment thereto, which said special school taxes shall be in excess of said one and one-fourth per centum (1 ¼%) herein provided for. Each election held under the provisions hereof shall be ordered, held, canvassed and may be contested in the same manner as is or may be provided by the law applicable to municipal corporations for elections to authorize the issuance of municipal bonds. The ballots used at such elections shall specify the purpose for which the proposed additional rate of taxation shall be authorized and shall contain the words "For ... % additional rate taxation"; and "Against ... % additional rate of taxation": the additional rate of taxation proposed to be shown in the blank space provided therefor. The voter shall record his choice, whether for or against the additional rate shown, by placing a cross mark before or after the words expressing his choice. The proceeds of any such additional tax so authorized at any such election shall be used only for the purpose for which the same shall be authorized at such election.

Elections to authorize the levy of such additional tax may be held as often as ordered by the governing body of the municipality, but when a proposition is submitted to the electors to levy such additional tax for a specific purpose and such proposition is defeated then no second election for the same purpose shall be held in one year thereafter.

This section (56, 1946) reflects the need for additional revenue to finance an expanding panoply of municipal services.

The insertion of the small percentage (1 ¼ percent) demonstrated the ongoing, grudging state attitude toward more activist local government, particularly when the programs were financed by property taxes.

Next follows what is perhaps the most controversial section of the Alabama Constitution. Popularly known as the "lid bill," it has been subject to more federal judicial challenges than any other section. As of late 2015, it had survived all of them unscathed.

SECTION 217.

(a) On and after October 1, 1978, all taxable property within this state, not exempt by law, shall be divided into the following classes for the purposes of ad valorem taxation:

Class I. All property of utilities used in the business of such utilities.

Class II. All property not otherwise classified.

Class III. All agricultural, forest and single-family owner-occupied residential property, and historic buildings and sites.

Class IV. All private passenger automobiles and motor trucks of the type commonly known as "pickups" or "pickup trucks" owned and operated by an individual for personal or private use and not for hire, rent or compensation.

(b) With respect to ad valorem taxes levied by the state, all taxable property shall be forever taxed at the same rate. On and after October 1, 1978, such property shall be assessed for ad valorem tax purposes according to the classes thereof as herein defined at the following ratios of assessed value to the fair and reasonable market value (except as otherwise provided in subsection (j) hereof) of such property:

Class I. 30 per-centum.

Class II. 20 per-centum.

Class III. 10 per-centum.

Class IV. 15 per-centum.

(c) With respect to ad valorem taxes levied by counties, municipalities or other taxing authorities, all taxable property shall be forever taxed at the same rate. On and after October 1, 1978, such property shall be assessed for ad valorem tax purposes according to the classes of property defined in subsection (a) hereof and at the same ratios of assessed value to the fair and reasonable market value thereof as fixed in subsection (b) hereof, except as otherwise provided in subsection (j) hereof and this subsection (such ratios being herein called "assessed ratios"). In connection with the ad valorem taxes that a county, municipality or other taxing authority is authorized or required to levy and collect pursuant to any provision of this Constitution, for the ad valorem tax year beginning October 1, 1978, any such taxing authority may, subject to criteria established by act of the legislature, by resolution of the governing body of that taxing authority, at any time not later than September 30, 1979, increase or decrease the assessment ratio applicable to any class of taxable property, such increase or decrease to be effective for ad valorem tax years beginning on and after October 1, 1978. If (1) a county, municipality or other taxing authority adjusts an assessment ratio pursuant to the preceding sentence and (2) the receipts from all ad valorem taxes levied by or with respect to such taxing authority during the ad valorem tax year beginning October 1, 1978, exceed by more than five percent, or are less than 95 percent, of the receipts from such ad valorem taxes for the ad valorem tax year beginning October 1, 1977, then at any time not later than September 30, 1980, for ad valorem tax years beginning on and after October 1, 1979, the taxing authority may, subject to criteria established by act of the legislature, by resolution of the governing body of any county, municipality or other taxing authority, subject to criteria established by act of the legislature, at any time increase or decrease the assessment ratio applicable to any class of taxable property; provided, that any proposed adjustment to an assessment ratio to be made pursuant to this sentence, whether an increase or decrease shall have been (1) proposed by the governing body of the taxing authority after a public hearing on such proposal, (2) thereafter approved by an act of the legislature, and (3) subsequently approved by a majority vote of the qualified electors residing in the taxing authority who vote on the proposal at a special election called and held in accordance with the law governing special elections. [transitional material] ... The legislature shall enact general laws applicable to all counties, municipalities and other taxing authorities regulating and establishing criteria for the exercise of the powers granted such taxing authorities to adjust assessment ratios as hereinabove provided. Such assessment ratios as herein authorized may vary among taxing authorities so long as each such assessment is uniform within a taxing authority. Any decrease in any assessment ratio pursuant to this subsection shall not jeopardize the payment of any bonded indebtedness secured by any tax levied by the taxing authority decreasing the assessment ratio. Any action authorized by this subsection to be taken by a taxing authority, or the governing body, thereof, shall, other than in the case of a municipality, be taken by resolution of the governing body of the county in which such taxing authority is located acting on behalf of such taxing authority.

(d) With respect to ad valorem taxes levied by the state or by any county, municipality or other taxing authority, no class of taxable property shall have an assessment ratio of less than five per centum nor more than 35 per centum.

(e) A county, municipality or other taxing authority may decrease any ad valorem tax rate at any time, provided such decrease shall not jeopardize the payment of any bonded indebtedness secured by such tax. [transitional material] ... It is further provided that all millage adjustments shall be made in increments of not less than one tenth (1/10) mill.

(f) On and after October 1, 1979, any county, municipality or other taxing authority may at any time increase the rate at which any ad valorem tax is levied above the limit otherwise provided in this Constitution; provided, that the proposed increase to be made pursuant to this subsection shall have been (1) proposed by the governing body of the taxing authority after a public hearing on such proposal, (2) thereafter approved by an act of the legislature, and (3) subsequently approved by a majority vote of the qualified electors residing in the taxing authority who vote on the proposal at a special election called and held in accordance with the law governing special elections. Any adjustments or other actions authorized to be made or taken by resolution of the governing body of such taxing authority, or if there is no such governing body and in the case of a taxing authority other than a municipality, by resolution of the governing body of the county in which such taxing authority is located acting on behalf of such taxing authority. The provisions of subsections (c), (e) and (f) of this section shall not apply to ad valorem taxes levied by the state.

(g) The legislature is authorized to enact legislation to implement the provisions of this section and may provide for exemptions from taxation, provided, that unless otherwise expressly provided, no amendment in this section shall be construed to repeal any statutory exemption existing on the effective date of any such amendment thereto.

(h) Wherever any constitutional provision or statute provides for, limits or measures the power or authority of any county, municipality or other taxing authority to levy taxes, borrow money or incur indebtedness in relation to the assessment of property therein for state taxes or for state and county taxes, such provision shall mean as assessed for county or municipal taxes, as the case may be.

... [local exceptions]

(i) Whenever the total amount of ad valorem property taxes otherwise payable by any taxpayer with respect to any item of taxable property shall exceed in any one ad valorem tax year the maximum amount of such taxes permitted by this section, such amount of taxes shall be reduced by subtracting that amount of tax due that is in excess of the amount of tax otherwise permissible under the Constitution. In connection with the taxation of any item of taxable property, the amount of tax to be subtracted with respect to each authority levying and collecting any ad valorem property tax shall be in the same proportion to the total amount of tax to be subtracted that the total number of mills on each dollar of taxable property situated in the taxing authority levied by such taxing authority bears to the total number levied by all taxing authorities with respect to such item of taxable property.

Before sending to any taxpayer any notice relating to the collection of ad valorem taxes, the tax collector in each county shall determine whether any portion of the amount of ad valorem property tax otherwise due with respect to any item of taxable property shall be subtracted pursuant to the provisions of this subsection and shall apportion the amount to be subtracted in accordance with the provisions of this subsection.

(j) Notwithstanding any other provisions of this section on and after October 1, 1978, taxable property defined in subsection (a) hereof as Class III property shall, upon application by the owner of such property, be assessed at the ratio of assessed value to the current use value of such taxable property and not the fair and reasonable market value of such property. The legislature may enact laws uniformly applicable to the state and all counties, municipalities and other taxing authorities establishing criteria and procedures for the determination of the current use value of any eligible taxable property and procedures for qualifying such property for assessment at its current use value. The legislature may also enact laws uniformly applicable to the state and all counties, municipalities and other taxing authorities providing for the ad valorem taxation of any taxable property ceasing to qualify for current use valuation; provided, however, that any additional tax on taxable property ceasing to qualify for current use valuation shall not apply to more than three ad valorem tax years immediately preceding such cessation of qualification (including as one such year the year in which cessation of qualification occurs).

(k) The following property shall be exempt from all ad valorem taxation: the real and personal property of the state, counties and municipalities and property devoted exclusively to religious, educational or charitable purposes, household and kitchen furniture, all farm tractors, all farming implements when used exclusively in connection with agricultural property and all stocks of goods, wares and merchandise.

(l) ... [transitional language]

(m) If any portion of this section should be declared invalid by any court of competent jurisdiction, such invalidity shall not affect the validity of any of the remaining portions of this section, which shall continue effective.

Amendments of the original 1901 Section 217 basically have taken their cues from the language of a federal circuit judge (John Godbold) and two district judges (Hobart Grooms and Frank Johnson) in declaring Alabama's old inconsistent system of property taxation unconstitutional. "Rather than establishing various classes of taxable property," the three-judge federal court observed in 1971, "the State of Alabama has chosen to place all taxable property within the state in a single class for ad valorem tax purposes." (Weissinger v. Boswell, 330 F. Supp. 615 (M.D. Ala. 1971)) This made the arbitrariness with which the "system" was administered by the sixty-seven counties that much more indefensible. Godbold, Grooms, and Johnson held that "the failure of state officers to properly administer the state's tax laws [offended] the due process and equal protection clauses of the fourteenth amendment." (Ibid.)

The rate of assessment of all property in Alabama was supposed to be 60 percent of its fair and reasonable market value (according to Sec. 40-8-1 of then applicable Alabama *Code* provisions) as mandated by this article. In fact, however, it was never more than about 30 percent, and only that high in the more urbanized counties with modern (and less highly politicized) arrangements for ascertaining the value of taxable property.

The language produced here is that of Amendment 373, ratified in 1978, at the time the "Proposition 13" tax revolt begun in California was spreading to other parts of the nation. Alabama property taxes were already very low. The amendment would help ensure that they would remain that way.

A prior revision of the original Section 217 had been made only six years earlier through Amendment 325 (1972). Implementing legislation allowing assessment of property taxes for the same type of property at different ratios among the sixty-seven counties was declared unconstitutional, however. In contrast, Amendment 373 (this provision, Section 217) mandates the assessment of all property at uniform ratios within the categories presented in the commentary to Section 217. (See McCarthy v. Jones, 449 F. Supp. 480 (1978); Howell v. Malone, 388 So. 2d 908 (1980).)

Property tax policy in Alabama is especially favorable toward agricultural and forest land and thus is beneficial to agribusiness/timber interests. Note that agricultural, forest, and single-family, owner-occupied residential properties are to be taxed according to *current* use rather than fair market value. The justification for the first two has been disputed most vehemently by those who are interested in increasing amounts of revenue for public services, particularly public education. The current use doctrine helps keep property tax bills of many affluent landed interests very low.

As the reader sees, the new Section 217 is also very anti–home rule in its requirement for critical state legislative involvement before local property taxes can be increased. To raise property taxes for a specific county-community-district, it is necessary not only to have a locally favorable popular vote (the success of which is generally doubtful at best), but a favorable vote of a majority of the legislature as well. Support of the local legislative delegation would be most crucial here.

Amendment 373 was held by both federal and state judges in the 1980s not to violate the equal protection clause of the Fourteenth Amendment. (Weissinger v. White, 733 F.2d 802 (1984), Howell v. Malone, 388 So. 2d 1908 (1980)) In 2014 a federal district court held, after trial, that neither ethnic group (blacks or whites) was unequally impacted by Section 217. Thus it was once again allowed to stand because no race-based equal protection claim could be constructed. (Lynch v. State, 2011 U.S. Dist. LEXIS 155012 (2011) and I.L. v. Alabama, 739 F. 3d 1273 (2014))

SECTION 218.

The legislature shall not have the power to require counties or other municipal corporations to pay any charges which are now payable out of the state treasury.

The aim of this section "was to prevent the shifting of existing debts and obligations of the state onto counties and municipalities." (Ex parte Stone, 101 So. 62 (1924))

SECTION 219.

[Transitional] ...The legislature of Alabama may provide for the assessment, levy and collection of a tax upon inheritances and for the levying of estate taxes not to exceed in the aggregate the amounts which may by law of the United States be allowed to be credited against or deducted from any similar tax upon inheritances or taxes on estates assessed or levied by the United States on the same subject. The legislature shall have the power to levy such inheritance or estate taxes in the state of Alabama only so long as and during the time an inheritance or estate tax is enforced by the United States against Alabama inheritances or estate [sic], and shall only be exercised or enforced to the extent of absorbing the amount of any deduction or credit which may be permitted by the laws of the United States now existing or hereafter enacted to be claimed by reason thereof as deduction or credit against such similar tax of the United States applicable to Alabama inheritances or estates.

The language reproduced here is that of Amendment 38, ratified in 1931. The original 1901 section allowed inheritance taxes, but not in excess of 2 ½ percent and only when the estate was passing to others besides the family of the deceased. The language here was necessitated because the federal inheritance tax law provided that the federal tax would be abated if the state had an acceptable inheritance tax law. The federal law was designed to moderate some of the harsher aspects of interstate competition and was aimed particularly at no-inheritance-tax states such as Florida, the most popular haven for retirees.

The Alabama treasury has multiple pots of money, the great majority of which are not filled anywhere near to the brim. The next section creates a game and fish fund.

SECTION 219.01.

There is hereby created and shall be a fund in the state treasury, which shall be known as the game and fish fund. This fund shall consist of:

a. All monies received from all occupational licenses or privilege taxes imposed by the state on any person, firm or corporation for engaging in any business or activity relating to taking, catching, capturing or killing any furbearing or game animal or game bird in this state or the taking, catching, capturing or killing of any freshwater fish or aquatic animal in the public waters of this state;

b. All monies derived from the levying or imposition upon any person, firm or corporation of any tax, license, permit, certificate, fee or any other charge, by whatsoever name called, pursuant to the game and fish laws of this state or rules and regulations promulgated thereunder;

c. All monies paid, derived, received or arising from fines, penalties and forfeitures pursuant to the game and fish laws of this state and the rules and regulations promulgated thereunder;

d. All monies derived from the administration and enforcement of the game and fish laws of this state or rules and regulations promulgated thereunder;

e. All monies derived from the sale of hunting and fishing licenses or permits;

f. All monies derived from the sale of lands, timber or other natural resources owned by the game and fish division of the department of conservation;

g. All monies accruing to the game and fish fund from any other source whatsoever.

No funds accruing to the game and fish fund of the state of Alabama from any source whatsoever shall be expended for any other purpose than the payment of administrative costs of the game and fish activities of the department of conservation and for the protection, propagation, preservation, investigation of game and fish and public use of the game and fish resources of this state.

This section (257, 1967) conforms to the usual Alabama practice of earmarking user-related revenues to support the activities from which they are mostly derived. Constitutionalizing these arrangements, as in this section, further ensures that the legislature, despite changing needs and priorities, will not be able to alter the distribution fixed herein. Alabama also earmarks nonuser revenues to a far greater extent than any other state.

As noted in the discussion of Article Two relating to state boundaries, who owned what are known as the tidelands off the Gulf Coast states was an issue in the 1952 presidential campaign. Because the Republican nominee, Dwight D. Eisenhower, supported state ownership, many erstwhile loyal Democrats were motivated to move to the GOP. To receive money from oil and gas leases, Alabama created a state savings account discussed in the next very long section. Its 3,851 words make it close to half (46 percent) as long as the entire Vermont Constitution.

SECTION 219.02.
Alabama Trust Fund.

Section 1. For the continuing benefit of the state of Alabama and the citizens thereof, there is hereby created an irrevocable, permanent trust fund named "the Alabama trust fund" which shall be funded and administered in accordance with the provisions of this amendment.

Section 2. As used in this amendment, the following words and phrases shall have the following respective meanings:

"BOARD" means the board of trustees of the trust fund.

"ELIGIBLE INVESTMENTS" means any of the following:

(1) Demand deposits (interest bearing) in federally insured banks and interest bearing deposits (whether or not evidenced by certificates of deposit) in federally insured banks; provided, however, that said deposits plus interest shall be fully secured by obligations described in subdivisions (2) and (3) of this definition, to the extent that said deposits plus interest exceed insurance available from the Federal Deposit Insurance Corporation or from any agency of the United States of America that may succeed to the functions of the Federal Deposit Insurance Corporation;

(2) Bonds, notes and other evidences of indebtedness that are direct obligations of the United States of America or that are unconditionally guaranteed as to both principal and interest by the United States of America;

(3) Bonds, debentures, notes or other evidences of indebtedness issued or guaranteed by any federal agencies or government-sponsored enterprises authorized to issue their own debt instruments, including, without limitation to, the following: Federal Farm Credit Bank, Federal Intermediate Credit Banks, the Export-Import Bank of the United States, Federal Land Banks, the Federal National Mortgage Association, the Tennessee Valley Authority, the Governmental National Mortgage Association, the Federal Financing Bank, Federal Banks for Cooperatives, Federal Home Loan Banks, Federal Home and Loan Mortgage Association or the Farmers Home Administration; [names of agencies are presented as in the original act]

(4) Repurchase agreements with federally insured banks or with government bond dealers reporting to and trading with the Federal Reserve Bank of New York, provided that such repurchase agreements are secured by obligations described in subdivisions (2) and (3) of this definition; and

(5) Interest bearing time deposits (whether or not evidenced by certificates of deposit) in savings and loan associations (a) the deposits of which are insured to the maximum extent possible by the Federal Savings and Loan Insurance Corporation or any agency of the United States of America that may succeed to its functions and (b) the principal office of which is located in the state; provided, however, that said deposits plus interest shall be secured by obligations described in subdivisions (2) and (3) of this definition, to the extent that said deposits plus interest exceed insurance available from the Federal Savings and Loan Insurance Corporation or from any agency of the United States of America that may succeed to the functions of the Federal Savings and Loan Insurance Corporation;

(6) Corporate securities, provided, however, that no more than a maximum of 25 percent of the trust capital may be invested in such securities by the Board at any time and provided further that no more than a maximum of one percent of the 25 percent may be invested in any one corporation. The legislature may provide authorization to the Board to invest up to a maximum of 40 percent in corporate securities by a three-fifths vote of the membership of both the house of representatives and the senate. All corporate securities shall at the time of purchase by the Board carry a rating of "A" or better by Moody's and/or Standard and Poors; provided, however, that if neither Moody's nor Standard and Poors is in existence or ceases to issue bond ratings, then, in that event, otherwise eligible corporate securities must carry one of the three highest grade or quality ratings issued by the securities rating firm that, in the opinion of the Board, is recognized as the most reputable.

"Federally insured bank" means any bank which has its principal office located in Alabama, whether organized under the laws of the United States of America or the laws of this state, and which is a member of the Federal Deposit Insurance Corporation or which obtains deposit insurance to the maximum extent possible from any agency of the United States of America that may succeed to the functions of the Federal Deposit Insurance Corporation.

"Fiscal year" means the fiscal year of the state as may from time to time be provided by law.

"Oil and gas capital payment" means any payment (including any royalty payment) received after August 1, 1984, by the state or any agency or instrumentality thereof as all or part of the consideration for the sale, leasing or other disposition by the state or any agency or instrumentality thereof of any right to explore and drill for or to produce oil, gas or other hydrocarbon minerals in any area on the water side of the high water mark of Mobile Bay or in any other offshore area and shall include any revenue by the state from federal oil and gas leases off the coast of Alabama. Any royalty or other payment, with the exception of any taxes heretofore or hereafter levied that is based upon or determined with respect to, the production of oil, gas or other hydrocarbon minerals and that is paid to the state or any agency or instrumentality thereof regardless of the time of such payment shall be considered an oil and gas capital payment.

"State" means the state of Alabama.

"Trust capital" means all assets of the trust fund other than trust income.

"Trust fund" means "the Alabama trust fund" created by this amendment.

"Trust income" means the net income received by the state, subsequent to the transfer of the initial trust capital by the state treasurer to the board, from the investment and reinvestment of all assets of the trust fund, determined in accordance with the provisions of this amendment.

"Trustee" means a member of the board of trustees of the trust fund.

Section 3.

(a) The trust fund shall be under the management and control of the board, and all powers necessary or appropriate for the management and control of the trust fund shall be vested solely in the board. The board shall have a membership of nine trustees consisting of the governor, the state treasurer, the director of finance (or such other official as may by law succeed to the responsibilities of the director of finance), three trustees appointed by the governor, two trustees appointed by the lieutenant governor, and one trustee appointed by the speaker of the house of representatives. The governor, the state treasurer and the director of finance shall each serve as a trustee ex officio, and the service of each such official as a trustee shall begin and end concurrently with the beginning and end of his or her tenure in such office.... [Transitional provisions] Thereafter, the term of office of each appointed trustee shall be six years, commencing at noon on October 1 on which the term of the immediate predecessor trustee shall end.

(b) If at any time there shall be a vacancy among the appointed trustees, a successor trustee shall be appointed to serve for the unexpired term applicable to such vacancy. The appointment of each appointed trustee (other than those initially appointed), whether for a full six-year term or to complete an unexpired term, shall be made by the same officer of the state who appointed the trustee whose term shall have expired or is to expire or in whose position on the board a vacancy otherwise exists and shall be made not earlier than 30 days prior to the date on which such trustee is to take office as such. Each appointed trustee shall hold office from the effective date of his or her appointment by and with the consent of the senate and shall hold office until his or her successor is appointed as provided for herein. Trustees shall be eligible for reappointment without limit as to the number of terms previously served.

(c) At the beginning of each session of the legislature the governor shall certify to the senate for confirmation the names of all who shall have been appointed as trustees since the commencement of the last session of the legislature.

(d) Each appointed trustee shall, at the time of his or her appointment and at all times during his or her term of office, be a qualified elector of the state, and a failure by any trustee to remain so qualified during such term shall cause a vacancy of the office of such trustee. Each appointed trustee shall have recognized competence and experience in the evaluation and management of investments. Any appointed trustee may be impeached and removed from office as a trustee in the same manner and on the same grounds provided in Section 174 of the Constitution of Alabama of 1901, or successor provision thereof, and the general laws of the state for impeachment and removal of the officers of the state subject to said Section 174 or successor provision thereof. The governor, the state treasurer and the director of finance may not be impeached and removed from office as trustees apart from their impeachment and removal from the respective offices by virtue of which, ex officio, they serve as trustees.

(e) The governor, the state treasurer and the director of finance shall be entitled to vote, and shall perform the duties of trustees, ex officio, without any compensation other than that to which they are respectively entitled as governor, state treasurer and director of finance. Appointed trustees shall be entitled to such compensation for their services as may from time to time be provided by law duly enacted by the legislature, but the power to provide compensation of appointed trustees shall be discretionary with the legislature and nothing in this amendment shall be construed to confer upon such trustees an absolute right to any compensation for their services. Each trustee shall be reimbursed for expenses actually incurred in the performance of his or her duties as a trustee.

(f) A majority of the trustees shall constitute a quorum for the transaction of business by the board, and decisions shall be made on the basis of a majority of the quorum then present and voting, with each trustee to have a single vote. No vacancy in the membership of the board or the voluntary disqualification or abstention of any trustee shall impair the right of a quorum to exercise all of the powers and duties of the board. The governor shall be the chairman and presiding officer of the board. The director of finance shall be vice chairman, and the state treasurer shall serve as secretary. The board may appoint such other officers to perform such duties, not inconsistent with the provisions of this amendment or applicable law, as the board shall deem necessary or appropriate. In addition to such regular meetings of the board as may be provided by law or by bylaws or rules duly adopted by the board, special meetings of the board may be called by the governor acting alone or by any three other trustees acting in concert, in each case upon two days' notice to each trustee given in person or by registered letter or telegram; provided, however, that such notice to each trustee may be waived by such trustee, either before or after the meeting with respect to which such notice would otherwise be required. Any meeting held by the board for any purpose shall be open to the public, except that executive sessions may be held by the board when the character or good name of a person is involved. All proceedings of the board, except executive sessions, shall be reduced to writing on behalf of the board and maintained in the permanent records of the board, a copy of which shall be filed in the principal office of the board and shall be open for public inspection there during regular business hours. The principal office of the board shall be the principal office of the director of finance.

(g) No trustee shall vote on or participate in the discussion or consideration of any matter coming before the board in which such trustee, personally or through family connections or business associations, has any direct or indirect pecuniary interest, including, but without limitation thereto, decisions of the board concerning the investment of moneys constituting part of the trust fund in any deposit or obligation of any bank or corporation in which such trustee may have such an interest. If there shall be brought before the board any matter in which a trustee shall have any interest which may conflict with his or her duties as a trustee, he or she shall immediately make a complete disclosure to the board of such interest and shall thereafter withdraw from participation in any deliberation and decision of the board with respect to such matter.

(h) The board shall have all of the powers necessary to carry out and effectuate the purposes and provisions of this amendment, including, without limiting the generality of the foregoing, the following powers:

(1) To adopt, alter and repeal bylaws, regulations and rules for the regulation and conduct of its affairs and business;

(2) To make, enter into and execute contracts, agreements and other instruments and to take such other actions as may be necessary or convenient to accomplish any purpose for which the trust fund was created or to exercise any power expressly, or by reasonable implication, granted by this amendment;

(3) To enter into contracts with, to accept aid and grants from, to cooperate with and to do any and all things that may be necessary in order to avail itself of the aid and cooperation of the United States of America, the state or any agency, instrumentality or political subdivision of either thereof in furtherance of the purposes of this amendment; and

(4) To appoint, employ and contract with such employees, agents, advisors and consultants, including, but not limited to, attorneys, accountants, financial experts and such other advisors, consultants and agents as may in its judgment be necessary or desirable, and to fix their compensation; provided, however, that any obligation created or assumed by the board shall not create any pecuniary obligation or liability of the state or the trust fund other than such as shall be payable out of moneys appropriated by the legislature to defray the expenses of the board in carrying out the purposes of this amendment. No lien or charge against any assets of the trust fund for any purpose whatsoever shall be created by or result from any law enacted by the legislature or any action taken by the board or any other department, agency or instrumentality of the state.

(i) The expenses of making and disposing of investments, such as brokerage commissions, legal expenses referable to a particular transaction, transfer taxes and other customary transactional expenses shall be payable out of any trust income of the trust fund. The legislature shall provide for the administrative and other necessary expenses of the board in the same manner as it provides for the expenses of operating other departments and agencies of the state.

Section 4....

Promptly following the effective date of this amendment, the state treasurer shall take all actions necessary to transfer to the board the possession, control and management of the initial trust capital. If at the time of such transfer into the trust fund all or part of the initial trust capital is invested in certificates of deposit or other investments which cannot be converted into cash prior to the maturity thereof without loss of interest or other penalty, the state treasurer shall directly transfer such certificates of deposit or other investments to the board as part of the initial trust capital without first converting the same into cash. In the event that any certificates of deposit or other investments shall be transferred into the trust fund, the initial trust capital shall not include the income or profit from such certificates of deposit or other investments that has been received by the state on or before such transfer or that constitutes accrued interest, amortized discount or other amounts which in accordance with generally accepted accounting principles, should be considered as having been earned by the state as of the date of such transfer....

(b)The trust capital shall be augmented by (i) such other moneys or assets as the legislature may by law appropriate and transfer to the trust fund as a permanent part thereof; (ii) such other moneys or assets as may be contributed to the trust fund from any source; and (iii) all proceeds of any oil and gas capital payments as defined in this amendment subsequent to August 14, 1984....

Section 5.

(a) The trust capital shall be held in perpetual trust and shall not be appropriated by the legislature or expended or disbursed for any purpose other than to acquire eligible investments in accordance with the provisions of this amendment. All eligible investments acquired, in whole or in part, with moneys constituting part of the trust capital shall to the extent of such moneys constitute part of the trust capital, but any trust income derived therefrom shall be paid directly into the general fund as it is received by the board, subject to appropriation and withdrawal by the legislature.

(b) To the extent practicable, the board shall keep all moneys at any time held in the trust fund invested in such eligible investments as shall, in its sole and uncontrolled judgment, produce the greatest trust income over the term of such investments while preserving the trust capital. In making any investment of moneys held in the trust fund, the board shall exercise the judgment and care, under the circumstances prevailing at the time of such investment, which an institutional investor of the highest standard of prudence, intelligence and financial expertise would exercise in the management and investment of large assets entrusted to it not for the purpose of speculative profit but for the permanent generation and disposition of funds, considering the probable safety of capital as well as the expected amount and frequency of income. The board shall have full power and authority to select the eligible investments in which moneys held in the trust fund shall at any time be invested, and, to the extent not inconsistent with any express provision of this amendment, the eligible investments so selected shall be acquired from such issuers, underwriters, brokers or other sellers on such terms and conditions; shall be acquired for purchase prices reflecting such discount below or premium above the par or face amount thereof; shall bear such dates and be in such form, denominations and series; shall mature or be subject to mandatory redemption on such dates; shall bear interest at such rate or rates payable at such intervals or, alternatively, shall provide income to the holder thereof in such manner (including, without limitation thereto, the purchase of such investments at a discount which represents all or part of the income or profit derived therefrom); shall be unsecured or secured in such manner and subject to the provisions of Section 2, paragraphs 2 and 3; shall contain such provisions for prepayment or redemption at the option of the issuer or obligor; and shall contain or be subject to such other provisions as shall, in all of the foregoing respects, be determined by the board in exercise of its sole and uncontrolled judgment. The board shall have full power and authority to invest the trust capital in any eligible investments producing trust income in accordance with such schedule as the board shall, in the exercise of its sole and uncontrolled judgment, determine to be in the best interests of the state, and in determining such schedule the board may emphasize future benefits in preference to near-term needs. The board shall have complete and uncontrolled discretion in making decisions as to when moneys in the trust fund shall be invested, as to the purchase price or other acquisition cost to be paid or incurred in acquiring investments for the trust fund, as to when investments constituting part of the trust fund shall be sold, liquidated or otherwise disposed of, and, as to the amount and nature of the price or other consideration to be received by the trust fund upon the sale, liquidation or other disposition of investments constituting part of the trust fund. No law shall be enacted nor any action taken by the executive department of the state which impairs or interferes with the power, authority and discretion conferred upon the board by this amendment with respect to the acquisition, management, control and disposition of investments at any time constituting part of the trust fund.

(c) To the extent appropriate and not at the time prohibited by law, the board shall use the facilities of the state treasurer in the administration of the trust fund, including, but without limitation thereto, the keeping of records, the management of bank accounts, the transfer of funds and the safekeeping of securities evidencing investments.

(d) The board shall cause an annual audit of the trust fund to be performed for each fiscal year by the state examiners of public accounts or, in the discretion of the board, by an independent certified public accounting firm and shall cause a report of such audit to be prepared in accordance with applicable accounting principles. The board shall cause to be prepared and publicized such financial and other information concerning the trust fund as may from time to time be provided by law duly enacted by the legislature, but in the absence of any law directing the preparation and publication of different reports, the board shall cause to be prepared and made public, within 30 days after the end of each quarterly period in each fiscal year, a report containing (i) a statement of the trust capital then held in the trust fund showing any changes thereto since the last quarterly report, (ii) a statement of the trust income received during the quarterly period in question, (iii) a statement of the investments then held in the trust fund including descriptions thereof and the respective values thereof, (iv) a statement of the trust income received to date during the current fiscal year, and (v) any other information determined by the board to reflect a full and complete disclosure of the financial operations of the fund.

Section 6.

An individual trustee shall not in any way be personally liable for any liability, loss or expense suffered by the trust fund unless such liability, loss or expense arises out of or results from the willful misconduct or wrongdoing of such trustee.

Section 7.

This amendment shall be self-executing, but the legislature shall have the right and power to enact laws supplemental to this amendment and in furtherance of the purposes and objectives thereof, provided that such laws are not inconsistent with the express provisions of this amendment.

This section (450, 1985) was proposed and ratified during Governor George Wallace's last term in office. Given the fact that an energy resources trust fund (now defunct) had already been created during the administration of Governor

Fob James (394, 1982), the adoption of Amendment 450 can best be explained on the basis of the mutual distrust between James and Wallace. James's "Alabama Heritage Trust Fund" and Wallace's "Alabama Trust Fund" are combined into Section 219.02 in the Recompiled Constitution. Amendment 450 represented the Wallace administration's plans for the use of funds received by the state from offshore oil and gas leases.

The main aspects of this mammoth section can be summarized as follows: (1) creation of the Alabama Trust Fund as the depository for oil, gas, and other hydrocarbon payments by companies seeking to drill off state coasts, (2) establishment of a board to administer the fund, (3) identification of appropriate investments for moneys received, (4) specification that the trust capital was to be held in perpetual trust, and (5) designation of the state general fund as the recipient of income received from trust investments.

The Wallace administration put the $347.5 million the state had received from the most recent leases prior to the adoption of this section into the newly created Alabama Trust Fund; the fund would also be the depository for future lease monies. Only the interest was to be spent for hard-pressed general fund items.

City and county officials opposed Amendment 450 because they had wanted a specific, constitutionally designated share of the interest from the fund. As we will see later, substate governments soon did get a portion of the interest, but then it was made conditional on the soundness of the trust fund. When the energy crisis of the 1970s and early 1980s period declined, leases such as those involved here proved to be much less the bonanza than had been hoped for. In the giddy spirit of that era, however, it was not infrequently predicted that energy revenues would for many years prevent any revenue shortfalls. This did not work out.

The next section adds flexibility in terms of the kinds of investments the trust fund board can make.

SECTION 219.03.

Any other provision of this Constitution to the contrary notwithstanding, trust capital and trust income held in either the Alabama heritage trust fund or the Alabama trust fund may be invested in such kinds of investments and in accordance with such conditions as shall from time to time be authorized by law for the investment of any of the trust funds of either the teachers' retirement system of Alabama or the employees' retirement system of Alabama; provided, however, that if any restrictive conditions at any time made applicable by law to either the teachers' retirement system of Alabama or the employees' retirement system of Alabama should prohibit investments that would otherwise be permitted for the Alabama trust fund by Amendment No. 450 to the Constitution of Alabama of 1901, then, notwithstanding the restrictive conditions applicable to said retirement systems, the investments permitted by said Amendment 450 shall be permitted for trust capital and trust income held in either the Alabama heritage trust fund or the Alabama trust fund; and provided further, that for purposes of implementing the preceding proviso with respect to the investment of funds held in the Alabama heritage trust fund, any provision of said Amendment No. 450 which refers to the whole or any percentage of the trust capital of the Alabama trust fund in connection with the investment thereof shall be deemed to refer to the trust capital of the Alabama heritage trust fund.

Any provision of this Constitution to the contrary notwithstanding, any capital gains realized from the sale of any investments forming a part of either the Alabama heritage trust fund or the Alabama trust fund shall become a part of the trust capital of the fund in which such investments were held and shall be subject to all restrictions applicable to the preservation of such trust capital.

This section (488, 1988) gave additional discretion to trustees of the oil and gas lease depository by allowing them to make any investments which the retirement systems could make at that time, specifically, in common stocks. It also merged the James fund into the Wallace trust fund.

The next section shows the success of municipal and county governments in getting shares of the money being accumulated in the Alabama Trust Fund. The Forever Wild program (to be presented later), the state docks, senior citizens, highways, economic development, and infrastructure needs of state agencies were also named as beneficiaries. (Forever Wild had actually been named the first recipient of money from the trust fund besides the general fund.)

SECTION 219.04.

Section 1. The Legislature finds that the capital improvements and technology required by many governmental programs could be more efficiently funded through the establishment of a special trust fund dedicated to funding such improvements. Additionally, municipal and county governments require assistance in the funding of capital improvements. In order to meet these requirements, it is necessary and prudent to redistribute a portion of the Oil and Gas Capital Payments now being paid into the Alabama Trust Fund under Amendment No. 450 to the Constitution of Alabama of 1901. Accordingly, this amendment establishes the County and Municipal Government Capital Improvement Trust Fund to be administered in accordance with the provisions of this amendment. Finally, the Legislature finds that it is necessary and desirable to issue general obligation bonds for the purposes of (i) making substantial capital improvements to the state dock facilities at the Port of Mobile, (ii) providing local government match monies required to issue federal grant revenue bonds for road and bridge improvements and (iv) providing funds to municipal governments for infrastructure improvements.

Section II. As used in this amendment, the following words and phrases shall have the following respective meanings:

"Alabama Trust Fund" means the irrevocable, permanent trust fund created by Amendment 450 to the Constitution of Alabama of 1901.

"Alabama Capital Improvement Trust Fund" means one of the special trust funds created by this amendment.

"Capital Improvements" means capital outlay projects that include the planning, designing, inspection, purchasing, construction, reconstruction, improvement, repair or renovation of permanent buildings, docks, structures and sites therefor for the executive, legislative or judicial branches of state government. The term "Capital Improvement" shall also mean the construction or improvement of roads and bridges in the highway system; payment of debt service on the bonded indebtedness issued by the State of Alabama; funding economic development and industrial recruitment activities; and the procurement of technical equipment, including computer and telecommunications equipment, required for the operation of any governmental entity.

"County and Municipal Capital Improvement Trust Fund" means one of the special trust funds created by this amendment.

"Docks Improvements" means the acquisition, development, construction, improvement, expansion and modernization of the state docks facilities (including without limitation, cargo handling facilities) at the Port of Mobile.

"Docks Improvement Costs" means all costs and expenses in connection with the Capital Improvements, including, without limitation, the following:

(a) The costs of acquiring, constructing, installing and equipping Docks Improvements, including all obligations incurred for labor and to contractors, subcontractors, builders and materialmen.

(b) The costs of acquiring land or rights to land and any costs incidental thereto, including recording fees.

(c) The costs of contract bonds and of insurance of all kinds that may be required or necessary during the acquisition, construction or installation of Docks Improvements.

(d) The costs of architectural and engineering services, including test borings, surveys, environmental mitigation, supervision of construction and the like with respect to Docks Improvements.

(e) The costs of acquiring and installing fixtures and equipment, excavation, removal and demolition of structures, and provisions for drainage, stormwater retention, installation of utilities, and similar facilities, and paving.

(f) Interest accruing with respect to General Obligation Bonds for a period of up to two years after the issuance of such General Obligation Bonds.

(g) All costs, expenses and fees incurred in connection with the issuance of General Obligation Bonds, including, without limitation, all legal, accounting, financial, printing, recording, filing and other fees and expenses.

(h) The costs for obtaining bond insurance, letters of credit, or other forms of credit enhancement or liquidity facilities. All other costs of a nature comparable to or required in connection with those described.

(i) Reimbursement to any person of any of the foregoing costs incurred by such person either for its own account, or for the account of the State of Alabama and without regard to when incurred.

"Economic Development Costs" means the costs and expenses incurred or to be incurred by the state in connection with economic development projects and the recruitment of industrial prospects to the state including, without limitation, site preparation and infrastructure improvements, the costs of training and educating workers in the state and acquiring and constructing training facilities in the state, together with the costs, expenses and fees incurred in connection with the issuance of General Obligation Bonds for such purposes and the costs for obtaining bond insurance and other forms of credit enhancement on General Obligation Bonds issued for such purposes, and the reimbursement to any person of any of the foregoing costs incurred by such person either for its own account or for the account of the State of Alabama, its agencies or authorities.

"Fiscal Year" means the period beginning October 1 and ending September 30 of the following calendar year.

"General Fund" means the general fund in the State Treasury of the State of Alabama.

"General Obligation Bonds" means bonds, including refunded bonds, to be issued by the State of Alabama for the purpose of financing Docks Improvements Costs, Economic Development Costs, Local Government Match Funds and Municipal Infrastructure Costs, as provided in this amendment.

"Local Government Match Funds" means the monies required to be provided by the State of Alabama as a condition to the issuance of federal grant revenue bonds for road and bridge improvements, together with the costs, expenses and fees incurred in connection with the issuance of General Obligation Bonds for such purposes and the costs of obtaining bonds insurance and other forms of credit enhancement on General Obligation Bonds for such purposes.

"Municipal Infrastructure Costs" means the cost of acquiring and constructing municipal infrastructure improvements through the Alabama Department of Transportation, together with the costs, expenses and fees incurred in connection with the issuance of General Obligation Bonds for such purposes and the costs of obtaining bond insurance and other forms of credit enhancement on General Obligation Bonds for such purposes.

"Oil and Gas Capital Payment" means any payment (including any royalty payment) received by the state or any agency or instrumentality thereof as all or part of the consideration for the sale, leasing or other disposition by the state or any agency or instrumentality thereof of any right to explore and drill for or to produce oil, gas or other hydrocarbon minerals in any area on the water wide of the high water mark of Mobile Bay or in any other offshore area and shall include any revenue by the state from federal oil and gas leases off the coast of Alabama. Any royalty or other payment, with the exception of any taxes heretofore or hereafter levied, that is based upon or determined with respect to, the production of oil, gas or other hydrocarbon minerals and that is paid to the state or any agency or instrumentality thereof regardless of the time of such payment shall be considered an oil and gas capital payment.

"Realized Capital Gains" means gains from the sale or exchange of assets of the Alabama Trust Fund, other than fixed income assets, to the extent they exceed losses from the sale of such assets. The amount of gain or loss on the sale of an asset shall be determined by subtracting from the proceeds of selling the asset its fair market value as of the end of the immediately preceding fiscal year, or, in the case of the fiscal year in which this amendment is ratified, its fair market value as of the first business day following ratification of this amendment.

"Trust Income" means the Trust Income as defined in Amendment Numbers 450 and 488 to the Constitution of Alabama of 1901.

"Unrealized Capital Gains" means the excess of the fair market value of the Alabama Trust Fund on the last day of the fiscal year over the fair market value of the Trust Fund on the last day of the immediately preceding fiscal year. The fair market value of the Trust Fund on the last day of a fiscal year shall be determined without including the Trust Income for the fiscal year; realized capital gains for the fiscal year; or the fair market value of fixed income assets. For the fiscal year beginning October 1, 2001, the fair market value of the assets on September 30, 2002, shall be determined without regard to the fair market value on the date of transfer of the assets transferred from the Alabama Heritage Trust Fund.

Section III. Distributions of Trust Income and capital gains earned by the Alabama Trust Fund shall be made annually in accordance with the following:

In any fiscal year in which the Trust Income exceeds $60,000,000, ten percent (10%) of the Trust Income shall be distributed to the Municipal Government Capital Improvement Fund created in Section 11-6-4, Code of Alabama 1975, and ten percent (10%) of the Trust Income shall be distributed to the County Government Capital Improvement Fund created in Section 11-29-4, Code of Alabama 1975. The Director of Finance shall certify such amounts to the State Comptroller, who shall make the required distributions not later than April 15 of the following fiscal year. The distributions provided for in this section shall be in lieu of and not in addition to the distributions required by Sections 11-29-5 and 11-66-5, Code of Alabama 1975. The remainder of the Trust Income shall be paid into the General Fund, except as provided by Amendment 543 to the Constitution of Alabama of 1901. Provided, however, the fiscal year following the first fiscal year that the Forever Wild Land Trust receives fifteen million dollars ($15,000,000) from the trust income of the Alabama Trust Fund, one-fourth (1/4) of one percent of the trust income from the Alabama Trust Fund shall be allocated to the Alabama Senior Services Trust Fund. This allocation shall increase each fiscal year by one-fourth (1/4) of one percent of the trust income earned from the Alabama Trust Fund; provided, however, that in no event shall such trust income paid to the Alabama Senior Services Trust Fund exceed five million dollars ($5,000,000) in any one fiscal year.

(a) Notwithstanding any other provision of this constitution, within 30 days following the end of each fiscal year, the Board of Trustees of the Alabama Trust Fund may transfer up to seventy-five percent (75%) of the realized capital gains for such fiscal year. The amount distributed shall be divided as follows: ten percent (10%) to the County Government Capital Improvement Fund created in Section 11-29-4, Code of Alabama 1975, and ten percent (10%) to the Municipal Government Capital Improvement Fund created in Section 11-66-4, Code of Alabama 1975, and the remainder of such realized capital gains shall be paid into the General Fund, except that a portion of such realized capital gains shall be distributed in the same manner as and deemed to be a part of trust income for purposes of the distributions required under Sections 7 and 13 of Amendment 543 to the Constitution of Alabama of 1901.

(b) Notwithstanding any other provision of this constitution, within 30 days following the end of each fiscal year, the Board of Trustees of the Alabama

Trust Fund may transfer up to seventy-five percent (75%) of the unrealized capital gains for such fiscal year. The amount distributed shall be divided as follows: ten percent (10%) to the County Government Capital Improvement Fund created in Section 11-29-4, Code of Alabama 1975, and ten percent (10%) to the Municipal Government Capital Improvement Fund created in Section 11-66-4, Code of Alabama 1975, and the remainder of such unrealized capital gains shall be distributed in the same manner as and deemed to be a part of trust income for purposes of the distributions required under Sections 7 and 13 of Amendment 543 to the Constitution of Alabama of 1901.

Section IV. Beginning on October 1 immediately following the ratification of this amendment, 35% of all Oil and Gas Capital Payments paid into the Alabama Trust Fund in any fiscal year shall be transferred by the State Treasurer to the special trust funds created by this amendment in the following manner: (a) an amount equal to seven percent (7%) of all Oil and Gas Capital Payments received by the Alabama Trust Fund during the preceding fiscal year shall be paid into the County and Municipal Government Capital Improvement Trust Fund; and (b) an amount equal to twenty-eight percent (28%) of all Oil and Gas Capital Payments received by the Alabama Trust Fund during the preceding fiscal year shall be paid into the Alabama Capital Improvement Trust Fund.

Section V.

(a) Funds in the Alabama Capital Improvement Trust Fund shall be invested by the Board of Trustees in such kinds of investments as are authorized for the investment of the Alabama Trust Fund. All income of such funds (determined in the same manner as Trust Income of the Alabama Trust Fund) shall be deposited into the General Fund.

(b) Funds in the County and Municipal Government Capital Improvement Trust Fund shall be invested by the Board of Trustees in such kinds of investments as are authorized for the investment of the Alabama Trust Fund. All income of such fund (as determined in the same manner as Trust Income of the Alabama Trust Fund) shall be deposited into the County and Municipal Government Capital Improvement Trust Fund subject to distribution pursuant to Section VI.

(c) The Board of Trustees shall determine from time to time the asset allocation of investments in the Alabama Trust Fund and shall determine the annual amount of Realized and Unrealized Capital Gains to be transferred to the General Fund. The Secretary-Treasurer of The Retirement Systems of Alabama shall be the initial manager of 50 percent of the assets, and financial institutions and other corporate entities with general trust powers shall be the initial manager or managers of 50 percent of the assets in the Alabama Trust Fund, subject to guidelines provided by the Board of Trustees. The Board of Trustees shall have the power to appoint another person or persons to manage all or any portion of the assets in the Alabama Trust Fund upon a two-thirds vote of the Board of Trustees.

Section VI. On April 1 of each year, the State Comptroller shall distribute one-half of all Trust Income earned during the preceding fiscal year from the investment of funds contained in the County and Municipal Capital Improvement Trust Fund to the Municipal Government Capital Improvement Fund created by Section 11-66-4, Code of Alabama 1975, and one-half of said Trust Income to the County

Government Capital Improvement Fund created by Section 11-29-4, Code of Alabama 1975. Distributions of Trust Income to the Municipal Government Capital Improvement Fund shall be administered in accordance with Section 11-66-6 Code of Alabama 1975. Distributions of Trust Income to the County Government Capital Improvement Fund shall be administered in accordance with Section 11-29-6, Code of Alabama 1975.

Section VII. Funds in the Alabama Capital Improvement Fund may be appropriated for Capital Improvements only upon the certification of the Governor, based upon the recommendation of the Director of Finance, that funds are needed for particular Capital Improvements. The Governor's certification for such Capital Improvements shall be contained in his or her budgets for the operation of state government submitted annually to the Legislature. Legislative appropriations from the Fund that are in excess of those contained in the Governor's certification must be accompanied by legislative findings of fact explaining the appropriations that differ from or are in excess of those certified by the Governor. The foregoing notwithstanding, the Legislature may appropriate funds from this trust fund for Capital Improvements upon a recorded majority vote of each house. . . .

Section IX. The Governor, the Director of Finance, the Commissioner of Revenue, the Chairman of the Senate Finance and Taxation General Fund Committee and the Chairman of the House Ways and Means General Fund Committee are hereby constituted a Bond Commission with full authority, except as herein specified or limited, to determine the terms and conditions of the General Obligation Bonds and to provide for the sale and issuance thereof. No member of the Bond Commission shall receive compensation in any form for any services performed by him or her in and about his or her duties as a member or officer of the Bond Commissions. The Bond Commission shall meet at the call of the Governor, who is hereby designated its chairman. Three members of the Bond Commission (at least one of which shall be the Chairman of the Senate Finance and Taxation-General Fund Committee or the Chairman of the Ways and Means-General Fund Committee) shall constitute a quorum for the transaction of business, and all proceedings of the Bond Commission shall be reduced to writing, recorded in a substantial record book and filed with the Director of Finance, who is hereby designated as the Secretary of the Bond Commission and who shall keep the records of the proceedings of the Bond Commission.

Section X. The proceeds of the General Obligation Bonds shall be paid into the State Treasury, shall be kept continually invested pending the expenditure thereof, and shall, together with the income derived from the investment and reinvestment thereof (including income derived from the investment and reinvestment of previously derived income), be retained in one or more separate accounts of the State Treasury until expended for the purposes authorized in this amendment, and in the manner provided by law. The proceeds of such General Obligation Bonds, together with the investment income derived from said proceeds, shall be used solely for the purpose of paying Docks Improvement Costs, Economic Development Costs, Local Government Match Funds and/or Municipal Infrastructure Costs. Not more than $50 million of the proceeds of such General Obligation Bonds shall be spent for local government match funds and not more than $15 million of such proceeds shall be spent for municipal infrastructure costs.

Section XI. There is hereby appropriated for the payment of the General Obligation Bonds such monies out of the Alabama Capital Improvement Fund as are necessary to pay principal of, interest on and redemption premium (if any) on the General Obligations Bonds. Monies in the Alabama Capital Improvement Trust Fund are also hereby appropriated for the payment of principal of, interest on and redemption premium (if any) on bonds authorized to be issued pursuant to Amendment Nos. 618, 619 and 620 of the Constitution of Alabama of 1901.

Counties and cities have had highly skilled lobbyists on the scene in Montgomery for many years as have other interests reflected in the significant expansion of beneficiaries from the Alabama Trust Fund authorized by this section. Like the Alabama Trust Fund section itself, this section is also specific to the nth degree, so it has not been litigated. However, another constitutional amendment was ratified in the fall of 2012 that may in the future restrict payments to beneficiaries previously made under the auspices of this section (856, 2012, Section 219.09).

SECTION 219.042.

(a) Anything in Amendment No. 666 to the Constitution of Alabama of 1901, as amended [Section 219.04], or Amendment No. 796 to the Constitution of Alabama of 1901, as amended [Section 219.041], to the contrary notwithstanding, the authority granted to the State of Alabama to become indebted and to sell and issue its interest-bearing general obligation bonds, in addition to all other bonds of the state, under Amendment No. 666 of the Constitution of Alabama of 1901 [Section 219.04], as amended by Amendment No. 796 to the Constitution of Alabama of 1901 [Section 219.041], shall not be subject to the limitations on aggregate principal amount imposed by Section VIII of said Amendment No. 666 to the Constitution of Alabama of 1901, as amended [Section 219.04], as modified by paragraph (a) of Amendment No. 796 to the Constitution of Alabama of 1901, as amended [Section 219.041]; provided, that at no time shall the aggregate principal amount of such general obligation bonds (including, without limitation, general obligation refunding bonds) then outstanding be in excess of $750 million.

(b) General obligation refunding bonds may be issued by the State from time to time pursuant to the authority contained in Amendment No. 666 to the Constitution of Alabama of 1901, as amended [Section 219.04], in aggregate principal amounts (which may exceed the principal amount of general obligation bonds being refunded) determined by the Bond Commission established pursuant to Section IX of Amendment No. 666 to the Constitution of Alabama of 1901, as amended [Section 219.04]; provided, however, that no such general obligation refunding bonds shall be issued unless (i) the present value of all debt service on such general obligation refunding bonds (computed with a discount rate equal to the true interest rate of such general obligation bonds and taking into account all underwriting discount and other issuance expenses) shall not be greater than 97 percent of the present value of all debt service on the general obligation bonds to be refunded (computed using the same discount rate and taking into account the underwriting discount and other issuance expenses originally applicable to such general obligation bonds to be refunded) determined as if such general obligation bonds to be refunded were paid and retired in accordance with the schedule of maturities (considering mandatory redemption as a scheduled maturity) provided at the time of their issuance; and (ii) the average maturity of such general obligation refunding bonds, as measured from the date of issuance of such general obligation refunding bonds, shall not exceed by more than three years the average maturity of the general obligation bonds to be refunded, as also measured from such date of issuance, with the average maturity of any principal amount of general obligation bonds to be determined by multiplying the principal of each maturity by the number of years (including any fractional part of a year) intervening between such date of issuance and each such maturity, taking the sum of all such products, and then dividing such sum by the aggregate principal amount of general obligation bonds which the average maturity is to be determined.

(c) The principal amount of general obligation bonds for which provision for payment has been made with proceeds of general obligation refunding bonds (including anticipated investment earnings thereon), shall not be deemed outstanding for purposes hereof.

(d) Except to the extent modified hereunder, the terms and provisions of Amendment No. 666 to the Constitution of Alabama of 1901, as amended [Section 219.04], and Amendment No. 796 to the Constitution of Alabama of 1901, as amended [Section 219.041], shall remain in full force and effect.

This section (880, 2012) provides yet another explanation for the ever-expanding Alabama Constitution. It gives the state increased additional authority to issue general obligation bonds and to issue general obligation refunding bonds as well. The expectation would be that the interest expense to the state would be significantly less in the newer bond issue.

SECTION 219.05.

(a) For the purposes of this amendment, the following terms shall have the following meanings:

1. FISCAL YEAR. The fiscal year of the state as may from time be provided by law.

2. COUNTY GOVERNMENT CAPITAL IMPROVEMENT FUND. The fund created in Section 11-29-4, Code of Alabama 1975.

3. MUNICIPAL GOVERNMENT CAPITAL IMPROVEMENT FUND. The fund created in Section 11-66-4, Code of Alabama 1975.

4. THE ALABAMA TRUST FUND OR TRUST FUND. The fund created by Amendment 450 of the Constitution of Alabama of 1901.

5. TRUST INCOME. The net income received by the state, subsequent to the transfer of the initial trust capital by the State Treasurer to the board of trustees of the trust fund, from the investment and reinvestment of all assets of the trust fund, determined in accordance with the provisions of Amendment 450 of the Constitution of Alabama of 1901. Trust income does not include income which become part of the trust capital of the trust fund, but the purpose of this amendment shall include the amounts allocated to the Forever Wild Land Trust Fund as provided in Section 7(d) of Amendment 543 of the Constitution of Alabama of 1901.

(b) Beginning October 1 of the fiscal year immediately following ratification of this amendment, in addition to all other appropriations heretofore or hereafter made, there is hereby annually appropriated from the State General Fund to the county government capital improvement fund and to the municipal government capital improvement fund each an amount equal to at least 10 percent of the trust income received by the state in the preceding fiscal year or exceeds sixty million dollars ($60,000,000) as calculated pursuant to Amendment 450 and Section 7(d) of Amendment 543 of the Constitution of Alabama of 1901. No funds shall be appropriated in any fiscal year for which in the previous fiscal year trust income received by the state was less than sixty million dollars ($60,000,000).

(c) The county government capital improvement fund appropriation shall be distributed to the several counties of the state and shall be paid on April 15 of the fiscal year for which each annual appropriation is made as follows:

Part of the funds to be paid to counties that is equal to 45.45 percent of the total of that portion shall be allocated equally among the 67 counties of the state; and the entire residue of the portion to be paid to counties, being an amount equal to 54.55 percent of that portion, shall be allocated among the 67 counties of the state on the basis of the ratio of the population of each county to the total population of the state according to the then next preceding federal decennial census.

(d) The municipal government capital improvement fund appropriation shall be distributed to the incorporated municipalities of the state and shall be paid on April 15 of the fiscal year for which each annual appropriation is made as follows:

(1) Each incorporated municipality in the state with a population of less than 1,000 shall receive one thousand dollars ($1,000); each incorporated municipality in the state with a population of 1,000 or more shall receive two thousand five hundred dollars ($2,500).

(2) The residue of the portion to be paid to the incorporated municipalities in the state shall be distributed among the incorporated municipalities in the state on the basis of the ratio of the population of each municipality incorporated to the total population of all the incorporated municipalities in the state according to the then next preceding federal decennial census.

(e) The county government capital improvement fund and the municipal county government capital improvement fund [sic] shall continue in existence until and unless extinguished by an amendment to the Constitution of Alabama of 1901.

(f) The State Comptroller shall make all allocations of funds and shall make the distribution and payments thereof pursuant to the allocations provided for in this amendment. All funds allocated to the county government capital improvement fund and to the municipal government capital improvement fund shall only be expended for any purposes as are now or hereafter authorized by general act of the Legislature.

This section (668, 2000) provided that counties and municipalities in the state would get at least 10 percent of the trust income from the Alabama Trust Fund whenever that fund's trust income was in excess of $60 million in the most recently completed fiscal year. (The Forever Wild program would also continue to receive trust fund income.)

However, Section 219.09 (856, 2012) stipulated that trustees of the Alabama Trust Fund could henceforth decrease the amounts to be allocated to counties and cities if doing so was necessary to safeguard the state's invested assets in that fund. The main stimulus for the adoption of Section 219.09 was to cover an anticipated shortfall in the general fund for the 2013 fiscal year.

SECTION 219.06.

(a) There shall be established and maintained the "penny trust fund" within the state treasury to promote the public health and the public schools. Citizens may make voluntary donations to the penny trust fund. All donations and funds received shall be held in perpetual trust and shall not be subject to legislative appropriation or otherwise expended.

Earnings, including accrued interest and dividends shall be retained in the penny trust fund, not subject to appropriation until the state treasurer certifies that sufficient moneys exist in the Fund or until the fiscal year which begins in 2000, whichever comes first, then and afterward, only 90 percent of the prior fiscal year's earnings to be subject to appropriation. Capital gains taken on the sale of any securities shall revert to the principal of the penny trust fund.

(b) Funds in the penny trust fund are to be managed and invested by the state treasurer who may receive funds from any source not prohibited by law.

(c) Fifty percent of the earnings subject to appropriation shall be dedicated to the programs and projects which promote the public health and 50 percent dedicated to the public schools.

(d) The legislature shall have power to implement this amendment by appropriate legislation.

This section (512, 1990) takes its lead from the oil- and gas-based trust fund discussed earlier. This trust fund is accurately named since it is expected to depend solely on voluntary contributions. This fund provides only a small percentage of the money available for public health/public school programs. By the end of fiscal year 2014 about $440,000 had been distributed to public health and public school programs.

The next section is close to double (7,128 words compared to 3,851) the length of the Alabama Trust Fund section. It is about 82 percent as long as the average state constitution (approximately 8,700 words). This is the Forever Wild section, one which is laudable in its objectives but abysmal in terms of its misuse of the Constitution to achieve them.

SECTION 219.07.

Section 1. The Legislature of Alabama finds that Alabama is endowed with a rich diversity of natural areas having unique ecological systems, plant and animal life, geological formations, wildlife habitats, recreational values and scenic beauty. As a part of the continuing growth of the population and the economic development of the state, it is necessary and desirable that certain lands and waters be set aside, managed and preserved for use as state parks, nature preserves, recreation areas, and wildlife management areas. In order to meet the State's outdoor recreation needs and to protect the natural heritage of Alabama for the benefit of present and future generations, it is the policy of the state to:

(a) Protect, manage, and enhance certain lands and waters of Alabama with full recognition that this generation is a trustee of the environment for succeeding generations;

(b) Protect, to the fullest extent practicable, recreational lands and areas of unique ecological, biological and geological importance; and

(c) Promote a proper balance among population growth, economic development, environmental protection, and ecological diversity.

Accordingly, there is hereby established the Alabama Forever Wild Land Trust for the purpose of identifying, acquiring, managing, protecting and preserving natural lands and waters that are of environmental or recreational importance.

Section 2.

(1) "Alabama Trust Fund" means the irrevocable, permanent trust fund created by Amendment 450 to this Alabama Constitution of 1901.

(2) "Alabama Trust Fund Board" means the board of trustees of the Alabama Trust Fund as established by Amendment 450 to this Alabama Constitution of 1901.

(3) "Appraised Value" means that price estimated in terms of money at which the property would change hands between a willing and financially able buyer and a willing seller, neither being under any compulsion to buy or sell.

(4) "Board" means the Board of Trustees of the Alabama Forever Wild Land Trust, as established by Section 4 of this Amendment.

(5) "Commissioner" means the Commissioner of the Alabama Department of Conservation and Natural Resources or any other officer of the state who, by law, shall succeed to his responsibilities.

(6) "Conservation Easement" means a right, whether or not stated in the form of restriction, easement, covenant or condition. In any deed, will, or other instrument executed by or on behalf of the owner of land providing for the retention of properties predominately [sic] in their natural scenic, open or wooded condition, or as suitable habitat for fish and wildlife, or as recreational lands.

(7) "Dedication" means the transfer to the state of an estate, interest, or right in a natural area to fulfil the purposes of this Amendment.

(8) "Department" means the Alabama Department of Conservation and Natural Resources or any other department or agency of the state that, by law, shall succeed to its functions and responsibilities.

(9) "Final Approval Committee" means the Committee, as established by Section 6 of this Amendment, to be composed of the Governor, the Lieutenant Governor and the Speaker of the House of Representatives.

(10) "Forever Wild Land Trust" means the Alabama Forever Wild Land Trust created by this Amendment.

(11) "Instrument of Dedication" means any written document by which an estate, interest, or right in a natural area is formally dedicated as a natural area preserve.

(12) "Land" or "lands" means real property and any interests therein, including, but not limited to, fee simple titles, ownership interests less than fee simple, leases, easements, licenses, restrictions and use agreements.

(13) "Natural Area" means any property, whether publicly or privately owned, (a) that retains or has generally reestablished its natural character, though it need not be completely natural and undisturbed, or (b) which is important in preserving rare or vanishing flora and fauna, native ecological systems, fish and wildlife habitats, geological, natural, scenic or similar features of scientific, recreational, or educational value benefitting the citizens of the state.

(14) "Natural Area Preserve" means a natural area that has been dedicated pursuant to Section 12 of this Amendment.

(15) "State" means the State of Alabama.

(16) "Stewardship" means the maintenance, protection, operation, enhancement, and management of lands acquired for the Forever Wild Land Trust.

(17) "Trustee" means a member of the Board of Trustees of the Forever Wild Land Trust.

(18) "Trust Income" means the net income received by the state from the investment and reinvestment of all assets of the Alabama Trust Fund, determined in accordance with the provisions of Amendment Number 450 of the Constitution of Alabama of 1901.

(19) In dividing the State into geographical regions:

(a) "Central District" means the following counties of the state: Autauga, Bibb, Chambers, Chilton, Clay, Coosa, Elmore, Greene, Hale, Jefferson, Lee, Perry, Pickens, Randolph, Shelby, Sumter, Talladega, Tallapoosa, and Tuscaloosa.

(b) "Northern District" means those counties in the geographical region of the state north of the Central District, as defined above.

(c) "Southern District" means those counties in the geographical region of the state south of the Central District, as defined above.

(20) "Person" means any individual, firm, corporation, trust, partnership or association.

Section 3.

(a) For the purposes set forth in this Amendment, there is hereby established the Alabama Forever Wild Land Trust, which shall be a permanent trust to be funded and administered in accordance with the provisions of this Amendment. Title to all properties acquired for the Forever Wild Land Trust shall be vested in the Alabama Trust Fund for the State of Alabama. The Department shall serve as the lead management agency with respect to all lands acquired and shall have the responsibility of providing to the Board administrative support as necessary.

(b) In order to protect the natural heritage and diversity of Alabama for future generations, the state, acting through the Forever Wild Land Trust, will acquire lands, the title of which shall be held in the Alabama Trust Fund, to ensure their protection and use for conservational, educational, recreational or aesthetic purposes. These lands may include, but shall not be limited to the following: wetlands, river corridors, lakes and streams, and the banks and shores thereof, springs, riverine, montane, plain, coastal, and other kinds of terrain, geological systems, areas supporting threatened or endangered species, sensitive and ecologically important lands, unusual habitat types, forests and woodlands, fish and wildlife habitats, wilderness areas, unusual assemblages of wildflowers, natural lands, waters or wetlands that will provide public hunting and fishing, lands having other distinctive natural or recreational characteristics, and lands that will constitute suitable additions to the state's system of parks and fish and wildlife management areas.

(c) Property purchased with Forever Wild Land Trust moneys or which becomes part of the trust property through dedication or by some other means shall be subject to the condemnation of easements, rights-of-way and other necessary rights and estates in property by or on behalf of corporations that construct, own or operate railroads, pipelines [sic] for the transportation of oil, gas, fuel or water, hydroelectric or other electric generating facilities and electric lines, telephone transmission lines and other communication facilities, or any other public utility or method of transportation which serves, or is intended to serve, the public convenience and necessity to the same extent and under the same conditions that such lands, if owned by private persons, would be subject to condemnation by such corporations under federal or state law now in effect or hereafter enacted. No use of any such lands as determined by the Board shall constitute a use thereof for public purposes that will require proof of actual necessity by any corporation seeking to condemn such lands.

(d) Notwithstanding any other provisions of this Amendment, no property shall be acquired for the Alabama Trust Fund or with moneys from the Forever Wild Land Trust through condemnation or the use of eminent domain.

a. No funds or assets of the Forever Wild Land Trust derived from any source shall be expended or used to construct or improve buildings, structures or facilities used for human lodging, feeding or entertainment, including without limitation thereto, hotels and other lodging facilities, restaurants, convention centers and meeting halls, golf courses, dancing or meeting pavilions, tennis courts, recreational dams, exhibition halls, and similar facilities that have a principal purpose not related to the stewardship of properties of the Forever Wild Land Trust, the title of which is held in the Alabama Trust Fund, in their natural state; provided, however, that nothing herein contained shall be constituted to prohibit the expenditure of funds allocated to the Stewardship Account for the construction and maintenance of roads, bridges, culverts, drainage facilities, hiking trails, boat launching ramps and other improvements located on Trust Lands to provide reasonable public access thereto, for the construction and maintenance of facilities and the acquisition of equipment necessary or appropriate in connection with the performance of stewardship responsibilities (including housing for custodial personnel), or for any other purpose reasonably related to the stewardship responsibilities of the Board.

Section 4.

(a) There is hereby established the Board of Trustees of the Alabama Forever Wild Land Trust, which shall consist of fifteen voting members as follows:

(1) One member shall be the Commissioner of the Department who shall also serve as Chairman of the Board.

(2) One member shall be the State Forester.

(3)Three members shall be appointed by the Alabama Commission on Higher Education from Departments of Biology, Zoology, Environmental Sciences and Wildlife Science from eligible four-year institutions of higher education in Alabama. An eligible institution shall consist of a public or private four-year college or university, offering a degree in biology or one of its divisions, and having an enrollment of at least 1,500 undergraduate students. There shall be one professional biologist appointed to the Board from eligible institutions in the Northern District of the state, one from such institutions in the Central District of the state, and one from such institutions in the Southern District of the state, as said districts are defined in Section 2 hereof. Each eligible institution in the appropriate geographical region shall be entitled to submit one nomination to the Alabama Commission on Higher Education for the professional biologist trustee from the region on the Board.

(4) One member shall be the Executive Director of the Marine Environmental Sciences Consortium.

(5)There shall be three members from each of the three geographical regions of the state as defined in Section 2 of this Amendment, as follows:

Provided, however, at least one appointee by the Governor, at least one appointee by the Lieutenant Governor and at least one appointee by the Speaker of the House of Representatives shall be black. If none of the recommending groups recommend a black to the appointing authority, said appointing authority shall appoint a black on his or her own initiative.

(A) One member from the Northern District shall be appointed by the Governor from a list of names presented by Group A and shall serve an initial term of six years. One member from the Northern District shall be appointed by the Lieutenant Governor from a list of names presented by Group B and shall serve an initial term of four years. One member from the Northern District shall be appointed by the Speaker of the House of Representatives from a list of names presented by Group C and shall serve an initial term of two years.

(B) One member from the Central District shall be appointed by the Lieutenant Governor from a list of names presented by Group C and shall serve an initial term of six years. One member from the Central District shall be appointed by the Speaker of the House of Representatives from a list of names presented by Group A and shall serve an initial term of four years. One member from the Central District shall be appointed by the Governor from a list of names presented by Group B and shall serve an initial term of two years.

(C) One member from the Southern District shall be appointed by the Speaker of the House of Representatives from a list of names presented by Group B and shall serve an initial term of six years. One member from the Southern District shall be appointed by the Governor from a list of names presented by Group C and shall serve an initial term of four years. One member from the Southern District shall be appointed by the Lieutenant Governor from a list of names presented by Group A and shall serve an initial term of two years.

(D) Any successor appointments and appointments to vacancies shall be made in the same manner as described in subparagraphs (A), (B) and (C) above, and members appointed after the initial term of that office has expired shall serve for six-year terms, except that no member shall serve consecutive six-year terms.

(E) It is the intent of this Amendment that the eastern and western areas of the three geographical regions of the State shall be represented on the Board of Trustees.

(6) Each person appointed to the Board shall be and remain an Alabama resident and shall have a demonstrated knowledge of and commitment to land acquisition for the purposes of conservation and recreation. Organizations making recommendations to the appointing officials shall be Alabama organizations or the Alabama chapter of national organizations in order to ensure that the decisions affecting Alabama's future are made by Alabama residents.

The recommending groups are composed as follows:

(A) "Group A" shall consist of non-profit organizations, each having its principal programs extending throughout the State, whose demonstrated primary concerns are environmental protection for the state and its citizens and non-consumptive use and preservation of natural areas, and whose membership exceeds 750 individual residents of Alabama, including but not limited to: The Nature Conservancy of Alabama, the Alabama Audubon Council (comprising the chapters in Alabama of the National Audubon Society), the Alabama Conservancy, the Alabama Chapter of the Sierra Club, and their respective successor organizations.

(B) "Group B" shall consist of business, industry, trade associations and professional organizations, each having its principal programs extending generally throughout the state, and having a demonstrated concern for balancing economic growth with protection for the environment and increased recreational opportunities, including, but not limited to, the Business Council of Alabama, the Alabama Forestry Association, Alabama Forest Resources Center, the Alabama Farmers Federation, the Petroleum Council of Alabama, the Association of County Commissions of Alabama, and their respective successor organizations.

(C) "Group C" shall consist of non-profit organizations, each having its principal programs extending generally throughout the state, whose demonstrated primary purposes are to promote hunting, fishing, camping or other comparable recreational activities or conservation for such purposes, and whose membership exceeds 750 individual residents of Alabama, including, but not limited to the Alabama Wildlife Federation, the Alabama State Advisory Council of Ducks Unlimited, Bowhunters of Alabama, Inc., the Coastal Land Trust, Inc., the Gulf Coast Conservation Association, the Tennessee Valley Waterfowl Association, the Alabama Rifle and Pistol Association, the Alabama Chapter of the Safari Club International (whether or not those named organizations meet the membership requirement), and their respective successor organizations.

(D) In order to qualify as a recommending organization, each organization not specifically listed in this section must file with the Secretary of State and with the named organizations within the same "group," by January 1 preceding the date of expiration of term of office of Trustees hereunder, a written statement of intent to nominate persons to serve on the Board.

This statement must include a request for designation of the "group" within which the organization plans to nominate Trustees and information demonstrating that the organization qualifies to make such nominations. It shall also include a copy of the organization's charter, stating its purpose. Should the Secretary of State or any of the named organizations within the same group oppose in writing the eligibility of the new organization to nominate members of the Board or the designation of the "group" within which it proposes to nominate members, then the Secretary of State shall determine the eligibility of the applying organization to submit nominations for membership on the Board and, if determined eligible, the "group" within which it shall submit nominations. In making this decision, the Secretary of State shall give due consideration to the views submitted to him by the organizations in the "group" within which the new organization proposes to submit nominations. An organization, together with its affiliates, cannot recommend names to the appointing officials as a member of more than one "group."

Each organization submitting nominations may submit, to the appropriate appointing official for the position on the Board, the names of not more than two of its members who have the qualifications to serve in the position for which they are being nominated. In the event that no organization with a group recommends names to the appointing official, then that official may appoint a Trustee from that group solely of his own choice.

(E) ...... Nominees of successor Trustees shall be made to the appropriate appointing officials not later than two months prior to the expiration of the Trustees' terms of office, and said officials shall appoint new Trustees within 30 calendar days after the expiration of said term.

(F) In the event a Trustee resigns or dies, or otherwise vacates his office, the Commissioner or the Secretary of State shall promptly notify the appropriate nominating organizations and shall publish notice of such vacancy once a week for three successive weeks in three newspapers of regional circulation in this state with a request for new nominations from any group that may qualify to do so under the provisions of this Amendment. Nominations for a replacement Trustee shall made to the appointing official during the 30 calendar days following such death, resignation or other vacation of office, and the appointing official shall appoint a replacement Trustee not later than the end of the next succeeding 30 calendar days thereafter. In the event the appropriate appointing official fails to make an initial appointment or an appointment within said 30-day periods for appointment after expiration of term of office or after death, resignation or other vacation of office, the right to make an appointment to fill that vacancy shall fall to the next appointing official in line of rotation of the Governor to the Lieutenant Governor to the Speaker of the House (with the governor then to follow the Speaker); and if that successor appointing official fails to make such appointment within 30 days then the right to make the appointment shall fall to the next succeeding appointing official, all to the end that there will, as nearly as possible, always be a full complement of Trustees on the Board. Trustees appointed to fill a vacancy other than by reason of expiration of term of office shall serve the remainder of the unexpired term of the Trustee being replaced.

Section 5.

(a) The Board is to meet at least quarterly each year for the transaction of its business and to review the progress of the Forever Wild Land Trust. It shall review written requests from state agencies, private organizations, and private citizens proposing that certain properties or interests be acquired. For purposes of establishing a quorum, there must be present at least three-fifths (3/5) of the members of the Board then in office at any Board meeting in order to conduct business; provided, however, that in the absence of a quorum, the members present, by majority vote, may adjourn the meeting from time to time until a quorum shall attend. Any Board action or recommendation must be approved by at least three-fifths (3/5) of the members of the entire Board then in office, unless specified otherwise in this Amendment. Using its own knowledge and expertise, as well as the knowledge and expertise of the scientific community and state and federal agencies, the Board shall adopt a priority list of properties to be considered for acquisition. Recognizing that real estate transactions must involve willing sellers and may involve complicated procedures that could affect the availability of property, the Department shall, to the extent practicable, follow the directions of the Board in acquiring lands or waters. Provided, however, the Forever Wild Land Trust may only purchase or acquire an interest in property from the priority list of properties adopted by the Board.

(b) In addition to the site-specific management and allowable use guidelines referred to in Section 9, the Board may recommend to the Department rules, regulations and management criteria, which the Board feels would be beneficial to carrying out the goals and purposes of this Amendment.

(c) The Board shall assist the Department in developing and maintaining an inventory of areas and sites which through acquisition become state natural and/or recreational areas and shall make public as desirable information regarding their location, management, regulation and permissible public uses.

(d) The Board shall prepare and submit to the Governor and the state Legislature, on or before February 1 of each year, a report which shall describe and account for all expenditures and acquisitions by the Forever Wild Land Trust for the preceding fiscal year, as well as plans for the current fiscal year. The Board shall present this annual report to the public at a public meeting to be held within ten days after February 1 of each year. The public meeting shall be an informal process to present information on the Forever Wild Land Trust to the public and give the public an opportunity to have a dialogue with the Board regarding its future plans and operations.

(e) Before purchasing or acquiring any interest in lands with moneys from the Forever Wild Land Trust, the Board, acting through the Commissioner, or the Commissioner on his own initiative, shall obtain at least two appraisals from certified real estate appraisers. In no event shall the Board expend more than the "appraised value," as defined in Section 2 of this Amendment, in purchasing such lands; provided, however, that by affirmative vote of at least three-fourths (3/4) of the members of the Board, the Board may expend up to 125 percent of the appraised value of such purchase where such action is necessary to accomplish the purposes and goals of this Amendment.

(f) The Board may assume indebtedness on behalf of the Forever Wild Land Trust that may be owed with respect to real or personal property given, donated, contributed or devised to the Forever Wild Land Trust, or that may be secured by a mortgage, deed of trust or security interest covering such property, and to agree to pay such indebtedness from current assets or future revenues of the Forever Wild Land Trust; provided that the present value of all installments of principal and of interest on such indebtedness at the time of the assumption thereof, determined in accordance with accepted principles as determined by an active public market for such property or an appraisal performed by an independent, professionally qualified appraiser.

(g) The Board may contract for the purchase of tracts or parcels of land in which the purchase price shall be payable in future installments, together with such rate of interest on the unpaid balance of such purchase price as the Board shall determine to be reasonable, and to secure the payment of such installments, together with the interest thereon, by purchase money mortgages on the land so acquired and by a pledge of future revenues committed to the Forever Wild Land Trust, including, without limitation thereto, any portion of the trust income allocated to said trust by Section 7 of this Amendment; provided that such installments shall in no event exceed 80% of the fair market value of such property determined as set forth in the preceding subsection and provided further that the total cumulative indebtedness assumed each year under the preceding subsection (f) together with the total cumulative indebtedness incurred each year by purchase money mortgages as provided in this subsection (g) shall be limited to no more than 25% of the trust income allocated to said trust for the preceding year.

(h) The Board may enter into contracts with any person, nonprofit organization, corporation, governmental entity or other entity concerning tracts or parcels of land that constitute desirable acquisitions for the Forever Wild Land Trust pursuant to which such person, nonprofit organization, corporation, governmental entity or other entity will agree to acquire and hold such land, or to hold such land if theretofore acquired by such person, nonprofit organization, corporation, governmental entity or other entity and to sell or donate such land to the Forever Wild Land Trust at some future date, in the interim preserving and managing such land in its natural state subject to such conditions, including the reimbursement of expenses, as the Board shall deem advantageous for the ultimate acquisition and preservation of such land.

(i) The Board may sell, lease or exchange specific properties or interests therein acquired or held by the Alabama Trust Fund or the Forever Wild Land Trust. Any such sale or exchange shall be made at not less than the "appraised value", as defined in Section 2 of this Amendment; provided, however, that by affirmative vote of at least three-fourths (3/4) of the members of the Board, the Board may authorize and direct the Commissioner to sell or exchange property of said trust for not less than 85 percent of the appraised value where such action is necessary to accomplish the purposes and goals of the Amendment. All moneys received from any such sale or lease shall be paid into the Forever Wild Land Trust.

(j) The Board shall establish a technical advisory committee, consisting of the State Forester, the President of the Alabama Chapter of the Wildlife Society, the State Geologist, and any other person whom the Board may desire to appoint for the purpose of obtaining advice and assistance in performing the Board's functions and duties under this Amendment.

(k) In addition, the Board is authorized at its discretion:

(1) to establish procedures relating to the confidentiality of information where necessary to accomplish the purposes and goals of this Amendment;

(2) to cooperate with any federal, state or local government agency, private organization, or individual to accomplish any of the purposes and goals of

this Amendment, paying any reasonable fees or expenses in connection with such cooperation or contracts from moneys held under or within the Forever Wild Land Trust;

(3) to recommend that moneys paid into the Forever Wild Land Trust be allowed to accumulate, with only the income thereon being spent, or that the corpus or principal of the Forever Wild Land Trust be expended in whole or in part;

(4) to do any and all things necessary to take advantage of federal, state, or local government or private funds donated or obtainable through the use of the Forever Wild Land Trust; and

(5) to adopt, alter and repeal bylaws, regulations and rules in accordance with the provisions of the Administrative Procedure Act for the regulation and conduct of its affairs and business in accordance with the provisions of the Alabama Administrative Procedures [sic] Act.

(l) Members of the Board and the technical advisory committee shall be entitled to receive the per diem allowance and travel expenses provided by law to state employees. These expense payments shall be for the sole purpose to travel to and from their places of residence to meetings and for travel involving official business of the Forever Wild Land Trust. Those members who are state officials or employees shall serve without compensation or expense allowances other than that to which they are otherwise entitled in the positions they hold.

Section 6. There is hereby established a Final Approval Committee to be composed of the Governor, the Lieutenant Governor, and the Speaker of the House of Representatives.

Before purchasing or leasing any property, or acquiring any interest therein, with any funds from the Forever Wild Land Trust or selling any properties previously purchased from the Forever Wild Land Trust, the Board shall submit to the Final Approval Committee a written proposal of the purchase, lease, sale or acquisition of [sic] any other interest in property. Said proposal shall include a legal description of the property to be purchased, leased or sold; the proposed purchase, lease or other interest therein. The Final Approval Committee shall approve or disapprove the proposal by a majority vote of the full membership of said Committee within 30 days after the date of the submission of the proposal. Failure of the Committee to act within 30 days of submission shall constitute approval of said proposal.

Section 7.

(a) Beginning with the state's 1992–1993 fiscal year, there shall be allocated and paid into the Forever Wild Land Trust the percentage of trust income earned from the Alabama Trust Fund under Section 4(c) of Amendment Number 450 [Section 219.02] to this Alabama Constitution of 1901. Notwithstanding Section 4(c) of Amendment 450 to the Alabama Constitution of 1901, the percentage of trust income earned from the Alabama Trust Fund shall be allocated to the Forever Wild Land Trust as follows:

(1)–(6) [transitional]

(7) Thereafter, ten percent (10%) of the trust income earned from the Alabama Trust Fund; provided, however, that in no event shall such trust income paid to the Forever Wild Land Trust exceed $15 million in any one fiscal year.

(b) The Alabama Trust Fund Board shall provide the Board of Trustees of the Forever Wild Land Trust with advice and assistance in the investment of funds in the Forever Wild Land Trust.

(c) Title to the property acquired from funds in the Forever Wild Land Trust shall be held in the Alabama Trust Fund for the State of Alabama. Provided, however, that the Alabama Trust Fund Board shall not have any responsibility for nor any control over the approving of disapproving of the acquisition, disposition or use of any such property. Nothing in this Amendment or Amendment 450 to this Alabama Constitution of 1901 shall be construed so as to require the Alabama Trust Fund Board to have a fiduciary responsibility for the investment of Forever Wild Land Trust funds or the production of income from property acquired by the Board of Trustees of the Forever Wild Land Trust.

(d) The amounts allocated to the Forever Wild Land Trust shall be included in determining whether the trust income received by the state from the Alabama Trust Fund equals or exceeds $60,000,000 provided for the purposes of the County Government Capital Improvement Act (codified at Sections 11-29-1 through 11-29-7 of the Code of Alabama, 1975, as amended) and the Municipal Government Capital Improvement Act (codified at Sections 11-66-1 through 11-66-7 of the Code of Alabama, 1975, as amended). In no event shall any provision hereof serve to decrease the amount of income from the Alabama Trust Fund which is to be appropriated to the Municipal Government Capital Improvement Fund and the County Government Capital Improvement Fund under the above-referenced acts.

Section 8. Any person making a donation of any property or any interest therein, to the state for the purposes of this Amendment, shall receive, irrespective of any other provisions of the income tax laws of the state, twice the ordinary deduction for state income tax purposes for the taxable year in which the property or interest is donated. Provided, however, the value of any such property or interest therein, subject to this double deduction, shall be limited to the actual value of the property, or any interest therein, donated to the state which shall not include any indebtedness, encumbrances or liens assumed by the Forever Wild Land Trust or the value of any interests or rights retained by the donor.

For the purposes of this section, the "actual value" of property shall be appraised for ad valorem taxation purposes, averaged over the preceding five years.

Section 9. The Alabama Trust Fund Board shall establish a separate account within the Alabama Trust Fund to be known as the Forever Wild Land Trust Stewardship Account. Whenever the Forever Wild Land Trust acquires property or an interest in property pursuant to this Amendment, the Board of Trustees of the Forever Wild Land Trust shall set aside an amount from the Forever Wild Land Trust equal to fifteen percent (15%) of the appraised value of the land acquired, or the land affected if less than a fee interest was acquired. The Alabama Trust Fund Board shall provide for the investment of the Stewardship Account. The Board of Trustees of the Alabama Forever Wild Land Trust may authorize the Department to expend any interest income generated from the investment of funds within the Stewardship Account by the Alabama Trust Fund Board. Provided, however, the Commissioner shall notify the Board of Trustees in writing if he determines that the interest income projected to be generated from the Forever Wild Land Trust Stewardship Account for the next fiscal year will be insufficient to properly manage property acquired by the Forever Wild Land Trust. The Board may authorize by a three-fifths (3/5) vote that funds within the corpus of the Forever Wild Land Trust Stewardship Account be expended by the Department for management purposes for the next fiscal year, provided that funds from the Stewardship Account may not be expended to purchase additional property or interests therein. Within one year after the Forever Wild Land Trust acquires any properties pursuant to this Amendment, the Board of Trustees of the Forever Wild Land Trust shall develop management and allowable use guidelines which shall be followed by the Department in the administration and stewardship of that piece of property.

The Lands Division of the Department shall, in accordance with such general directions as may be given by the Board of Trustees, coordinate management of properties acquired pursuant to this Amendment and expenditures from the Stewardship Account. All lands will be managed under the multiple-use management principle; to insure that all resource values including recreation, hunting, fishing, boating, hiking, aesthetics, soil, water, forest management and minerals are protected and enhanced. No use will be allowed that is not compatible with the primary purpose for acquiring the land. In coordinating such management within the Department, the Game and Fish Division of the Department shall manage wildlife and fisheries programs; the State Parks Division of the Department shall manage parks programs; the Lands Division of the Department shall manage natural areas programs through its Natural Heritage Program; and the Lands Division of the Department shall manage other activities and programs relating to the Forever Wild Land Trust properties. The Forestry Commission shall serve as consultant to the Department for the purpose of managing the forest and forestry resources programs. Any income that may be generated from the property or from any use of said property acquired through the Forever Wild Land Trust shall be treated as interest income of the Alabama Trust Fund and shall accrue to the credit of the general fund of the State of Alabama.

The right of the public to hunt and fish on the lands and easements acquired under the provisions of this act shall not be abridged or restricted, subject to such rules, regulations, seasons and limits as are established by the Department of Conservation and Natural Resources.

Section 10.

(a) No conservation restriction or easement as defined in Section 2 of this Amendment held by any governmental body shall be unenforceable on account of lack of privity of estate or contract or lack of benefit to particular land or on account of the benefit being assignable to or being assigned to any other governmental body with like purposes. All such restrictions and easements shall be duly recorded and indexed in the manner of other conveyances of interests in land, and shall describe the land subject to the restrictions or easements by adequate legal description or by reference to a recorded plat showing its boundaries. Such conservation restrictions are interests in land and may be acquired by any governmental body which has power to acquire interests in land, in the same manner as it may acquire other interests in land. Such a restriction or easement may be enforced by injunction or proceeding in equity, and shall entitle the holder of it to enter the land in a reasonable manner and at reasonable times to assure compliance. Such a restriction or easement may be released in whole or in part, by the holder for such consideration, if any, as the holder may determine, in the same manner as the holder may dispose of land or other interest in land, subject to such conditions as may have been imposed at the time of creation of the restriction.

This section shall not be construed to imply that any restriction, easement, covenant or condition which does not have the benefit of this section shall, on account of any provision hereof, be unenforceable. Nothing in this Amendment shall diminish the powers granted by any law to acquire by purchase, gift, eminent domain or otherwise as restricting the use of an existing or future easement, express or implied, in favor of any utility or other holder of an easement for public purpose. The existence of conservation easements or restrictions shall not of itself be proof of value as a measure of damages in any eminent domain proceedings.

(b) When a conservation restriction or easement is held by a public body under the program established by this Amendment, the real property subject thereto shall be assessed for taxation purposes on the basis of the true cash value of the property or as otherwise provided by law, less such reduction in value as may result from the granting of the conservation restriction or easement. The value of the interest held by the public body shall be exempt from property taxation to the same extent as other public property.

Section 11.

(a) The Alabama Natural Heritage Program is hereby established as part of the Lands Division of the Department, or its duly designated successor, and shall be funded from the Forever Wild Land Trust or the Forever Wild Land Trust Stewardship Account as provided by the Board, and from private donations.

(b) For purposes of this program, the Department, subject to approval by the Board, shall:

(1) Produce an inventory of Alabama's natural heritage resources, including their location and ecological status.

(2) Maintain a natural heritage data bank of inventory data and other relevant information for ecologically significant sites supporting natural heritage resources. Information for this data bank may be made available to public agencies and to private institutions or individuals for environmental assessment and land management purposes.

(3) Develop a Natural Heritage Plan which suggests priorities for the protection, acquisition and management of dedicated natural area preserves.

(4) Establish procedures relating to the confidentiality of data and inquiries for information in order to protect natural resources and encourage use by public agencies and private organizations and individuals in planning or conducting their activities.

Section 12.

(a) The Department shall, in the name of the State, and upon the recommendation of the Board, accept the dedication of natural areas on lands deemed by the Board and the Commissioner to qualify as natural area preserves under the provisions of this Amendment. Natural area preserves may be offered for dedication by voluntary act of the owner. The owner of a qualified natural area may transfer fee simple title or other interest in land to the State. Natural area preserves may be acquired by gift, grant or purchase.

(b) Dedication of a natural area preserve shall become effective only upon acceptance of the instrument of dedication by the Board and the Commissioner.

(c) The instrument of dedication may:

(1) Contain restrictions and other provisions relating to management, use, development, transfer, and public access, and may contain any other restrictions and provisions as may be necessary or advisable to further the purposes of this Amendment;

(2) Define, consistent with the purposes of this Amendment, the respective rights and duties of the owner and of the state and provide procedures to be followed in cases of violations of the restrictions;

(3) Recognize and create reversionary rights, transfers upon condition or with limitations, and gifts over; and

(4) Vary in provisions from one natural area preserve to another in accordance with differences in the characteristics and conditions of the several areas.

(d) Public departments, commissions, boards, counties, municipalities, corporations, colleges, universities and all other agencies and instrumentalities of the state and its political subdivisions may dedicate suitable areas within their jurisdictions as natural area preserves in accordance with the powers and authorities granted to such organizations by existing state legislation.

(e) The Board may enter into amendments to the instrument of dedication upon finding that such amendments will not permit an impairment, disturbance, use or development of the area inconsistent with the provisions of this Amendment. If the fee simple estate in the natural area preserve is not held by the state under this article, no amendment may be made without the written consent of the owner of the other interests therein.

Section 13. Beginning with the state's 2012–2013 fiscal year and each succeeding fiscal year, all moneys paid into the Forever Wild Land Trust shall be paid to the Alabama Trust Fund in the event the Legislature has not provided for the continuation of payments into the Forever Wild Land Trust Fund as provided for in this section, provided that 2.5% of the trust income earned from the investment of funds in the Alabama Trust Fund shall continue to be paid to the Forever Wild Stewardship Account established in Section 9 of this Amendment until such time as the Legislature, by legislative act, determines that interest income earned from the investment of funds within the corpus of the Stewardship Account is sufficient for the proper administration and stewardship of properties acquired from the Forever Wild Land Trust. And provided further, that the Legislature, by legislative act, or by the enactment of a constitutional amendment [sic] may continue payment of the revenues provided in Section 7 hereof, or at any time provide for the payment of other revenues, into the Forever Wild Land Trust shall cease, the percentage of trust income accruing to said trust fund shall be paid into the Alabama Trust Fund each year to become a part of the corpus of the Alabama Trust Fund.

Section 14. This Amendment shall be self-executing, but the Legislature shall have the right and power to enact laws supplemental hereto and in furtherance of the purposes and objectives hereof, provided that such laws are not inconsistent with the provisions of this Amendment.

Section 15. If any provision of this Amendment or the application of any provision to any entity, person, or circumstance is for any reason adjudged by a court of competent jurisdiction to be invalid, the remainder of this Amendment and its application shall not be affected.

While Forever Wild is totally contrary to the principle of the state constitution as fundamental law, it does have the laudable objective of setting aside substantial portions of land in Alabama for preservation and regulated recreation.

The five major aspects of Forever Wild may be summarized as follows: (1) establishing the goal of protecting "the natural heritage of Alabama for the benefit of present and future generations," (2) setting up the Alabama Natural Heritage Program to produce an inventory of the state's natural heritage resources, (3) creating the Alabama Forever Wild Land Trust to buy available natural areas to assure their continuation in this condition, (4) setting up a broadly representative board of trustees to administer the wilderness land trust and increase its holdings whenever this is feasible, and (5) tapping into the Alabama Trust Fund to accomplish the goals of Forever Wild.

In the year following its ratification, lands not already in state hands began to be purchased with interest money from oil and gas leases which otherwise would have been deposited in the capital fund. This program was the first to redirect money from the Alabama Trust Fund. The renewal of the program is treated in the next section.

SECTION 219.08.

All monies paid to the Forever Wild Land Trust pursuant to Section 7 of Amendment 543 of the Constitution of Alabama of 1901, now appearing as Section 7 of Section 219.07 of the Official Recompilation of the Constitution of Alabama of 1901, as amended, shall continue to be paid for a 20-year period beginning with the 2012–2013 fiscal year retroactive to October 1, 2012, and ending in the fiscal year 2031–2032.

This section (860, 2012) reauthorized the Forever Wild program for an additional twenty years. Voters overwhelmingly approved of this environmentally progressive state activity, giving it a 75 percent favorable vote.

The following section represents something of a pullback from doling out money from the accumulations of the Alabama Trust Fund to a variety of recipients and a feeling that there had been a loss of focus on providing money for the state general fund as originally contemplated.

SECTION 219.09.

Section 1.

(a) Notwithstanding any other provision of this constitution, beginning with the state's 2012–2013 fiscal year, the following distributions shall be made annually from the Alabama Trust Fund in lieu of any other distributions of trust income, realized capital gains, or unrealized capital gains provided by law:

(1) An amount equal to thirty-three (33%) of the oil and gas capital payment paid to the Alabama Trust Fund for the fiscal year ending one year prior to the beginning of the fiscal year for the fiscal year for which the distribution is being made plus five percent (5%) of the average market value of invested assets of the Alabama Trust Fund as of the end of the three fiscal years ending one, two, and three years prior to the beginning of the fiscal year for which the distribution is being made shall be distributed as follows:

a. Ten percent (10%) of the amount distributed shall be paid to the County Government Capital Improvement Fund and shall be distributed pursuant to Section 11-29-6, Code of Alabama 1975, as amended.

b. Ten percent (10%) of the amount distributed shall be made to the Municipal Government Capital Improvement Fund and shall be distributed pursuant to Section 11-66-6, Code of Alabama 1975, as amended.

c. If the constitutional amendment proposed by Act 2011-315 is ratified, then ten percent (10%) of the amount distributed, but not more than fifteen million dollars ($15,000,000) in any one fiscal year, shall be paid to the Forever Wild Land Trust. This distribution shall continue through the fiscal year ending September 30, 2032, and shall not be made after the end of that fiscal year....

d. One percent (1%) of the amount distributed, but not more than five million dollars ($5,000,000) in any one fiscal year, shall be paid to the Alabama Senior Services Trust Fund.

e. The remainder of the amount distributed shall be paid to the State General Fund.

(b) Beginning with the state's 2012–2013 fiscal year, an amount equal to five percent (5%) of the average market value of invested assets of the County and Municipal Government Capital Improvement Trust Fund as of the end of the three fiscal years ending one, two, and three years prior to the beginning of the fiscal year for which the distribution is being made shall be distributed as follows:

(1) Fifty percent (50%) of the amount distributed shall be paid to the County Government Capital Improvement Fund and shall be distributed pursuant to Section 11-29-6, Code of Alabama 1975, as amended.

(2) Fifty percent (50%) of the amount distributed shall be paid to the Municipal Government Capital Improvement Trust Fund and shall be distributed pursuant to Section 11-66-6, Code of Alabama 1975, as amended.

(c) Notwithstanding the provisions of subsections (a) and (b) of this Section, if market or financial conditions dictate that distributing the entire amounts authorized by this amendment would be detrimental to the preservation of the invested assets of the Alabama Trust Fund, the preservation of the County and Municipal Government Capital Improvement Trust Fund, or both, the Board of Trustees of the Alabama Trust Fund in its sole discretion may, by a two-thirds recorded vote of the entire membership of the Board, elect to distribute a smaller percentage of the oil and gas capital payments, a smaller percentage of the average amount of invested assets, or both. The Board shall make this election at least six months prior to the beginning of the fiscal year for which the distributions will be made.

(d) For purposes of this amendment, "invested assets" means all assets which are invested in accordance with the investment policy statement adopted by the Board of Trustees of the Alabama Trust Fund. Invested assets shall not include investments in land or properties acquired for the Forever Wild Land Trust and vested in the Alabama Trust Fund and shall not include any outstanding and unpaid amounts due to the Education Trust Fund Rainy Day Account or to the General Fund Rainy Day Account.

Section 2. A County and Municipal Government Capital Improvement Trust Fund Advisory Committee is created. The Committee shall be composed of three members appointed by the Alabama League of Municipalities and three members appointed by the County Commissions of Alabama. The Committee shall serve in an advisory role, and the Board of Trustees of the Alabama Trust Fund shall define the duties of the Committee.

Section 3. Beginning with the state's 2012–2013 fiscal year, whenever funds are withdrawn from the Education Trust Fund Rainy Day Account or the General Fund Rainy Day Account, there shall not be any additional transfer of funds into the County and Municipal Government Capital Improvement Trust Fund, and investment income earned on amounts repaid to the Education Trust Fund Rainy Day Account and the General Fund Rainy Day Account shall not be distributed to the State General Fund ... [obsolete language omitted]

Section 5. All laws or parts of laws in conflict with this amendment are repealed, including, but not limited to: Those portions of Amendment 450, 543, and 666 to the Constitution of Alabama of 1901, relating to the distribution of trust income, realized capital gains, and unrealized capital gains; Amendment 668 to the Constitution of Alabama of 1901, relating to the distribution of trust income; those portions of Amendment 803 to the Constitution of Alabama of 1901, relating to additional transfers to the County and Municipal Government Capital Improvement Fund and the distribution of investment income on repayments to the Education Trust Fund and State General Fund Rainy Day Accounts; and Sections 11-66-5 and 11-29-5 of the Code of Alabama 1975, as amended, relating to appropriations of trust income to the County and Municipal Government Capital Improvement Trust Funds.

This section was ratified as Amendment 856 on September 18, 2012, and, in the minds of skeptics, represented another unjustified delay in levying new general fund taxes to meet state spending burdens by following the easier course of borrowing from the Alabama Trust Fund. The money borrowed is supposed to be paid back by the mid-2020s. As noted at the outset, however, it also cautioned the multiple authorized recipients of funds from the state savings account outside the realm of general fund agencies that they might not receive the money they initially thought they would get.

Article XII

Corporations

MUNICIPAL CORPORATIONS

SECTION 220.

No person, firm, association, or corporation shall be authorized or permitted to use the streets, avenues, alleys, or public places of any city, town, or village for the construction or operation of any public utility or private enterprise, without first obtaining the consent of the proper authorities of such city, town, or village.

This section and the one following have been identified as something "in the nature of a bill of rights" for municipalities. (Birmingham Interurban Taxicab Service Corp. v. McLendon, 98 So. 578 (1923))

The Court views this provision as allowing a municipality "to control its streets by guaranteeing that the city has at least a veto power over what may be placed on its streets." (Alabama Power Co. v. Citizens of State, 527 So. 2d 678 (1988)) Within the municipality the Court most recently has shown deference to the council as opposed to the mayor. (Town of Boligee v. Greene County Water & Sewer Auth. 77 So. 3d 1166 (2011))

SECTION 221.

The legislature shall not enact any law which will permit any person, firm, corporation, or association to pay a privilege, license, or other tax to the State of Alabama, and relieve him or it from the payment of all other privilege and license taxes in the state.

This section ensures that counties and municipalities will not be prevented from reaping the benefits of this potentially important revenue source. It was directed at preventing "discrimination against counties and municipalities by levying a tax for the sole benefit of the state to the exclusion and prejudice of the counties and municipalities." (See Bozeman v. State, 61 So. 604 (App. 1913).)

SECTION 222.

The legislature, after the ratification of this Constitution, shall have authority to pass general laws authorizing the counties, cities, towns, villages, districts, or other political subdivisions of counties to issue bonds, but no bonds shall be issued under authority of a general law unless such issue of bonds be first authorized by a majority vote by ballot of the qualified voters of such county, city, town, village, district, or other political subdivision of a county, voting upon such proposition. The ballot used at such election shall contain the words: "For ...... bond issue," and "Against ...... bond issue" (the character of the bond to be shown in the blank space), and the voter shall indicate his choice by placing a cross mark before or after the one or the other. This section shall not apply to the renewal, refunding, or reissue of bonds lawfully issued ... nor shall this section apply to obligations incurred or bonds to be issued to procure means to pay for street and sidewalk improvements or sanitary or storm sewers, the cost of which is to be assessed, in whole or in part, against the property abutting said improvements or drained by such sanitary or storm water sewers.

This section was last used to decide a case in 2010 when the Court reaffirmed its prohibitions and declined to make a distinction between bonds and warrants issued by a local entity (in this instance a county school board). (Ex parte Monroe County Bd. of Educ., 48 So. 3d 621, overruling Kimmons v. Jefferson County Board of Education, 85 So. 774 (1920))

The requirement of a referendum on the issuance of bonds, except for the categories mentioned, has led to several constitutional amendments whose sponsors desired that the projects they were supporting not face the risk of rejection at the polls.

SECTION 222.01.

Revenue bonds and other revenue securities at any time issued by a municipality for the purpose of extending, enlarging or improving any water, sewer, gas or electric system then owned by such municipality shall not be deemed to constitute bonds or indebtedness of such municipality within the meaning of sections 222 and 225 of this Constitution if by their terms such bonds or other securities are not made a charge on the general credit or tax revenues of the issuing municipality and are made payable solely out of revenues derived from the operation of any one or more of such systems.

This section (107, 1954) gives more flexibility to municipalities attempting to respond to increasing citizen-consumer service demands. Once again it was necessary to circumvent excessively restrictive municipal debt limitations as found in the original 1901 Constitution.

SECTION 222.02.

Each public corporation hereafter organized or created in this state pursuant to authorization or determination by any municipality or municipalities, or county or counties, or the governing body of any one or more thereof, shall for the purpose of sections 222, 224, and 225 of this Constitution be deemed to be a separate entity from such municipality or municipalities, or county or counties. Bonds and other securities heretofore or hereafter issued by any public corporation so organized shall not be deemed to constitute bonds of indebtedness within the meaning of said sections even though property, whether or not capable of producing income, may have been transferred to such public corporation by any one or more of such municipalities or counties either with or without the payment of pecuniary consideration.

This section (108, 1954), ratified on the same day as Section 122.07 (107, 1954), provides further freedom for municipalities and also counties to avoid constitutional debt limits by setting up public corporations whose financial outlays would not be chargeable to the municipality or county. Such corporations would be used most notably to encourage industrial development.

SECTION 222.04.

Revenue bonds at any time issued by a municipality (a) for the purpose of enlarging, improving or expanding any manufacturing, industrial or commercial project then owned by such municipality and acquired by it pursuant to the provisions of Act No.756 enacted at the 1951 regular session of the legislature of Alabama as heretofore amended, or (b) for the combined purpose of so enlarging, improving or expanding any such project and of refunding any revenue bonds theretofore issued by it under said Act 756 shall not be deemed to constitute bonds or indebtedness of such municipality within the meaning of sections 222 and 225 of this Constitution if by their terms such bonds are not made a charge on the general credit or tax revenues of the issuing municipality and are made payable solely out of revenues to be derived by such municipality from the leasing of such project as so enlarged, improved or expanded. Each municipality in the state is hereby authorized to issue such revenue bonds, for either or both of such purposes, at any time and from time to time and on the same terms and conditions, with the necessary changes in details, as prescribed in said Act No. 756 for the issuance of revenue bonds for the purpose of acquiring such a project, anything in the Constitution of this state or in said Act No.756 to the contrary notwithstanding.

This section (228, 1965) encourages what the framers of the 1901 Constitution were determined to discourage—activist local government in behalf of economic development. Unusually generous bond-issuing authorization is granted to municipalities as part of the industry-promoting strategy originally contained in legislation co-sponsored in the early 1950s by state representative George C. Wallace.

SECTION 222.05.

Revenue bonds or other revenue securities at any time issued by a county for the purpose of extending, enlarging or improving any water, sewer, gas or electric system then owned by such county shall not be deemed to constitute bonds or indebtedness of such county within the meaning of Sections 222, 224 or [the new Section 224] of this Constitution, if by their terms such bonds or other securities are not made a charge on the general credit or tax revenues of the issuing county and are made payable solely out of revenues derived from the operation of any one or more of such systems.

Yet another section (398, 1982) provides debt relief for counties. This section particularly reflects the growing importance of counties as providers of urban services rather than merely being geographically decentralized subunits of state government. Section 224 (342, 1976), providing for a limited general debt limit increase for counties, had been ratified only six years prior to this section.

SECTION 223.

No city, town, or other municipality shall make any assessment for the cost of sidewalks or street paving, or for the cost of the construction of any sewers against property abutting on such street or sidewalk so paved, or drained by such sewers, in excess of the increased value of such property by reason of the special benefits derived from such improvements.

This section contains a general protection to those assessed for public improvements. However, the Court has said that "the conclusions of the tribunals as to the benefits accruing will not be weighed with delicate scales." (Harton v. Avondale, 41 So. 934 (1906))

SECTION 224.

No county shall become indebted in an amount[,] including present indebtedness, greater than three and one-half per centum of the assessed value of the property therein ... [Transitional language omitted] Nothing herein contained shall prevent any county from issuing bonds, or other obligations, to fund or refund any indebtedness now existing or authorized by existing laws to be created.

This section is another reflection of the fear of debt on the part of the framers of 1901. In order to get around the very specific language contained here, it has been necessary to amend the Constitution. For example, Sections 215.03 (76, 1949) and Section 222.05 (398, 1982) were specifically designed to avoid the constraints of this section, along with many other amendments, most strictly local, not reproduced in this volume. The most important of the amendments was this one, 342 (1976), which increased the maximum general county debt limit to 5 percent of the assessed value of the property within the county.

Eight years after the Constitution of 1901 went into effect, the Court observed that the main purpose of this section "was to curb the improvident creation of debts by counties, and thus protect the taxpayers against excessive and unnecessary burdens." (Hagan v. Commissioners, 49 So. 417 (1909)) The Court has ruled, however, that this section "does not apply to current obligations necessary for governmental operations required by law to be paid, and necessary for them to continue to function." (Jefferson County v. Carmichael, 170 So. 70 (1936))

The creation of public corporations and quasi-corporations has been a way to get around constitutional debt limits. The Court holds that the debts of these entities are not state subdivision debts. (Coxe v. Water Works Board, 261 So. 2d 12 (1972)) In 1994 the Court ruled that a law permitting the issuing of warrants and securing for their payment a special tax did not amount to "indebtedness" as defined in Section 224. (Taxpayers & Citizens v. Acker, 641 So. 2d 259)

SECTION 225.

No city, town or other municipal corporation having a population of less than six thousand, except as hereafter provided, shall become indebted in an amount, including present indebtedness, exceeding twenty per centum of the assessed value of the property therein, except for the construction of waterworks, gas or electric lighting plants, or sewerage, or for the improvement of streets, for which purpose an additional indebtedness not exceeding three per centum may be created; provided, this limitation shall not affect ... any temporary loans to be paid within one year, made in anticipation of the collection of taxes, not exceeding one fourth of the annual revenues of such city or town. All towns and cities having a population of six thousand or more are hereby authorized to become indebted in an amount, including present indebtedness, not exceeding twenty per centum of the assessed valuation of the property therein, provided that there shall not be included in the limitation of the indebtedness of such last described cities and towns the following classes of indebtedness, to-wit: Temporary loans, to be paid within one year, made in anticipation of the collection of taxes and not exceeding one fourth of the general revenues, bonds, or other obligations ... [Transitional] which may hereafter be issued for the purpose of acquiring, providing, or constructing school houses, waterworks, and sewers; and obligations incurred and bonds issued for street or sidewalk improvements, where the cost of the same, in whole or in part, is to be assessed against the property abutting said improvements; provided, that the proceeds of all obligations issued as herein provided in excess of said twenty per centum shall not be used for any purpose other than that for which said obligations are issued.

Nothing contained in this article shall prevent the funding or refunding of valid obligations existing at the time of such funding or refunding.... [Local exceptions.]

The limitations specified in this section shall not be applicable to any obligations or indebtedness that may be exempted from the said limitations by the provisions of this Constitution, including any amendment thereto at any time adopted.

This section (268, 1967) in a very elaborate manner, indicates the debt limits for two classes of municipalities, those below 6,000 and those having a population of 6,000 or more. The 1967 modification of the original section gives both somewhat more flexibility in the creation of debt, particularly for public improvements.

The Court has advised that bonds sold by an industrial development board do not create a municipal indebtedness as contemplated by this section. (Opinion of the Justices, 49 So. 2d 175 (1959)) Nevertheless, those who lend cities money must be aware of this section. They are not obligated to pay up if it means a violation of it. (Oppenheim v. Florence, 155 So. 859 (1934))

SECTION 225.01.

Obligations hereafter incurred and securities hereafter issued for any of the following purposes and under the following circumstances by a municipality having a population of less than six thousand inhabitants shall not be deemed to constitute indebtedness of such municipality within the meaning of section 225 of this Constitution: (a) for the purpose of acquiring, providing or constructing sanitary or storm water sewers or abutting such improvements; or (b) for the purpose of acquiring, providing or constructing school houses, provided that there shall be pledged for payment of the principal of and interest on such obligations or securities a tax which the governing body of such municipality shall have determined, upon the basis of its estimate of the revenues from said tax, will be sufficient to pay said principal and interest at their respective maturities.

This section (126, 1957) provides constitutional debt limit relief for smaller communities. These municipalities were also confronting rapidly rising service demands at the time this addition was adopted in the mid-1950s.

SECTION 227.

Any person, firm, association, or corporation, who may construct or operate any public utility along or across the streets of any city, town, or village, under any privilege or franchise permitting such construction or operation, shall be liable to abutting proprietors for the actual damage done to the abutting property on account of such construction or operation.

This is clearly statutory material but is as much a part of the Constitution as the Declaration of Rights. Its language is clear, and it not been the basis for deciding a case since 1917 (Sudduth v. Central of G.R. Co., 77 So. 350).

SECTION 228.

No city or town having a population of more than six thousand shall have authority to grant to any person, firm, corporation, or association the right to use its streets, avenues, alleys, or public places for the construction or operation of water works, gas works, telephone or telegraph lines, electric light or power plants, steam or other heating plants ... or any other public utility ... for a longer period than thirty years.

With the information revolution since the 1960s this section has become more significant. Cable television and telephone companies (along with other communication-related firms) are presently fierce competitors for access to increasingly lucrative urban electronic markets.

SECTION 228.01

Part I.

As used in this amendment, the following terms shall have the following meanings:

(a) AUTHORIZED CITY. Any city in which the voters have authorized the establishment of one or more trust funds in the manner provided in this amendment, notwithstanding Section 94 of this Constitution.

(b) AUTHORIZED INVESTMENT. Any investment authorized by law for the investment of any of the trust funds of either theTeachers' Retirement System of Alabama or the Employees' Retirement System of Alabama.

(c) AUTHORIZING ORDINANCE. An ordinance of an authorized city adopted in accordance with this amendment.

(d) CITY. Any city with a population of 150,000 or more according to the latest federal decennial census.

(e) GOVERNING BODY. The city council, city commission, or other legislative body authorized under general law to adopt ordinances for the operation and governance of a city.

(f) INVESTMENT POLICY. A written statement setting forth the mode and manner for investing the assets of a trust fund in authorized investments, establishing benchmarks and criteria for measuring investment performance and compliance with the investment policy, and specifying a requirement for the preparation and publication of periodic reports on investment performance and investment policy compliance.

(g) TRUST FUND. A fund established pursuant to this amendment.

Part II.

The governing body of any authorized city may establish by ordinance one or more trust funds for the continuing benefit of the authorized city and its citizens which shall be funded and administered in accordance with the ordinance and this amendment.

Part III.

The authorizing ordinance shall include the following provisions:

(a) The amount and source of funds to be initially set aside in the trust fund.

(b) The conditions of expenditure of the principal of or earnings on the assets of the trust fund, or any other conditions, which conditions may include a request by the mayor, approval by any specified number of members of the governing body of the authorized city greater than a simple majority of the members, or any other conditions.

(c) An investment policy for the trust fund.

(d) Provision for the custody of the assets of the trust fund by the finance director of the authorized city, or a bank, savings association or trust company with a place of business in Alabama, which is organized and existing under the laws of this state, any other state of the United States, or the United States and which is authorized pursuant to the laws of this state or the United States, to conduct, and is conducting in this state, the business of a trust company, or with respect to a bank or savings association, the business of making loans and taking deposits, selected in a manner specified in the authorizing ordinance.

(e) Any other provisions, not inconsistent with this amendment, as may be deemed appropriate by the governing body.

Part IV.

An authorizing ordinance once adopted may be subsequently amended only as proposed in an ordinance adopted by the governing body, approved by the mayor, and approved by a majority of the qualified electors of an authorized city voting at an election called for such purpose. Approval by a majority of the qualified electors shall not be required for an amendment to an authorizing ordinance for the sole purpose of providing for the deposit of additional funds or authorized investments into a previously established trust fund. An authorized city may call and pay the expenses of elections for the purpose of considering amendments to an authorizing ordinance.

Part V.

In the event this amendment is approved and a majority of the qualified electors of a city who vote thereon vote in favor of the adoption of this amendment when it is submitted to them for approval, the governing body may establish one or more trust funds as provided in this amendment. In the event this amendment is approved and a majority of the qualified electors of a city who vote thereon vote against the adoption of this amendment when it is submitted to them for approval, the authority to establish one or more trust funds as provided herein shall not be given unless the question of authority to establish trust funds is again submitted to a vote of the qualified electors of a city and voted in the affirmative by a majority of those voting at the election. Each such election shall be ordered, held, canvassed, and may be contested in the same manner as is provided by law applicable to the city for elections to authorize the issuance of municipal bonds. In the event the authority to establish trust funds is defeated, subsequent elections for the approval of the authority may be held again, but no election shall be held within one year of any previous election. Once authority to establish trust funds has been approved, no further election shall be required thereon.

Part VI.

The authority and powers conferred by this amendment are intended to be in addition to, and not in derogation of, authority and powers otherwise provided by law.

Part VII.

This amendment is intended to supersede any conflicting constitutional provisions or statutes. Notwithstanding the foregoing, the Legislature may enact laws supplemental to this amendment and in furtherance of the purposes and objectives thereof, provided that those laws are not inconsistent with the express provisions of this amendment.

This section was adopted as Amendment 623 in 1998. Following the pattern being pursued at the state level, it allows cities also to establish trust funds. Although the section has been a part of the Constitution for close to a decade, there is no evidence that cash-strapped municipalities have taken advantage of the authority they now have to establish trust funds.

PRIVATE CORPORATIONS

SECTION 229.

The Legislature shall pass general laws under which corporations and other entities may be organized, authorized to do business or conduct their affairs, operated, dissolved, and regulated; such laws, now existing or hereafter passed, shall be subject to amendment or repeal by general law. The Legislature, by general law, shall provide for payment to the State of Alabama of a tax on the privilege of doing business in Alabama or being organized, incorporated, qualified, or registered under the laws of Alabama. Strictly benevolent, educational, or religious corporations shall not be required to pay such tax on their withdrawable or repurchasable share to the extent they have such shares.

The language reproduced here is that of Amendment 872, ratified in 2012. It replaced Amendment 27 (1935), the purpose of which was to exempt the new Depression-era federally chartered savings and loans from having to pay a franchise tax. In 1999, however, the Court ruled that the franchise tax on corporations chartered out of state had made an unacceptable distinction between them and domestic corporations: The foreign corporation franchise tax was based on the amount of its capital invested in Alabama rather than simply its capital stock which was the standard for domestic corporations. (South Cent. Bell Tel. Co. v. State, 789 So. 2d 133) This decision necessitated the 2012 constitutional change.

SECTION 235.

Municipal and other corporations and individuals vested with the privilege of taking property for public use, shall make just compensation, to be ascertained as may be provided by law, for the property taken, injured, or destroyed by the construction or enlargement of its works, highways or improvements, which compensation shall be paid before such taking, injury, or destruction. The legislature is hereby prohibited from denying the right of appeal from any preliminary assessment of damages against any such corporations or individuals made by viewers or otherwise, but such appeal shall not deprive those who have obtained the judgment of condemnation from a right of entry, provided the amount of damages assessed shall have been paid into court in money, and a bond shall have been given in not less than double the amount of the damages assessed, with good and sufficient sureties, to pay such damages as the property owner may sustain; and the amount of damages in all cases of appeals shall on demand of either party, be determined by a jury according to law.

Eminent domain is initially treated in Section 23. This section has not been judicially expanded beyond the categories identified at the outset. Thus "[i]t does not apply to eminent domain proceedings initiated by the state." (Markstein v. Birmingham, 243 So. 2d 551 (1971)) (It does include counties.) The federal government is, of course, also exempt.

The definition of "public use" has expanded with the times. Thus it now includes off-street parking. (Florence v. Williams, 439 So. 2d 83 (1983))

SECTION 238.

The legislature shall have the power to alter, amend, or revoke any charter of incorporation now existing and revocable at the ratification of this Constitution, or any that may be hereafter created, whenever, in its opinion, such charter may be injurious to the citizens of the state, in such manner, however, that no injustice shall be done to the stockholders.

This section is very similar to that which appeared in the Constitution of 1875. One of the cases decided based on it refers back to the classic Dartmouth College v. Woodward decision of the U.S. Supreme Court (4 Wheat. 518 (1819)). That case was Alabama Traction Co. v. Selma Trust & Savings Bank (104 So. 517 (1925)), which endorsed Chief Justice Taney's view that, while corporations have rights, they must operate in the public interest or face the loss of them.

SECTION 239.

Any association or corporation organized for the purpose, or an individual, shall have the right to construct and maintain lines of telegraph and telephone within this state, and connect the same with other lines; and the legislature shall, by general law of uniform operation, provide reasonable regulations to give full effect to this section.

This section was substituted for the original section by Amendment 872 in 2012. Its effective date was January 1, 2014, and it has not been litigated. The original section had forbidden consolidations and mergers of communication companies.

SECTION 240.

All corporations shall have the right to sue, and shall be subject to be sued, in all courts in like cases as natural persons.

Dues from private corporations shall be secured by such means as may be prescribed by law; but in no case shall any stockholder be individually liable otherwise than for the unpaid stock unpaid by him or her.

This section (also 872, 2012) was part of a larger measure submitted for voter consideration at a general election. It basically cleaned up portions of the Constitution dealing with private corporations by reaffirming the legislature's authority to regulate them, including levying a tax for the privilege of doing business in the state which was fair to both in-state and "foreign" corporations. Voters also approved ridding the Constitution of obsolete provisions related to railroads and canals.

SECTION 241.

The term "corporation," as used in this article shall be construed to include all joint stock companies, and all associations having any of the powers or privileges of corporations not possessed by individuals or partnerships.

This section defining "corporations" is very clear. It has never been the basis for deciding a case.

RAILROADS AND CANALS

SECTION 242.

All railroads and canals, not constructed and used exclusively for private purposes, shall be public highways, and all railroad and canal companies shall be common carriers. Any association or corporation organized for the purpose shall have the right to construct and operate a railway between any points in this state, and connect at the state line, with the railroads of other states. Every railroad company shall have the right with its road to intersect, connect with, or cross any other railroad, and each shall receive and transport the freight, passengers, and cars, loaded or empty, of the others, without delay or discrimination.

The last part of Article XII is headed, "Railroads and Canals." The framers of 1901 focused on the modes of transport for humans and cargo which were dominant at the time they wrote rather than on transportation generally. Thus much of the material in this part of the Constitution is very time-dated and of little interest today. Further, in the case of rail transport, most important regulatory authority is now exercised by federal officials. The initial section in this group states a general principle of conduct mainly applicable to railroads. They are "public highways" and "common carriers" and are required to accommodate to each other's needs in performing their corporate functions.

Article XIII

Banks and Banking

SECTION 247.
Authority of Legislature.

(a) The Legislature shall not have the power to establish or incorporate any bank or banking company or moneyed institution for the purpose of issuing bills of credit or bills payable to order or bearer, except under the conditions prescribed in this Constitution. No bank shall be established otherwise than under a general banking law.

(b) There shall be no limit of time for the duration of a corporation organized as a bank or banking company, and it shall not be necessary to renew or extend the life or charter of any such corporation now existing. All extensions of the life or charter of any such corporations are ratified and confirmed.

(c) Neither the state, nor any political subdivision thereof, shall be a stockholder in any bank, nor shall the credit of the state or any political subdivision thereof be given or lent to any banking company, banking association, or banking corporation.

(d) The Legislature, by appropriate laws, shall provide for the examination, by some public officer, of all banks and banking institutions and trust companies engaged in banking business in this state; and each of such banks and banking companies or institutions, through its president, or such other officer as the Legislature may designate, shall make a report under oath of its resources and liabilities at least twice a year.

Amendment 873, adopted in November 2012, basically substituted this new, simplified banking article for the older, much more detailed one contained in the original 1901 Constitution. Its most important aspects are those (1) chartering banks under general rather than special laws, (2) making these charters extend indefinitely rather than for a defined period of time, (3) prohibiting governments from being stockholders in banks or otherwise supporting them, and (4) having banks examined as to the propriety of their business practices at least twice yearly.

Article XIV

Education

SECTION 256.

The legislature shall establish, organize, and maintain a liberal system of public schools throughout the state for the benefit of the children thereof between the ages of seven and twenty-one years.... [obsolete and unconstitutional material omitted]

This portion of the original section was restored by the federal court in the case of Smith v. Dallas Board of Education (480 F. Supp. 1324 (S.D. 1979)). Segregationists had sought to substitute for it another section designed to perpetuate racially separate public and private schools, but this effort was doomed from the outset. The word "liberal" was crucial for the finding of Circuit Judge Eugene Reese in 1993 (Alabama Coalition for Equity v. Folsom, Case No. CV-90-883-R) that the state had not funded public elementary and secondary schools at constitutionally acceptable levels. The Supreme Court, however, declined to intervene in this area—unlike the highest tribunals in some other states such as New Jersey. (See, for example, Abbott v. Burke, 149 N.J. 145 (1997).) As noted previously, the federal district court has found that the segregative effects of property tax provisions of the Alabama Constitution were, in 2007, too weak to warrant judicial intervention. (Knight v. Alabama, 4776 F. 3d 1219)

SECTION 257.

The principal of all funds arising from the sale or other disposition of lands or other property, which has been or may hereafter be granted or entrusted to this state or given by the United States for educational purposes shall be preserved inviolate and undiminished; and the income arising therefrom shall be faithfully applied to the specific object of the original grants or appropriations.

This original section was untarnished during the era of massive resistance to maintain segregated education despite the decision of the U.S. Supreme Court in Brown v. Board of Education. It is almost identical to one in the Constitution of 1875.

SECTION 258.

All lands or other property given by individuals, or appropriated by the state for educational purposes, and all estates of deceased persons who die without leaving a will or heir, shall be used or applied to the furtherance of education.

The language reproduced here is that of Amendment 111, added in 1956, much of which is probably unconstitutional because its overriding purpose was to maintain a segregated system of public education in Alabama. It is included here because it has not been stricken by either federal or state judicial review. The new section substituted "education" for "public education." Some die-hard segregationists were looking to a time when private, segregated schools would take the place of public schools.

SECTION 260.

The income arising from the sixteenth section trust fund, the surplus revenue fund, until it is called for by the United States government, and the funds enumerated in sections 257 and 258 of this Constitution, together with a special annual tax of thirty cents on each one hundred dollars of taxable property in this state, which the legislature shall levy, shall be applied to the support and furtherance of education and it shall be the duty of the legislature to increase the educational fund from time to time as the necessity therefor and the condition of the treasury and the resources of the state may justify; provided, that nothing herein contained shall be so construed as to authorize the legislature to levy in any one year a greater rate of state taxation for all purposes, including schools, than sixty-five cents on each one hundred dollars' worth of taxable property; and provided further, that nothing herein contained shall prevent the legislature from first providing for the payment of the bonded indebtedness of the state and interest thereon out of all the revenue of the state. Except as they may be specifically set aside in trust funds or otherwise applied to the payment of indebtedness, all proceeds of income or other taxes levied by the state, and of all special ad valorem or other taxes levied by counties and other municipalities, or school districts, pursuant to the Constitution, as heretofore amended, for public school purposes, shall be applied to the support and furtherance of education pursuant to section 256 of the Constitution as amended.

This section, like Section 258, was amended during the massive resistance era (1956) to allow the appropriation of income from the sources mentioned to "education," not simply to the "public schools," as the original section required. It has not been formally declared unconstitutional because funds have not in fact been appropriated to segregated nonpublic schools. The 1901 section was originally amended by Amendment 3 to allow for additional county property taxes in aid of public education. The "sixteenth section" lands originated in legislation passed by Congress in 1785 and 1787. In the Northwest Territory grants, lot 16 in every township had to be devoted to the maintenance of public schools in that township. In order to win Congress's approval for statehood, Alabama also had to agree to make a similar pledge. So undeveloped was any notion of a local public school system in the early years, however, that the state took jurisdiction from the United States of sixteenth section lands for the use intended by Congress. (See State v. Schmidt, 61 So. 293 (1913).) Reference to these lands was included in the original 1819 Constitution and all five subsequent charters.

As previously noted, a federal court has recently held that the ad valorem property tax provisions of the Alabama Constitution, as lamentable as they are in terms of adequate public education funding, did not unconstitutionally discriminate in their effects as between blacks and whites. (Lynch v. State, No. 08-450-NE U.S. Dist. N.D. Ala. LEXIS 155012 (2011))

What now follows is another pullback from generous appropriations from the state savings account, the Alabama Trust Fund.

SECTION 260.02.

Section I. Amendment 709 [2002] to the Constitution of Alabama of 1901, now appearing as Section 260.01 of the Official Recompilation of the Constitution of Alabama of 1901, as amended, is hereby repealed.

Section II. As used in this amendment, the following words and phrases shall have the following respective meanings:

"Alabama Trust Fund" means the irrevocable, permanent trust fund created by Amendment No. 450 to the Constitution of Alabama of 1901, now appearing as Section 219.02 of the Official Recompilation of the Constitution of Alabama of 1901, as amended.

"Education Trust Fund Rainy Day Account" or "General Fund Rainy Day Account" means the special accounts created by this amendment.

"Oil and Gas Capital Payment" means any payment (including any royalty payment) received by the state or any agency or instrumentality thereof as all or part of the consideration for the sale, leasing or other disposition by the state or any agency or instrumentality thereof of any right to explore and drill for or to produce oil, gas or other hydrocarbon minerals in any area on the water side of the high water mark of Mobile Bay or in any other offshore area and shall include any revenue by the state from federal oil and gas leases off the coast of Alabama. Any royalty or other payment, with the exception of any taxes heretofore or hereafter levied, that is based upon or determined with respect to the production of oil, gas or other hydrocarbon minerals and that is paid to the state or any agency or instrumentality thereof, regardless of the time of such payment, shall be considered an oil and gas capital payment.

Section III.

(a) Within thirty days following ratification of this constitutional amendment there shall be created within the Alabama Trust Fund the Education Trust Fund Rainy Day Account and the General Fund Rainy Day Account. In any year in which the Governor certifies to the state comptroller and notifies the Legislature that proration would occur in appropriations from the Education Trust Fund or the State General Fund, the Education Trust Fund Rainy Day Account or the General Fund Rainy Day Account shall be credited with Oil and Gas Capital Payments previously transferred into the Alabama Trust Fund in the amount required to fund withdrawals from the Account of the amounts authorized by this section. However, the amount withdrawn from the Education Trust Fund Rainy Day Account in a fiscal year may not exceed six and one-half percent of the previous fiscal year's Education Trust Fund appropriations less the total amount of any prior years' withdrawals from the Account which have not been repaid to the Account, as provided for in subsections (b), (c), and (e). The amount withdrawn from the General Fund Rainy Day Account in a fiscal year may not exceed ten percent of the previous fiscal year's General Fund appropriations less the total amount of any prior years' withdrawals from the Account which have not been repaid to the Account, as provided for in subsections (b), (c), and (e). Funds from the Education Trust Fund or the General Fund Rainy Day Account may be withdrawn only to prevent proration of the appropriations from the Education Trust Fund or the General Fund. [Transitional] ... Beginning in the fiscal year beginning October 1, 2009, withdrawals from the Education Trust Fund Rainy Day Account and the General Fund Rainy Day Account shall be limited to an amount necessary to reach the average of the estimated available revenue for each Fund which is to be certified by the Finance Director and the Legislative Fiscal Officer prior to the third legislative day of each Regular Session. The Governor shall certify to the state comptroller and notify the Legislature that proration would occur in appropriations from the Education Trust Fund or the General Fund in accordance with this constitution. Upon the certification by the Governor, and after all other sources available to be used to offset proration have been utilized, withdrawals from the Education Trust Fund Rainy Day Account or the General Fund Rainy Day Account may be made; however, withdrawals shall be limited to the amount of the anticipated proration and funds allotted only to the extent necessary to avoid proration of appropriations from the Education Trust Fund or the General Fund as limited by this section. In the event funds are withdrawn from the Education Trust Fund or the General Fund Rainy Day Account an additional amount equal to twenty-five percent of the Education Trust Fund or the General Fund transfer amount shall be transferred from the Alabama Trust Fund to the County and Municipal Government Capital Improvement Fund.

The Finance Director shall ensure that if during the fiscal year, receipts to the Education Trust Fund or the General Fund (net of the Education Trust Fund or the General Fund Rainy Day Account payments) are sufficient to reduce anticipated proration which has been certified by the Governor to the state comptroller and for which funds have been withdrawn, then the amount corresponding to the reduced anticipated proration percentage shall be transferred back to the Education Trust Fund or the General Fund Rainy Day Account within the Alabama Trust Fund within thirty days after the end of the fiscal year in which the withdrawals were made. Any amount transferred back to the Education Trust Fund or the General Fund Rainy Day Account shall necessitate a transfer of an additional amount equal to twenty-five percent of that amount from the County and Municipal Government Capital Improvement Fund into the Education Trust Fund or the General Fund Rainy Day Account within the Alabama Trust Fund.

(c) The Legislature may provide by statute for the replenishment of the Education Trust Fund or the General Fund Rainy Day Account within the Alabama Trust Fund from sources other than the Alabama Trust Fund or Oil and Gas Capital Payments. The earnings from the investment of funds due to the replenishment shall be deposited into the State General Fund.

(d) The allocations to the Alabama Capital Improvement Trust Fund and to the County and Municipal Government Capital Improvement Fund as provided in Amendment 666 to the Constitution of Alabama of 1901, now appearing as Section 219.04 of the Official Recompilation of the Constitution of Alabama of 1901, as amended, shall not be diminished by the application of this [section].

(e) The Legislature must replenish the accounts within six (6) years after withdrawal of any funds from the Education Trust Fund Rainy Day Account and within ten (10) years after withdrawal of any funds from the General Fund Rainy Day Account pursuant to the provisions of this [section]. After the complete replenishment of the Education Trust Fund or the General Fund Rainy Day Account, any excess funds shall be designated to repay any lost interest earnings to the trust established under Amendment 543 to the Constitution of Alabama of 1901, now appearing as Section 219.07 of the Official Recompilation of the Constitution of Alabama of 1901, as amended, due to any withdrawal from the Education Trust Fund or the General Fund Rainy Day Account.

As previously noted, Section 219.09 (856, 2012) took away the assurance counties and cities previously had regarding their getting sizable amounts of Alabama Trust Fund interest on a regular basis (666, 2000). Whether they could or would not was to be dependent on the feelings of the trustees of the omnibus fund about the security of its investments. This section (803, 2008) was also imperiled by 219.09. It provided that infusions to the education rainy day fund established by this section as a safeguard against proration would also depend on judgments of the Alabama Trust Fund trustees about the status of its invested assets.

SECTION 261.

Not more than four per cent. of all moneys raised or which may hereafter be appropriated for the support of public schools, shall be used or expended otherwise than for the payment of teachers employed in such schools; provided, that the legislature may, by a vote of two-thirds of each house, suspend the operation of this section.

This section relating to teacher pay does not constitute a serious limitation on legislative discretion. Education budgets, after much debate and bargaining, regularly pass by overwhelming margins. As in any large, labor-intensive system, salaries for employees take the lion's share of monies expended.

Now follows a switch between the state board of education and the state superintendent of education in terms of the manner of their selection.

SECTION 262.

1. General supervision of the public schools in Alabama shall be vested in a state board of education, which shall be elected in such manner as the legislature may provide.

2. The chief state school officer shall be the state superintendent of education, who shall be appointed by the state board of education and serve at its pleasure. The authority and duties of the superintendent of education shall be determined by the state board of education according to such regulations as the legislature may prescribe. The superintendent of education shall receive an annual salary which shall be fixed by the legislature of Alabama and shall be paid from the state treasury in installments as the salaries of other state officers are paid.

3. The legislature shall enact appropriate laws to implement or enforce this article of amendment.

4. The provisions of article V and XIV of the Constitution of Alabama as amended in conflict with this article are expressly repealed ...

Prior to this section (284, 1969) the state board of education was appointed by the governor and the superintendent of education was elected by the voters. It is commendably flexible in leaving it to the legislature to specify how the board would now be elected and would appoint and direct the newly constituted office of superintendent of education. Due to federal pressure, eight board members are elected from single-member districts specifically drawn to ensure that the state will have a board fairly representative of its white and black citizens. The governor is the ninth member of the board ex officio and also serves as its president.

SECTION 263.

No money raised for the support of the public schools shall be appropriated to or used for the support of any sectarian or denominational school.

This section, which is almost identical with one included in the Constitution of 1875, enunciated a commitment to the principle of separation of church and state. The concept expressed here is fully in accord with the establishment of religion clause of the First Amendment as interpreted by the U.S. Supreme Court.

The next two sections of the Education Article deal with the composition and selection of boards of trustees of Alabama's two major universities, the University of Alabama and Auburn University.

SECTION 264.

The state university shall be under the management and control of a board of trustees, which shall consist of two members from each congressional district in the state, an additional member from the congressional district which includes the site of the first campus of the university, the superintendent of education, and the governor, who shall be ex officio president of the board.... The additional trustees provided for by this amendment shall be elected by the existing members of the board, and confirmed by the senate in the manner provided below, for initial terms of not more than six years established by the board so that one term shall expire each three years in each congressional district. Successors to the terms of the existing and additional trustees shall hold office for a term of six years, and shall not serve more than three consecutive full six-year terms on the board; provided, however that a trustee shall retire from the board and vacate office at the annual meeting of the board following that trustee's seventieth birthday. Election of additional and successor trustees or of trustees to fill any vacancy created by the expiration of a term or by the death or resignation of any member or from any other cause shall be by the remaining members of the board by secret ballot; provided, that any trustee so elected shall hold office from the date of election until confirmation or rejection by the senate, and, if confirmed, until the expiration of the term for which elected, and until a successor is elected. At every meeting of the legislature the superintendent of education shall certify to the senate the names of all who shall have been so elected since the last session of the legislature, and the senate shall confirm or reject them, as it shall determine is for the best interest of the university. If it rejects the names of any members, it shall thereupon elect trustees in the stead of those rejected. No trustee shall receive any pay or emolument other than his actual expenses incurred in the discharge of his duties as such. Upon the vacation of office by a trustee, the board, if it desires, may bestow upon a trustee the honorary title of trustee emeritus, but such status shall confer no responsibilities, duties, rights, or privileges as such.

The language here is that of Amendment 399 (1982), which superseded the original 1901 section. It did not alter the basically self-perpetuating character of the board, but it did seek to make the board somewhat more open to new ideas and individuals by: (1) increasing the number of trustees from the central campus congressional district from two to three, (2) (more importantly) significantly enlarging the board by doubling the number of members from the other congressional districts from one to two, (3) decreasing the length of trustees' terms from twelve to six years, (4) limiting members to three consecutive terms (formerly there were no limits), and (5) forcing members to leave the board after age seventy (formerly there was no retirement age). Furthermore, the Alabama Senate has at times shown itself quite willing to substitute its own choices for trustees for those of the existing board. For example, in 1981 the Senate, at the urging of Lieutenant Governor George McMillan, rejected four nominees. The main problem for the majority of senators was that no African American had yet been named to the board.

SECTION 265.

After the ratification of this Constitution there shall be paid out of the treasury of this state at the time and in the manner provided by law, the sum of not less than thirty-six thousand dollars per annum as interest on the funds of the University of Alabama, heretofore covered into the treasury, for the maintenance and

> support of said institution; provided, that the legislature shall have the power at any time they deem proper for the best interest of said university to abolish the military system at said institution or reduce the said system to a department of instruction, and that such action on the part of the legislature shall not cause any diminution of the amount of the annual interest payable out of the treasury for the support and maintenance of said university.

The University of Alabama was essentially a military academy until June 1903, when the military system was terminated. This followed a student rebellion on December 7, 1900. This section provided that a minuscule amount of funding (by twenty-first-century standards) would not be terminated for the university should its military nature be changed.

SECTION 266.

> Section 1. Auburn University shall be under the management and control of a board of trustees. The board of trustees shall consist of one member from each of the congressional districts in the state as the same were constituted on the first day of January, 1961, one member from Lee County, two at-large members both of whom shall be a resident of the continental United States, ... one additional at-large member who shall be a resident of the continental United States and the governor, who shall be ex officio president of the board.
>
> ... [T]he trustees from each congressional district, from Lee County, and all ... at-large trustees ... shall be appointed by the appointing committee created herein, by and with the advice and consent of the senate. The appointment of members to fill a vacated position with a partially expired term of office shall also be made by the appointing committee as provided herein.
>
> A board of trustees appointing committee is established composed of the following members:
>
> > The President Pro Tem of the Board of Trustees of Auburn University or the designee of the President Pro Tem. The designee shall be a member of the Board of Trustees of Auburn University.
> >
> > A member of the Board of Trustees of Auburn University selected by the board of Trustees.
> >
> > Two members of the Auburn Alumni Association Board of Directors, who are not current employees of Auburn University, selected by the Auburn Alumni Association Board of Directors.
> >
> > The Governor or a designee of the Governor who is an alumnus of Auburn University but who is not a current member of the Auburn Board of Trustees nor a current member of the Auburn Alumni Association Board of Directors nor a current employee of Auburn University.
> >
> > The Governor, or the designee of the Governor, shall serve as chairperson of the appointing committee. If the chairperson fails to call a meeting within 90 days prior to the expiration of the term of a sitting board member or within 30 days following the creation of a vacancy by death, resignation, or other cause, a majority of the committee, in writing, may call a meeting giving at least 10 days' notice. In the absence of the chairperson or another member designated by the chairperson to preside, the majority of the committee shall choose its own chairperson.

When appropriate, the appointing committee shall meet to address the appointment of ... [p]ersons to fill an expired or soon-to-be expired term of office of any member of the Board of Trustees of Auburn University ...

The appointing committee, by majority vote, shall appoint an individual to fill the respective position on the board of trustees. The committee shall ensure that appointments are solicited from all constituencies, are inclusive, and reflect the racial, gender, and economic diversity of the state. A person may not be appointed to the Board of Trustees of Auburn University while serving on the appointing committee.

A trustee shall hold office for a term of seven years, and may serve no more than two full seven-year terms of office. Appointment and service for a portion of an unexpired term shall not be considered in applying the two-term limit ...

No person shall be appointed as a member of the board of trustees after having reached 70 years of age....

One more than half of the members of the board shall constitute a quorum, but a smaller number may adjourn from day to day until a quorum is present.

No trustee shall receive any pay or emolument other than his or her actual expenses incurred in the discharge of duties as such.

No employee of Auburn University shall be eligible to serve as a member of the board of trustees.

The appointing committee ... shall submit the name of the person selected for appointment to the Secretary of the Senate, who shall inform the Senate of the receipt of such submission. If the Senate is in regular session at that time, the submission shall be made by the conclusion of the next legislative day following the appointment.

If the Senate is not in regular session at the time of the appointment, the submission shall be made before the commencement of the next regular session.

If the entire Senate, by majority vote, confirms the submission, the appointee shall immediately assume office.

An appointee may not begin service prior to Senate confirmation.

If the submission is not confirmed by the entire Senate by a majority vote by the conclusion of the legislative session, the submission shall be considered rejected.

A submission to the Senate may be withdrawn at any time by the appointing committee in regard to appointments made by the committee.

Upon the rejection of a submission or the withdrawal of a submission, the appointment and confirmation process specified in this amendment shall begin anew.

The same name may be submitted to the Senate for the same position on the board more than one time.

Upon the expiration of a term of office, a member of the board of trustees shall continue to serve until a successor is appointed pursuant to this amendment, is confirmed by the entire Senate by majority vote, and assumes office. If a successor is not confirmed by the conclusion of the regular session in which one or more names for the position were initially submitted, the former holder of the position may continue to serve until a successor is appointed and confirmed, but in no case until this continuation be longer than one year after completion of the term of office.

If any position on the board of trustees becomes vacant during a term of office by reason of death, resignation, or other cause, a person shall be appointed by the appointing committee to fill the remainder of the unexpired term of office pursuant to the procedure provided for other appointments made by the appointing committee. The position shall be considered vacant until a person is confirmed by a majority vote of the entire Senate.

Section 2. Section 266 of article 14 of the Constitution of Alabama 1901 is hereby repealed. [Ellipses represent temporary, transition procedures.]

Prior to the adoption of this section (670, 2000) the Auburn Board of Trustees, like that of most state institutions of higher learning aside from the University of Alabama, was simply appointed by the governor with Senate consent. The elaborate appointive procedure now provided for and the expanded membership (especially the at-large members) reflect much dissatisfaction among many Auburn alumni with regard to choices governors had made to fill vacancies on the board of trustees (most notably men who had made generous contributions to their winning gubernatorial campaigns).

SECTION 267.

The legislature shall not have power to change the location of the state university, or of the Alabama Polytechnic Institute, or of the Alabama Schools for the Deaf and Blind, or the Alabama Girls' Industrial School, as now established by law, except upon a vote of two-thirds of the legislature taken by yeas and nays and entered upon the journals.

Just as is the case with courthouses, this original 1901 section reflects the determination of local interests not to lose out on the sites of the three named institutions with their important economic, political, social, and other benefits.

SECTION 268.

The legislature shall provide for taking a school census by townships and districts throughout the state not oftener than once in two years, and shall provide for the punishment of all persons or officers making false or fraudulent enumerations and returns; provided, the state superintendent of education may order and supervise the taking of a new census in any township, district, or county, whenever he may have reasonable cause to believe that false or fraudulent returns have been made.

As part of its regular bureaucratic operation, the state department of education maintains elaborate sets of statistics pertaining to the operation of schools in Alabama. It does not need this constitutional mandate to ensure that the simplistic sort of survey contemplated here is made with the frequency directed.

SECTION 269.

The several counties in this state shall have power to levy and collect a special tax not exceeding ten cents on each one hundred dollars of taxable property in such counties, for the support and furtherance of education in such manner as may be authorized by the legislature; provided, that the rate of such tax, the time it is to continue, and the purpose thereof, shall have been first submitted to a vote of the qualified electors of the county, and voted for by three-fifths of those voting at such election; but the rate of such special tax shall not increase the rate of taxation, state and county combined, in any one year, to more than one dollar and twenty-five cents on each one hundred dollars of taxable property; excluding, however, all special county taxes for public buildings, roads, [and] bridges ...

This is the fifth of the original sections of the Constitution's Education Article which were revised by the legislative architects of Alabama's massive resistance policy (111, 1956). Again the key change from the original section was to provide that "education," not simply "public schools," could receive tax money. Nonpublic schools do in fact regularly receive small appropriations out of the education trust fund, but these grants do not represent any attempt to perpetuate segregation. From the perspective of public schools, a federal district judge ruled in 2014 that neither Section 269 nor other challenged sections of the Alabama Constitution currently had a racially discriminatory effect. (I.L. v. Alabama, 739 F. 3d 1273 (2014))

The following section, adopted as Amendment 3 in 1916, was the first to promote increased funding for public education at the local level.

SECTION 269.01.

The several counties in the state shall have power to levy and collect a special county tax not exceeding thirty cents on each one hundred dollars worth of taxable property in such counties in addition to that now authorized or that may hereafter be authorized for public school purposes, and in addition to that now authorized under section 260 of article XIV of the Constitution; provided, that the rate of such tax, the time it is to continue and the purpose thereof shall have been first submitted to the vote of the qualified electors of the county, and voted for by a majority of those voting at such election.

This section also, when challenged in federal district court, was held not to have a racially segregative, and therefore unconstitutional, impact. (Lynch v. State, 2011 U.S. Dist. LEXIS 155012 (Nov. 7, 2011), modified I.L. v. Alabama,—F. 3d—, 2014 U.S. App. LEXIS 503 (Jan. 10, 1914))

SECTION 269.02.

The several school districts of any county in the state shall have power to levy and collect a special district tax not exceeding thirty cents on each one hundred dollars worth of taxable property in such district for public school purposes; provided, that a school district under the meaning of this section shall include incorporated cities or towns, or any school district of which an incorporated city or town is a part, or such other school districts now existing or hereafter formed as may be approved by the county board of education; provided further, that the rate of such tax, the time it is to continue and the purpose thereof shall have been first submitted to the vote of the qualified electors of the district and voted for by a majority of those voting at such election ...

See the comment for Section 269.01.

SECTION 269.03.

The funds arising from the special county school tax levied and collected by any county shall be apportioned and expended as the law may direct, and the funds arising from the special school tax levied in any district which votes the same independently of the county shall be expended for the exclusive benefit of the district, as the law may direct.

These sections, ratified in the World War I era (3, 1916), clearly permit county and subcounty school district property taxes in addition to those very conservatively authorized in Section 269 in the Constitution approved in 1901. Permission for school districts to levy their three-mill tax was initially conditioned on the larger territory, the county, already having instituted its tax. (This prerequisite was later removed.) See the comment for Section 269.01.

SECTION 269.04.

The court of county commissioners, board of revenue, or other like governing body of each of the several counties in the state shall have the power to levy and collect a special county tax of not to exceed fifty cents on each one hundred dollars of taxable property, in addition to all other taxes now or hereafter authorized by the Constitution and laws of Alabama, for educational purposes, on the value of the taxable property in the county as assessed for state taxation, provided the purpose thereof, and the time such tax is proposed to be continued shall have been first submitted to a vote of the qualified electors of the county and voted for by a majority of those voting at such election. If any proposal to levy the tax is defeated in any election, subsequent elections thereon may be held at any time. The election provided for herein shall be called, held, conducted, paid for, and governed otherwise in the manner provided for an election on the school district tax authorized in constitutional amendment III [Sections 269.01–269.03].

Instead of giving county commissioners the right to decide what amount of increase in property taxes would be needed to improve educational programs to the desired level and then submit this figure for voter approval, this section (202, 1962) typically specifies the exact amount for all counties along with the other restrictive conditions stated here. (As previously noted, many local amendments have authorized specific taxes for designated school jurisdictions.)

SECTION 269.05.

In addition to any and all taxes now authorized, or that may be hereafter authorized by the Constitution and laws of Alabama, the several school districts of any [sic] in the state shall have power to levy and collect an additional special district school tax not exceeding thirty cents on each one hundred dollars worth of taxable property in such district for public school purposes in addition to that now authorized or that may hereafter be authorized for public school purposes; provided, that a school district under this section shall include incorporated cities or towns, or any school district of which an incorporated city or town is a part, or such other school districts now existing or hereafter formed as may be approved by the county board of education; provided, further, that the rate of such tax, the time it is to continue and the purpose thereof shall have been first submitted to the vote of the qualified electors of the district, and voted for [sic] a majority of those voting at such election.

This section (382, 1989) represents another grudging increase in state constitutional authorization to local governments generally to try to bolster school revenue by a small amount, providing they can secure voter approval. (Experience shows that the overwhelming majority of the time, school tax referenda, except for tax renewals, will fail.)

SECTION 269.06.

Any provision of the Constitution of Alabama 1901, as amended, to the contrary notwithstanding, all ad valorem taxes for public school or education purposes in the state of Alabama which have been approved by a majority vote of the appropriate electorate prior to March 1, 1990, and the levy and collection thereof from the date of the initial levy thereof, are hereby authorized, ratified and confirmed regardless of any statutory or constitutional defects, mistakes, errors or ambiguities in the authorization or levy thereof or the election thereon, or in any act of the legislature with respect thereto ...

This section (525, 1990) gives retroactive approval to school taxes passed in referenda prior to 1990. It was proposed by several local school systems which were fearful that, in previous local votes, they had not followed to the letter the stringent procedures called for in Section 217 (373, 1978), also known as the "lid bill."

SECTION 269.07.

The provision contained in Section 2 of Amendment No. 3 to this constitution [Section 269.02] relating to district school taxes and providing that no district school tax shall be voted upon or collected except in those counties that are levying and collecting not less than a three-mill special county school tax is hereby repealed. Notwithstanding any other provision of this constitution or any law to the contrary, the levy of a countywide tax shall not be required as a condition precedent for the levy and collection of any district school tax in any school district in the state.

This section (669, 2001) represents an acknowledgment of the continuing failure of efforts to induce counties to provide a larger share of the funding for K–12 schools. It repeals a previous (1916) stipulation that local school districts could not levy additional taxes unless the county in which they were located had a minimum three-mill countywide tax.

What concludes the Education Article is the most recent (2006) state constitutional encouragement of better funding for public education by local school districts.

SECTION 269.08.

(a) There is hereby authorized and there shall be levied and collected for general public school purposes, for the ad valorem tax year commencing October 1, 2006, and for each ad valorem tax year thereafter, in each school district of the state, in addition to all other taxes, a special ad valorem school property tax at a rate equal to the difference between ten dollars on each one thousand dollars of taxable property in such district and the sum of the rates per thousand of all the ad valorem property taxes described in Section (b) hereof otherwise levied and collected for general public school purposes in such school district and required or permitted by the terms of this [section] to be taken into account for purposes of determining the rate of said tax. The County Commission or other like governing body of each county in the State is hereby directed to compute and determine annually the rate or rates of, and to levy and collect in and for the benefit of each school district within such county, the additional ad valorem property tax authorized hereby, in compliance with the provisions of this [section]. The proceeds from said tax shall not, any provisions of any law or of this constitution to the contrary notwithstanding, be subject to any fees, charges or commissions for assessment or collection by any person whatever, it being the intent hereof that the full amounts of the proceeds of said tax collected shall be used for general public school purposes.

(b) The following described ad valorem property taxes, to the extent the use of the proceeds thereof is not lawfully restricted, earmarked or otherwise designated for a purpose or purposes more particular than general public school purposes, now or hereafter levied and collected in each school district of the State, shall be taken into account annually in determining the rate of the tax required to be levied each year pursuant to the provisions of Section (a) of this amendment:

(1) countywide ad valorem property taxes levied and collected for public school or educational purposes under the provisions of Section 269 of, or Amendments 3 [Section 269.04] or 202 [Sections 269.01–269.03] to, the Constitution of Alabama of 1901 or any amendment thereto adopted subsequent to the adoption of this amendment similarly authorizing the levy of such taxes,

(2) countywide ad valorem property taxes levied and collected for public school or educational purposes,

(3) that portion, expressed as an ad valorem tax millage rate, of any local countywide ad valorem property tax or taxes levied and collected in any county of the state for general purposes that is paid or required to be distributed to or used for the benefit of the respective public school system or

systems of the county to which the school district has reference, and that is designated by official action of the taxing authority levying the same as creditable for purposes of Section (a) of this amendment, provided that any such portion of such tax once so designated may not thereafter be designated for other than general school purposes and shall be recorded as a school tax that may be levied and collected without limit as to time,

(4) school district ad valorem property taxes levied and collected under the provisions of Amendments 3 [Sections 269.01–269.03] or 382 [Section 269.05] to the Constitution of 1901, or the provisions of any constitutional amendment applicable only to the county (or part thereof) in which the school district is located authorizing the levy of an ad valorem property tax in the school district, and

(5) any ad valorem property taxes otherwise levied by and collected in any municipality of the state for public school purposes the proceeds of which are paid or required to be used for the benefit of the school system of such municipality, and that are designated by the taxing authority levying the tax as creditable for purposes of Section (a) of this amendment, provided that any such tax once so designated may not thereafter be designated for other than general school purposes and shall be recorded as a school tax that may be levied and collected without limit as to time.

(c) Each local taxing authority in the State levying ad valorem property taxes for public school purposes shall annually notify the Alabama Department of Revenue, the Alabama State Superintendent of Education, and the Director of Finance of all ad valorem property taxes so levied by such authority for school purposes (including the tax authorized to be levied hereby), of the authority under which such taxes were levied and collected, the provisions of any referendum at which they were approved pertaining to the rates thereof, the time they are to continue, the purposes for which they were approved, and the particular constitutional authority under which they were submitted for referendum, if applicable.

(d) The levy and collection of the additional ad valorem property tax authorized and required to be levied and collected pursuant to the provisions of this amendment shall not affect or reduce any authorization heretofore or hereafter otherwise existing for the levy of any school district or countywide ad valorem property tax or taxes, whether such levy is subject to approval by the qualified electors of the jurisdiction in which the tax may be levied at a referendum election or otherwise.

(e) The tax levied pursuant to this amendment may be pledged for payment of any debt obligations incurred for public school purposes for which any other ad valorem property tax levied in the school district in which the tax is levied is or may be pledged for repayment. No provision of this amendment shall affect or impair the validity of any pledge of any local ad valorem property tax heretofore or hereafter made for the payment of any indebtedness of any type whatever.

(f) Any provision of the Constitution of Alabama of 1901, as amended, to the contrary notwithstanding, all ad valorem property taxes for public school or education purposes in the state of Alabama the levy of which has been approved by a majority vote of the appropriate electorate prior to the ratification of this amendment by the qualified electors of the State, and the levy and collection of any such tax from the date of the initial levy thereof, are hereby authorized, ratified

> and confirmed regardless of any statutory or constitutional defects, mistakes, errors or ambiguities in the authorization or levy thereof or the election thereon, or in any act of the Legislature with respect thereto ...

This section (778, 2006) required school districts which were then levying an ad valorem tax of less than ten mills to increase tax revenues to that figure. It would be permissible to substitute sales tax revenue, so long as the total district revenue was the equivalent of ten mills of ad valorem property taxes.

Article XV

Militia

SECTION 271.

The legislature shall have power to declare who shall constitute the militia of the state, and to provide for organizing, arming, and disciplining the same; and the legislature may provide for the organization of a state and naval militia.

This section provides the constitutional basis for state Army, Air Force, and Naval components of the National Guard. In the early years of American history, every able-bodied male was deemed a member of his state's unorganized militia.

SECTION 272.

The legislature, in providing for the organization, equipment, and discipline of the state military forces, shall conform as nearly as practicable to the regulations of the department of defense of the United States, and the laws of the United States, governing the armed forces of the United States. All affairs pertaining to the state military forces shall be administered by a state military department, which shall be headed by the adjutant general, and who shall be responsible to the governor as commander-in-chief.

SECTION 273.

Officers of the state military forces, including the adjutant general, shall be appointed and shall be subject to suspension, discharge, removal, or compulsory retirement as such, solely on the basis of military proficiency, character and service as determined by department of defense regulations and military usages sanctioned by the military laws of the United States, anything in this Constitution to the contrary notwithstanding. The qualifications of personnel of the federally recognized national guard shall be as prescribed in pertinent regulations and policies of the United States department of defense.

Sections 272, 273, and 276 were parts of Amendment 89 (1951). Sections 272 and 273 in particular reflect the desire to depoliticize the process of leadership appointments to positions within the National Guard. This has not been fully achieved, however, and occasionally complaints are heard from those passed over that they failed to get appointments they desired on account of political considerations.

SECTION 274.

Volunteer organizations of infantry, cavalry, and artillery and naval militia may be formed in such manner and under such restrictions and with such privileges as may be provided by law.

Military values are not as fully subscribed to in today's culture as they used to be. Consequently, there is little interest in doing what the Constitution here authorizes. The interest of this type today is in clubs which from time to time stage reenactments of Civil War battles. This old section is identical to one in the Constitution of 1875.

SECTION 275.

The militia and volunteer forces shall, in all cases, except treason, felony, and breach of the peace, be privileged from arrest during their attendance at musters, parades, and elections, and in going to and returning from the same.

This section is practically the same as that in the Constitution of 1868. It lacks relevance in an era when military "musters" and parades are most infrequent.

SECTION 276.

The governor shall, with the advice and consent of the senate, appoint the adjutant general and all general officers. The governor shall appoint his own staff, as may be provided by law.

This is the last of the three original military sections to be changed by Amendment 89 (1951). The primary change was to remove a reference to four years as the term of the National Guard officers to be appointed by the governor.

SECTION 277.

The legislature shall provide for the safe keeping of the arms, ammunition, accoutrements, and military records, banners, and relics of the state.

SECTION 278.

The officers and men of the militia and volunteer forces shall not be entitled to or receive any pay, rations, or emoluments when not in active service.

This section, if enforced, would address a remaining part of the problem of double-dipping. That it has not been is attested to by what some see as a problem in high-ranking Guard officers receiving pay for military activity while also being compensated for other public employment.

Article XVI

Oath of Office

SECTION 279.

All members of the legislature and all officers, executive and judicial, before they enter upon the execution of the duties of their respective offices, shall take the following oath or affirmation:

> "I ...., solemnly swear (or affirm, as the case may be) that I will support the Constitution of the United States, and the Constitution of the State of Alabama, so long as I continue a citizen thereof; and that I will faithfully and honestly discharge the duties of the office upon which I am about to enter, to the best of my ability. So help me God."

The oath may be administered by the presiding officer of either house of the legislature, or by any officer authorized by law to administer an oath. The oath clearly recognizes the supreme obligation these officers have to uphold the U.S. Constitution. It also makes reference to the Supreme Being, which the federal Constitution does not. (In practice, federal oath-takers do add "So help me God" to their pledges.) The subjects of the oath have been defined as those "persons invested with the sovereign power of the State of Alabama." (State v. Coats, 500 So. 2d 1 (1986), quoting trial court opinion) Within the executive departments, this includes agency heads but not their assistants.

Article XVII

Miscellaneous Provisions

SECTION 280.

No person holding an office of profit under the United States, except postmasters, whose annual salaries do not exceed two hundred dollars, shall during his continuance in such office, hold any office of profit under this state; nor, unless otherwise provided in this Constitution, shall any person hold two offices of profit at one and the same time under this state, except justices of the peace, constables, notaries public, and commissioner of deeds.

Judicial definitions stress applicability of the provisions enumerated here to individuals who are invested with a portion of the "sovereign powers of the state." (Alexander v. State, 150 2d. 204 (1963))

The original motivation behind this section has been identified as trying "to preserve a pure public policy." (See Shepherd v. Sartain, 185 Ala. 430 (1913), quoting Attorney General v. Oakman, 86 N.W. 151. (1901).) The constitutional stipulation is generally enforced when the designee to a second office automatically gives up the first public office he or she was holding at the time the second office is secured.

SECTION 281.

The salary, fees, or compensation of any officer holding any civil office of profit under this state or any county or municipality thereof, [sic] shall not be increased or diminished during the term for which he shall have been elected or appointed.

The motivation for this section has been identified as that of calling a halt to "a practice, which had long prevailed in the state, of changing the salaries, fees and compensation of state, county and municipal officers during the term for which they were elected [in order to] secure some stability and certainty as to the amount of compensation such officers should receive at least during the given term for which they were elected." (State v. Sanders, 65 So. 378 (1914))

To reduce the compensation of an incumbent might be an effective way to drive him or her from office without following fair procedures for achieving this objective. Still, while such a move as this is prohibited, the legislature could abolish any office it had created. (Hard v. State, 157 So. 77 (1934))

The Court ruled, in the depths of the Great Depression, that the legislature could not "compel, by reduction of salaries of constitutional and statutory officials, proration of all appropriations where revenues are insufficient." (Abramson v. Hard, 155 So. 633 (1934)) This relieves some of the anxiety of these officials during periods of proration. This section does not apply to merit system employees. They do not serve "terms" as contemplated by the language here.

SECTION 282.

It is made the duty of the legislature to enact all laws necessary to give effect to the provisions of this Constitution.

This section is one of the most bizarre. It originated in the Constitution of 1875. The judiciary has not attempted to use the section to compel the legislature to do anything it has been disinclined to do to implement the hundreds of (frequently conflicting) provisions of the Alabama Constitution of 1901 as amended close to 900 times.

Article XVIII

Mode of Amending the Constitution

SECTION 284.

Amendments may be proposed to this Constitution by the legislature in the manner following: The proposed amendments shall be read in the house in which they originate on three separate days, and, if upon the third reading thereof, three-fifths of all the members elected to that house shall vote in favor thereof, the proposed amendments shall be sent to the other house, in which they shall likewise be read on three several days, and if upon the third reading three-fifths of all the members elected to that house shall vote in favor of the proposed amendments, the legislature shall order an election by the qualified electors of the state upon such proposed amendments, to be held either at the general election next succeeding the session of the legislature at which the amendments are proposed or upon another day appointed by the legislature, not less than three months after the final adjournment of the session of the legislature at which the amendments were proposed. Notice of such election, together with the proposed amendments, shall be given by proclamation of the governor, which shall be published in every county in such manner as the legislature shall direct, for at least four successive weeks next preceding the day appointed for such election. On the day so appointed an election shall be held for the vote of the qualified electors of the state upon the proposed amendments. If such election be held on the day of the general election, the officers of such general election shall open a poll for the vote of the qualified electors upon the proposed amendments; if it be held on a day other than that of the general election, officers for such election shall be appointed; and the election shall be held in all things in accordance with the law governing general elections. In all elections upon such proposed amendments, the votes cast thereat shall be canvassed, tabulated and returns thereof be made to the secretary of state, and counted, in the same manner as in elections for representatives in the legislature; and if it shall thereupon appear that a majority of the qualified electors who voted at such election upon the proposed amendments voted in favor of the same, such amendments shall be valid to all intents and purposes as parts of this Constitution. The result of such election shall be made known by proclamation of the governor. Representation in the legislature shall be based upon population, and such basis of representation shall not be changed by constitutional amendments.

It will be noted that while in the U.S. Congress a two-thirds majority of a quorum in each house proposes amendments, in Alabama the requirement is a three-fifths majority of the total membership of the chamber. Only a majority of the voters actually balloting on a particular amendment is needed to approve the amendment.

The last sentence of the section reflects the fears of whites in heavily black areas of south Alabama that whites in the north might continue to seek to get representation changed to number of voters. This would seriously jeopardize the position of Black Belt whites who either did not permit blacks to vote (the most common pattern after the Constitution went into effect) or manipulated the blacks to favor white, not black, interests. The language reproduced here is that of Amendment 24, ratified in 1933. The only change made at that time was to reduce the number of advance publications for amendments from eight to four.

Frustrating recent efforts at limited constitutional reform, the Court has asserted that Sections 284–287 "define the exclusive means by which the Alabama Constitution may be changed." Thus, "Until the people decide to delegate the power of complete revision of the Constitution to the legislature, the provisions of ss 286 . . . must be observed in proposing a new Constitution." (State v. Manley, 441 So. 2d 864 (1983)) This section, then, acted to prevent the legislature from proposing a new, cleaned-up Constitution as a single amendment in 1983. "Until such time as [a change is made] the legislature's power to initiate proceedings leading toward a new Constitution is limited to the provisions of 286." (Ibid.)

What follows is one of the most questionable provisions of the Constitution. As the reader will see, it allows one small part of the state to change what ideally should be the fundamental law of the entire state.

SECTION 284.01.

(a) Any proposed constitutional amendment which affects or applies to only one county shall be adopted as a valid part of the constitution by a favorable vote of a majority of the qualified electors of the affected county who vote on the amendment. Any proposed constitutional amendment which affects or applies to only one political subdivision within a county or counties shall be adopted as a valid part of the constitution by a favorable vote of a majority of the qualified electors of both the county and the political subdivision affected by the amendment who vote on the amendment. The proposed amendment may provide for a separate referendum in a political subdivision of less than a county if a simultaneous referendum is not possible because of conflicting voting precincts.

(b) The proposed amendment shall first be approved by at least a three-fifths vote of the elected members of each house of the Legislature with no dissenting vote cast and approved by a majority vote of the Local Constitutional Amendment Commission. The commission shall be composed of the Governor, Presiding Officer of the Senate, Attorney General, Secretary of State, and Speaker of the House of Representatives. The Legislature may by general act specify procedures for the Local Constitutional Amendment Commission, but may not expand its role beyond deciding whether the amendment affects more than one county or more than one political subdivision in one or more counties.

(c) Notice of the election, together with the proposed amendment, shall be given by proclamation of the Governor, which proclamation shall be published once a week for four successive weeks next preceding the day appointed for the election in each newspaper qualified to run legal notices in the county or counties affected.

(d) In the event any constitutional amendment proposed for adoption pursuant to this amendment is approved by at least a three-fifths vote of the elected members of each house of the Legislature but with one or more dissenting votes cast, the amendment shall be treated as a statewide amendment as described in subsection (e).

(e) If after having been approved by at least a three-fifths vote of the elected members of each house of the Legislature without a dissenting vote cast the proposed amendment is not approved by a majority vote of the Local Constitutional Amendment Commission, it shall automatically be submitted in a statewide referendum in accordance with the procedures for proposed statewide constitutional amendments under Sections 284 and 285 of the Constitution of Alabama of 1901. If the proposed amendment is submitted in a statewide referendum, it shall not become effective unless approved at a referendum by a majority of the qualified voters of the affected county voting on the proposition and the affected political subdivision voting on the proposition, if it affects less than the whole county. The referendum in a political subdivision may be held at the same time as the election for the ratification of the proposed amendment, or at another time if provided by the proposed amendment.

(f) Notwithstanding any provision of the Constitution of Alabama of 1901, to the contrary, all constitutional amendments which have been adopted by a majority vote of the appropriate electorate pursuant to [this section as added by] Amendment No. 425 to the Constitution of Alabama of 1901, are hereby ratified and confirmed.

This section (555, 1994) was designed to remedy an earlier procedure specifically for approving local amendments (425, 1982) which smacked of racial unfairness. It kept the practice of having local constitutional amendments being voted on only by the county impacted by them. (If the impact is subcounty, both the county and the subdivision must approve.) However, for an amendment to be classified as local there should have been no dissenting votes in the House and Senate. Then it should be approved by a majority of what is termed the Local

Constitutional Amendment Commission, the commission consisting of five ex officio members. The commission is to make no other judgment than to determine the scope of the amendment. One member of this body could not prevent submission of a proposed amendment based on alleged defects. A U.S. Justice Department review of the original workings of the commission found them to be adverse to the interests of African-American legislators.

SECTION 285.

Upon the ballots used at all elections provided for in section 284 of this Constitution the substance or subject matter of each proposed amendment shall be so printed that the nature thereof shall be clearly indicated. Following each proposed amendment on the ballot shall be printed the word "Yes" and immediately under that shall be printed the word "No." The choice of the elector shall be indicated by a cross mark made by him or under his direction, opposite the word expressing his desire, and no amendment shall be adopted unless it receives the affirmative vote of a majority of all the qualified electors who vote at such election.

This section provides for a synopsis of a proposed amendment to be placed on the ballot, which proposal is then approved if a majority of those voting on it react positively.

SECTION 286.

No convention shall hereafter be held for the purpose of altering or amending the Constitution of this state, unless after the legislature by a vote of a majority of all the members elected to each house has passed an act or resolution calling a convention shall be first submitted to a vote of all the qualified electors of the state and approved by a majority of those voting at such election. No act or resolution of the legislature calling a convention for the purpose of altering or amending the Constitution of this state, [sic] shall be repealed, except upon the vote of the majority of all the members elected to each house at the same session at which such act or resolution was passed; provided, nothing herein contained shall be construed as restricting the jurisdiction and power of the convention, when duly assembled in pursuance of this section, to establish such ordinances and to do and perform such things as to the convention may seem necessary or proper for the purpose of altering, revising, or amending the existing Constitution.

See notes on Section 284 above.

It is interesting that this section begins in a negative vein, that is, "no convention." The 1901 framers were not interested in further, general constitutional change which might upset their handiwork designed to minimize the political role of blacks in Alabama. However, once a convention assembled under the procedures specified here, it would not be limited in terms of the subjects it could consider for reform.

SECTION 286.01.

Any proposed Constitution of Alabama adopted to replace the Constitution of Alabama of 1901, whether adopted by a constitutional convention pursuant to Section 286 or by any other constitutionally authorized method now in existence or subsequently adopted, shall become effective only if the proposed constitution is ratified by a majority of the qualified electors of the state voting on the question of such ratification.

Prior to the ratification election, the text of the proposed constitution shall be published in the same manner as the proclamation of the election.The proposed constitution shall be published on a separate sheet or sheets and circulated with the newspapers in which the proclamation is published.The Legislature may also provide for other methods of publishing the text of the proposed constitution.

The result of the election shall be made known by proclamation of the Governor. If the proposed constitution is ratified as provided in this amendment, it shall become effective on the first day of January following ratification, unless otherwise provided in the ratified constitution. If the ratified constitution provides otherwise, the effective date shall be as provided in the ratified constitution.

The Legislature shall provide for the notice, and procedures related to the election, canvassing, proclamation, and costs which are in conformity with this amendment. If proposed by convention, the election shall be held at the next general election not less than 90 days following adjournment of the convention at which it was proposed.

This section (714, 2002) was adopted to allay one fear of opponents of constitutional reform: A convention would proclaim a new constitution it had drafted in effect without submitting it to a popular vote. This had happened in the past—for example, the 1875 Constitution. Proponents of constitutional reform had hoped that this would do away with a major obstacle to fundamental change. However, a new constitution for Alabama is no more likely now than it was before this section was adopted.

SECTION 287.

All votes of the legislature upon proposed amendments to this Constitution and upon bills or resolutions calling a convention for the purpose of altering or amending the Constitution of this state, shall be taken by yeas and nays and entered on the journals. No act or resolution of the legislature passed in accordance with the provisions of this article, proposing amendments to this Constitution, or calling a convention for the purpose of altering or amending the Constitution of this state, shall be submitted for the approval of the governor, but shall be valid without his approval.

Transitional sections here (and elsewhere in the Constitution) and names of convention delegates are omitted.

APPENDIX

Explanation for Completely Excluded Sections and Amendments (Supplemental to Previously Stated Reasons)

Section	Reason for Exclusion
138.02	Authorized Activity Completed
213.02, 213.10–213.13, 213.19–213.34, 213.36, 213.38–213.41, 219.04 (Section VIII), 222.03	Bond Issue Being/or Has Been Paid Off
213.08, 213.35	Dormant Project or Proposal
102	In Conflict with Federal Law
162	One-Time Action
49, 230–234, 236–237, 243–246, 248, 249, 255.01	Repealed
48, 102, 163–164, 165–172, 174, 178–196, 202–203, 214, 248–255, 259, 261, 283	Replaced or Superseded by Federal Constitution or Subsequent State Constitutional Provision
202, 203, 214, 216.02–216.03, 226, 248, 250, 259, 261, 283	Substantially Local
119, 180, 187, 202–203	Transitional

BIBLIOGRAPHY

PART ONE: THE HISTORY OF THE ALABAMA CONSTITUTION

Abernethy, Thomas P. 1965. *The Formative Period in Alabama, 1815–1828.* Tuscaloosa: University of Alabama Press.

"Constitution of Alabama, 1819." 1969. *Alabama Historical Quarterly,* 31 (7–38).

Constitutional Conventions of Alabama (1819–1901). 1903. Department of Archives and History, Montgomery (with bibliography).

Hackney, Sheldon. 1969. *Populism to Progressivism in Alabama.* Princeton, N.J.: Princeton University Press.

Holloway, William V., and Smith, Charles W., Jr. 1941. *Government and Politics in Alabama.* Tuscaloosa: University Supply Store.

Jones, Walter B. "Survivors Constitutional Convention." 1940. *Alabama Historical Quarterly,* 2 (309–17).

"Journal of the Constitutional Convention, 1819." 1969. *Alabama Historical Quarterly,* 31 (41–42).

"Journal of the Constitutional Convention, 1819: As Reported in the Alabama Republican." 1969. *Alabama Historical Quarterly,* 31 (129–50).

Journal of the Constitutional Convention of the State of Alabama. 1875. Montgomery: W. W. Screws, State Printer.

Journal of the Convention of the Alabama Territory. 1819. Huntsville: John Boardman, Printer.

Journal of the Proceedings of the Constitutional Convention of the State of Alabama. 1901. Montgomery: Brown Printing Company.

Lee, McDowell, and others. 1978. *The Role of the Senate in Alabama History.* Troy: Troy University Press.

McMillan, Malcolm C. 1951. "The Alabama Constitution of 1819: A Study of Constitution-Making on the Frontier." *Alabama Lawyer,* 12 (74–91).

______. 1955. *Constitutional Development in Alabama, 1798–1901: A Study in Politics, the Negro and Sectionalism.* Chapel Hill: University of North Carolina Press.

______. 1969. "The Original Draft of the Alabama Constitution of 1901 as Reported by the Committee of Fifteen." *Alabama Historical Quarterly,* 31 (93–128).

Martin, David L. 1994. *Alabama's State and Local Governments.* 3d ed. Tuscaloosa: University of Alabama Press.

Moore, A. B. 1927. *History of Alabama and Her People.* Vol. I. Chicago and New York: American Historical Society.

Pruitt, Paul M., Jr. 1981. "Defender of the Voteless: Joseph C. Manning Views the Disfranchisement Era in Alabama." *Alabama Historical Quarterly*, 43 (171–85).

Reynolds, H. G. 1972. "The Alabama Constitution: The Antithesis of States' Rights After Seventy-one Years." *Cumberland Law Review*, 3 (33–69).

Rodabaugh, Karl L. 1972. "Fusion, Confusion, Defeat, and Disfranchisement: The Fadeout of Populism in Alabama." *Alabama Historical Quarterly*, 34 (131–53).

Stewart, William H. *The Alabama Constitutional Commission*. 1975. Tuscaloosa: University of Alabama Press.

Thomas, W. H. 1950. "Birth and Growth of the Constitution of Alabama." *Alabama Lawyer*, 11 (104–09).

■ PART TWO: THE ALABAMA CONSTITUTION AND COMMENTARY

Articles

Adams, J. P. 1969. "Legislation by Census: The Alabama Experience." *Alabama Law Review*, 21 (401–26).

B. N. and A. M., Jr. 1972. "Inferior Courts in Alabama." *Alabama Law Review*, 24 (509–62).

Bell Willis V. 1949. "Negro Suffrage—Voting Qualifications." *Alabama Law Review*, 1 (262–65).

Brewer, Albert P. "Constitutional Revision in Alabama." 1997. *Alabama Law Review*, 48 (583–612).

C. W. 1974. "To Catch the Elusive Conscience of the King: The Status of the Doctrine of Sovereign Immunity in Alabama." *Alabama Law Review*, 26 (463–84).

Carpenter, Joseph T. 1969. "Alabama Constitutional Restrictions on Local Government Indebtedness." *Alabama Law Review*, 21 (427–35).

Citizens' Conference on Alabama's Judicial System. 1966. "Consensus State of the Citizens' Conference on Alabama's Judicial System." *Alabama Lawyer*, 28 (190–92).

Clark, Charles E. 1973. "Right to Jury Trial in Alabama." *Cumberland Law Review*, 4 (317–26).

Cole, Charles D. 1973. "Judicial Commission of Alabama: Procedural Rules." *Alabama Lawyer*, 34 (80–92).

______. 1973. "Judicial Reform in Alabama: A Survey." *Cumberland Law Review*, 4 (41–72).

Dean, Joseph L. 1975. "Homestead for Survivors in Alabama." *Alabama Law Review*, 27 (443–75).

Erdreich, Ben L. 1962. "Alabama's Unrepresentative Legislature." *Alabama Law Review*, 14 (403–22).

Fair, Bryan K. 2002. "Equality for All: The Case for a New Declaration of Rights Article of the Alabama Constitution." *Cumberland Law Review*, 33 (339–85).

Freyer, Tony A., and Pruitt, Paul M., Jr. 2001. "Transforming the Judiciary under Alabama's Constitution." *Alabama Law Review*, 53 (77–134).

Gardner, James A. 1998. "Southern Character, Confederate Nationalism, and the Interpretation of State Constitutions." *Texas Law Review*, 86 (1219–92).

Grooms, H. H. 1965. "The Origin and Development of Trial by Jury." *Alabama Lawyer*, 26 (162–71).

Hamilton, Drayton N. 1973. "The Legal Viewpoint: Article VI—The Judicial Department." *Alabama Municipal Journal*, 30 (no. 11, p. 13).

______. 1974. "The Legal Viewpoint: Proposed Constitutional Article on Local Government." *Alabama Municipal Journal*, 32 (no. 3, p. 18).

______. 1974. "The Legal Viewpoint: Proposed Constitutional Article on Taxation." *Alabama Municipal Journal*, 32 (no. 3, p. 18).

Hammons, Christopher W. 1999. "Was James Madison Wrong? Rethinking the American Preference for Short, Framework-Oriented Constitutions." *American Political Science Review* 93 (837–49).

Heflin, Howell T. 1977. "The Judicial Implementation Act." *Alabama Law Review*, 28 (215–41).

Jackson, William P. 1962. "Eminent Domain Procedure in Alabama State Courts." *Alabama Law Review*, 28 (215–41).

Jones, Walter B. 1943. "Constitutional Convention of 1901 and Poll Taxes." *Alabama Lawyer*, 4 (3–22).

Lucie, Patricia A. 1987. "White Rights as a Model for Black: Or—Who's Afraid of the Privileges and Immunities Clause." *Syracuse Law Review*, 38 (859–77) (Alabama freedom of speech clause differs from federal Constitution).

Maxman, Mellia H. 1987. "In Defense of the Constitution's Judicial Impeachment Standard." *Michigan Law Review*, 86 (420–63) (Alabama Constitution excludes legislature from judicial impeachment process).

Norrell, Robert J. 2001. "Law in a White Man's Democracy: A History of the Alabama State Judiciary." *Cumberland Law Review*, 32 (135–64).

Reynolds, H. G. 1972. "A Proposed Revision of Article III of the Alabama Constitution of 1901: Distribution of the Powers of Government." *Cumberland Law Review*, 3 (402–08).

Roquemore, Perry C. 1978. "The Legal Viewpoint: The Impact of Peddycoart." *Alabama Municipal Journal*, 35 (no. 9, p. 18).

______. 1976. "The Legal Viewpoint: The Municipal Court under the Judicial Article." *Alabama Municipal Journal*, 33 (no. 12, p. 20).

Roth, John Herbert. 2003. "Education Funding and the Alabama Example: Another Player on a Crowded Field." *BYU Education & Law Journal*, 2003 (739–70).

Sands, C. Dallas. 1951, "Government by Judiciary—Advisory Opinions in Alabama." *Alabama Law Review*, 4 (1–43).

Shores, Janie L., and others. 1997. "Tributes to Senator Howell Heflin." *Alabama Law Review*, 48 (417–40).

Smith, T. L. 1954. "Separation of Church and State in Public Schools." *Alabama Law Review*, 7 (99–107).

Spence, Susan Thompson. 1999. "The Usurpation of Legislative Power by the Alabama Judiciary." *Alabama Law Review*, 50 (929–68).

Staff. 1992. "General Powers of Municipalities." *Alabama Municipal Journal*, 50 (no. 4, p. 8).

______. 1975. "League Committee Opposes 'Lid Law.'" *Alabama Municipal Journal*, 33 (no. 5, p. 8).

Thomas, W. K. 1977. "Eminent Domain: A Survey of Alabama Law." *Alabama Law Review*, 28 (399–446).

Walter, James N., Jr. 1980. "Local Legislation in Alabama: The Impact of Peddycoart v. Birmingham." *Alabama Law Review*, 32 (167–96).

Walthall, Howard P., Sr. 2004. "A Doubtful Mind: Understanding Alabama's State Constitution." *Cumberland Law Review*, 35 (7–100).

Watkins, John. 1957. "Patrolling the Legal Boundaries." *Alabama Municipal Journal*, 15 (no. 8, p. 18) (essay on the Alabama Constitution and laws concerning debt limits and their election requirements).

______. 1963. "The Legal Viewpoint: Liberty and Domestic Tranquility." *Alabama Municipal Journal*, 20 (no. 8, p. 14) (essay on Preamble to Alabama Constitution).

Williams, Robert F. 2000. "Foreword: Tort Reform and State Constitutional Law." *Rutgers Law Journal*, 32 (897–906).

Work, James E. "Judicial Compensation, Retirement and Removal." 1967. *Alabama Lawyer*, 28 (160–67).

Books and Monographs

Alabama. 1943. *Constitution*. Wetumpka Printing Co. (as adopted November 11, 1901).

Alabama. Legislature. Legislative Reform Study Committee. 1970. *Improving the Alabama Legislature*. Montgomery: By the Committee.

Alabama. Secretary of State. 1983. *Proposed New Constitution for Alabama: Act No. 83-683*. Montgomery.

Alabama Administrative Office of Courts. N.D. *Alabama Courts Come to Order: The Unified Judicial System*. Montgomery.

Alabama Constitutional Commission. 1973. *Proposed Constitution of Alabama: Report of the Constitutional Commission*. Montgomery.

______. *Reprint of Commentaries on the Proposed Constitution for Alabama*. 1974. Montgomery.

Alabama Constitutional Convention (1901) Proceedings of the Constitutional Convention of the State of Alabama. 1940. Wetumpka: Wetumpka Printing Company (index).

Alabama Legislative Fiscal Office. 1985. *A Legislator's Guide to Alabama's Taxes: A Brief Summary of the Major Revenue Sources of the State of Alabama.* Montgomery: By the Office.

Beard, Charles Austin. 1910. *American Government and Politics.* New York: Macmillan Company.

Brewer, Albert P., and Cole, Charles D. 1992. *Brewer and Cole: Alabama Constitutional Law.* Birmingham: Samford University Press.

Bullock, Charles S., and Rozell, Mark J. (eds.) 3rd ed. 2006. *The New Politics of the Old South.* Lanham, Md.: Rowman & Littlefield.

Farmer, Hallie. 1949. *The Legislative Process in Alabama.* Tuscaloosa: Bureau of Public Administration, University of Alabama.

Frye, Robert J. 1969. *The Alabama Supreme Court: An Institutional View.* Tuscaloosa: Bureau of Public Administration, University of Alabama.

Institute for Government Research. 1932. *Organization and Administration of the State Government of Alabama: Report on a Survey Submitted to Governor B. M. Miller.* Vol. 1, Part 1. Washington, D.C.: Brookings Institution.

______. 1932. *Taxation: Report on a Survey Submitted to Governor B. M. Miller.* Vol. 4, Part 3.

McCurley, Robert C. (ed.) 13th ed. 2010. *Alabama Government Manual* Tuscaloosa: Alabama Law Institute.

Mayfield, James J. 1904. *Constitutions of 1875 and 1901.* Nashville: Marshall and Bruce Co.

Novkov, Julie. 2008. *Racial Union: Law, Intimacy, and the White State in Alabama, 1865–1954.* Ann Arbor: University of Michigan Press.

Orlando, Justin. 2012. *Constitutional Preambles: At a Crossroads between Politics and Law,* Santarcangelo: Maggoli Editore.

Skinner, Thomas E. 1938. *Alabama Constitution Annotated.* Birmingham: Birmingham Printing Company.

Tarr, G. Alan. 2000. *Understanding State Constitutions.* Princeton, N.J.: Princeton University Press.

Tarr, G. Alan, and Porter, Mary Cornelia. 1990. *State Supreme Courts in State and Nation.* New Haven: Yale University Press.

Thomas, James D. 1974. *Government in Alabama.* Tuscaloosa: Bureau of Public Administration, University of Alabama.

Thomas, James D., and Stewart, William H. *Government and Politics of Alabama.* 1988. Lincoln: University of Nebraska Press.

TABLE OF CASES

A

B

C

D

E

F

G

H

L

M

N

O

T

U

W

Y

■ INDEX

About the Author

WILLIAM H. STEWART, Former Chairman of the Department of Political Science and Director of the Doctoral Program in Public Administration, University of Alabama, has specialized in the study of Alabama politics, government, and constitutional history. His previous books include: *Alabama Government and Politics* (co-author) (1988), *Concepts of Federalism* (1984), The Alabama State Constitution: A Reference Guide (1st ed., 1994), and *The Alabama Constitutional Commission* (1975).

www.ingramcontent.com/pod-product-compliance
Lightning Source LLC
LaVergne TN
LVHW011751200926
848484LV00003B/668
* 9 7 8 0 1 9 9 8 9 6 3 9 4 *